VOLUME 492   JULY 1987

THE ANNALS

of The American Academy *of* Political *and* Social Science

RICHARD D. LAMBERT, *Editor*
ALAN W. HESTON, *Associate Editor*

UNEMPLOYMENT: A GLOBAL CHALLENGE

Special Editors of this Volume

BERTRAM GROSS

University of California
Berkeley

ALFRED PFALLER

Friedrich Ebert Foundation
Bonn
West Germany

Ⓢ SAGE PUBLICATIONS *NEWBURY PARK BEVERLY HILLS LONDON NEW DELHI*

THE ANNALS

Editorial Office: 3937 Chestnut Street, Philadelphia, Pennsylvania 19104.

For information about membership* (individuals only) and subscriptions (institutions), address:

SAGE PUBLICATIONS, INC.

2111 West Hillcrest Drive   275 South Beverly Drive
Newbury Park, CA 91320   Beverly Hills, CA 90212

From India and South Asia,   *From the UK, Europe, the Middle*
write to: *East and Africa, write to:*

SAGE PUBLICATIONS INDIA Pvt. Ltd.   SAGE PUBLICATIONS LTD
P.O. Box 4215   28 Banner Street
New Delhi 110 048   London EC1Y 8QE
INDIA   ENGLAND

SAGE Production Editor: JACQUELINE SYROP
**Please note that members of The Academy receive THE ANNALS with their membership.*

Library of Congress Catalog Card Number 86-061222
International Standard Serial Number ISSN 0002-7162
International Standard Book Number ISBN 0-8039-2934-X (Vol. 492, 1987 paper)
International Standard Book Number ISBN 0-8039-2933-1 (Vol. 492, 1987 cloth)
Manufactured in the United States of America. First printing, July 1987.

The articles appearing in THE ANNALS are indexed in *Book Review Index; Public Affairs Information Service Bulletin; Social Sciences Index; Monthly Periodical Index; Current Contents; Behavioral, Social Management Sciences;* and *Combined Retrospective Index Sets.* They are also abstracted and indexed in *ABC Pol Sci, Historical Abstracts, Human Resources Abstracts, Social Sciences Citation Index, United States Political Science Documents, Social Work Research & Abstracts, Peace Research Reviews, Sage Urban Studies Abstracts, International Political Science Abstracts, America: History and Life,* and/or *Family Resources Database.*

Information about membership rates, institutional subscriptions, and back issue prices may be found on the facing page.

Advertising. Current rates and specifications may be obtained by writing to THE ANNALS Advertising and Promotion Manager at the Newbury Park office (address above).

Claims. Claims for undelivered copies must be made no later than three months following month of publication. The publisher will supply missing copies when losses have been sustained in transit and when the reserve stock will permit.

Change of Address. Six weeks' advance notice must be given when notifying of change of address to insure proper identification. Please specify name of journal. Send change of address to: THE ANNALS, c/o Sage Publications, Inc., 2111 West Hillcrest Drive, Newbury Park, CA 91320.

Origin and Purpose. The Academy was organized December 14, 1889, to promote the progress of political and social science, especially through publications and meetings. The Academy does not take sides in controverted questions, but seeks to gather and present reliable information to assist the public in forming an intelligent and accurate judgment.

Meetings. The Academy holds an annual meeting in the spring extending over two days.

Publications. THE ANNALS is the bimonthly publication of The Academy. Each issue contains articles on some prominent social or political problem, written at the invitation of the editors. Also, monographs are published from time to time, numbers of which are distributed to pertinent professional organizations. These volumes constitute important reference works on the topics with which they deal, and they are extensively cited by authorities throughout the United States and abroad. The papers presented at the meetings of The Academy are included in THE ANNALS.

Membership. Each member of The Academy receives THE ANNALS and may attend the meetings of The Academy. Membership is open only to individuals. Annual dues: $26.00 for the regular paperbound edition (clothbound, $40.00). Add $9.00 per year for membership outside the U.S.A. Members may also purchase single issues of THE ANNALS for $6.95 each (clothbound, $10.00).

Subscriptions. THE ANNALS (ISSN 0002-7162) is published six times annually—in January, March, May, July, September, and November. Institutions may subscribe to THE ANNALS at the annual rate: $52.00 (clothbound, $68.00). Add $9.00 per year for subscriptions outside the U.S.A. Institutional rates for single issues: $10.00 each (clothbound, $15.00).

Second class postage paid at Philadelphia, Pennsylvania, and at additional mailing offices.

Single issues of THE ANNALS may be obtained by individuals who are not members of The Academy for $7.95 each (clothbound, $15.00). Single issues of THE ANNALS have proven to be excellent supplementary texts for classroom use. Direct inquiries regarding adoptions to THE ANNALS c/o Sage Publications (address below).

All correspondence concerning membership in The Academy, dues renewals, inquiries about membership status, and/or purchase of single issues of THE ANNALS should be sent to THE ANNALS c/o Sage Publications, Inc., 2111 West Hillcrest Drive, Newbury Park, CA 91320. *Please note that orders under $20 must be prepaid.* Sage affiliates in London and India will assist institutional subscribers abroad with regard to orders, claims, and inquiries for both subscriptions and single issues.

THE ANNALS

of The American Academy *of* Political *and* Social Science

RICHARD D. LAMBERT, *Editor*
ALAN W. HESTON, *Associate Editor*

---------- **FORTHCOMING** ----------

THE INFORMAL ECONOMY
Special Editors: Louis A. Ferman, Stuart Henry and Michele Hoyman
Volume 493   September 1987

A NEIGHBORHOOD, FAMILY, AND EMPLOYMENT POLICY TO PREVENT CRIME
Special Editor: Lynn A. Curtis
Volume 494   November 1987

TELESCIENCE: SCIENTIFIC COMMUNICATION IN THE INFORMATION AGE
Special Editor: Murray Aborn
Volume 495   January 1988

See page 3 for information on Academy membership and
purchase of single volumes of **The Annals.**

CONTENTS

BOOK DEPARTMENT CONTENTS

ECONOMICS

PREFACE

Social conditions have been changed profoundly since 1945, by technology and by decolonization to take two prominent influences, but they stubbornly resist change in other areas.[1]

A sad example of resistance to change has been the failure of the United Nations to respond to the plague of global unemployment, underemployment, and job insecurity. The organization and its members have not only underestimated the magnitude of the problem. They have failed to piece together the many storm warnings of future disaster: the debt crisis, austerity policies, new labor-displacing technologies, enormous overcapacity in agriculture and industry, beggar-thy-neighbor nationalism, self-centered regionalism, and recessions or depressions in many economic sectors and geographical areas. They have ignored the complex intertwinings that have brought capitalist, socialist, and developing countries together into a mysterious world order that cannot be well enough understood through the conventional concepts of classical, Marxist, Keynesian, or post-Keynesian economics. In the light of the full employment pledges in the U.N. Charter, the Universal Declaration of Human Rights, and the International Covenant on Economic and Social Rights, these failures are not merely sad. They are tragic.

In 1984 the Friedrich Ebert Foundation invited the contributors to this volume of *The Annals* to an unprecedented—and long overdue—conference, "Global Unemployment: Challenge to Policy-Makers." Since meeting in Bonn, we have refined our findings and have produced this volume.

Our purpose is ambitious: to help initiate a process of overcoming the resistance to change that has undermined earlier commitments to full employment. It is therefore a challenge to top policymakers in both governments and transnational agencies in all parts of the world.

It is also a challenge to many others—not only economists, but to all other social scientists and to professionals, labor unions, business leaders, and the civil servants of national governments and the U.N. family.

We are under no illusions about the difficulty of the task. This is made clear by the tentative nature of many findings and suggestions and by the many aspects of the problem that we have not had time or space to explore. We have had to omit several papers presented at Bonn. Among them are papers by Rashmi Mayur of Bombay, India, and Miguel Teubal of Buenos Aires, Argentina, on Third World unemployment, and a paper on transnational politics prepared by Ralph Goldman, who was the first to suggest the holding of our conference. Nor have we been able to include the generational approach to unemployment as presented to us in a preliminary paper by Ezio Tarantelli, head of the Institute for the Study of Labor

1. United Nations Secretariat, Department of International Economic and Social Affairs, Office for Development Research and Policy Analysis, *1985 Report on the World Social Situation*, E/CN.51985/2 (1985).

Economics in Rome. On 27 March 1985, Professor Tarantelli was assassinated by terrorists who objected to his views on cost-of-living escalators. If any of us had any doubts on the subject, this loss of a brilliant colleague dramatized the fact that our subject matter is much more than a mere academic exercise. Rather, it is at the very heart of powerful interest conflicts and power struggles that churn beneath the surface and, when suddenly erupting into the open, can uproot civilized society.

A civilized approach to these conflicts is to bring them frankly into the open. One might thus look forward to the kind of analysis that would uncover the full diversity of both the mutual and the conflicting interests surrounding the growth of labor supply and surplus labor.

This would involve a frank recognition of multiple impacts. Thus lower wages and higher profits can both promote more employment and, by reducing purchasing power and market demands, undermine longer-term employment and profitability. New technologies of computerization and advanced robotics have the dual impact of creating some jobs and destroying others. Job security can both motivate people to work more productively and, as demonstrated in many socialist countries and capitalist bureaucracies, remove incentives for productive labor and produce hidden unemployment in the form of unemployment on the job.[2] Which outcome is stronger depends on many other variables, including a country's power structure, social policies, managerial practices, and transnational relations. An understanding of these many variables requires a nonideological view of the actual workings of—to use U.N. terminology—"developed market economies," "centrally planned economies," and "developing countries." This, in turn, would be helped by the invention of world economy models dealing directly with labor supply, surplus labor, informal sectors, and transnational movements of labor, capital, and information.

In contrast to such difficult undertakings, more modest steps forward will occur to many readers of this volume. One step would be the inclusion of unemployment problems on the agendas of professional associations. Thus, in the wake of the Bonn conference, Dr. Hans Berglind of the University of Stockholm and Dr. Katherine Briar of the University of Washington organized the International Network on Unemployment and Social Work. This led to the subject's consideration by the International Council on Social Welfare at its 1985 and 1986 conferences in Finland and Japan, respectively, and the council's publication of *The Unemployed: Policies and Services*.[3] Similar steps may be expected by other professional, scientific, or research organizations.

A major contribution to such activities could be made if the United Nations' General Assembly or secretary general would ask each of the specialized agencies to

---

2. "Unemployment on the job," according to Janos Kornai, is one of "the immanent regularities of a socialist economy." Kornai, *Growth, Shortage and Efficiency: A Macrodynamic Model of the Socialist Economy* (Berkeley: University of California Press, 1982). In concentrating on labor redundancy in Eastern Europe, however, Kornai fails to recognize that in capitalist countries stretch-outs on the job—both organized and unorganized—are regular responses to the well-founded fear that working more productively would mean working oneself out of a job.

3. Report from The International Council on Social Welfare, Working Group 9, 13th Regional Symposium on Social Welfare, Turku, Finland, 9-14 June 1985.

face up to the global challenge. The potential role of the International Labor Organization—particularly in working with representatives of both employers and labor—is obvious. But equally important contributions could be made by the U.N. agencies in agriculture, health, education, housing, the environment, industrial development, trade, disarmament, and, above all, the International Monetary Fund and the World Bank. Most of these agencies have ignored problems of unemployment, underemployment, and job insecurity. Some—often unwittingly—have helped make the situation worse. If *National and International Measures for Full Employment,* the 1949 report of a U.N. group of experts, is ever to be updated, it would have to deal with all these areas.

In the meantime, a more immediate task would be an upgrading of data collection and analysis. As documented in this volume, the labor force concept developed decades ago in the United States was never designed for use in either centrally planned economies or developing countries with massive underemployment. The global use of this concept by U.N. agencies is another sad example of resistance to change. Considerable conceptual progress is a necessary precondition of more adequate estimation of the full labor supply, the labor surplus—including the many forms of underemployment in both wage and nonwage sectors—and the social costs and benefits to various societal sectors of failures to move toward fuller employment and more job security. Toward this end, it would seem obvious that a U.N. Group of Experts—with membership from so-called First, Second, and Third World countries—be charged with the task of recommending a staged approach to improved measurements of labor supply, employment, unemployment, underemployment, and job security.

Finally, in preparing its next report on the world social situation, the United Nations' Office for Development Research and Policy Analysis could build on the panoramic analysis of its 1985 report and probe more deeply into the facts and trends on labor supply and surplus labor. Its 1988 report could thus become part of a fortieth-anniversary evaluation of progress and regress under the 1948 Declaration of Human Rights.

BERTRAM GROSS

Introduction: The Global Dimensions of the Employment Issue

By ALFRED PFALLER

ABSTRACT: The resurgence of mass unemployment on a global scale is closely associated with the slowdown of worldwide economic growth to which the labor markets have not yet adjusted. The global character of the problem can be approached under the perspective of increased interdependence of national economies, which might require more coordinated growth policies. On the other hand, lack of coordination appears as less central to those who diagnose the breakdown of the whole postwar syndrome of mutually reinforcing growth-conducive conditions. To reestablish a new growth syndrome might even require restrictions on the trend toward internationalization. Either approach is represented in various shades among the articles in this volume, some of which also focus on the adjustment of national labor markets to the condition of slow worldwide growth. An additional theme brought up in this volume is the importance of political priorities for dealing with the challenge of global unemployment.

Alfred Pfaller studied sociology and economics in Munich, Mannheim, and Pittsburgh, where he received a Ph.D. in 1973. He worked for five years as a research fellow of the West German Friedrich Ebert Foundation in Chile and Ecuador and is currently head of the foundation's Research Group on International Economics and Development Policies in Bonn. His scientific interest focuses on the relationship between international economic dynamics and national societies and on the politics of economic policymaking in the West and the South.

"WORLD out of work" is the suggestive title of a book by Giles Merritt that was published in 1982. Four years later the International Labor Organization specified that 47 million jobs would have to be created in each one of the next forty years if the global work force were to be fully employed. Large-scale underemployment has been common in the less developed part of the world—the South—for a long time. Indeed, it has been considered by many as an essential characteristic of underdevelopment. But the industrialized Western nations have grown accustomed to the view that full employment is the normal state of affairs and that an appropriate kit of policy instruments is available to restitute this state in case of disturbances. It is for the West that the reappearance of mass unemployment in the 1970s and 1980s has been a tremendous shock. Now, after more than ten years of crisis, Western societies seem to have absorbed the shock. But the problem of unemployment is far from being solved. Now that accommodation rather than solution becomes a widespread response, it constitutes more than ever a challenge for policymaking.

From being a problem specific to certain countries, unemployment has turned into a worldwide phenomenon. But we cannot postulate that it is *eo ipso* a problem that requires a global policy approach. Only a thorough analysis could warrant such a conclusion, which deviates somewhat from the widely held view of full employment as the responsibility of national economic policymakers. It is precisely the purpose of the following articles to inquire into the international and transnational dimensions of the challenge of unemployment: the origins of the problem and the constraints it imposes on solutions.

The resurgence of mass unemployment in the West is closely associated with the generally much slower pace of economic growth since the early 1970s. In this short period, there have been considerable lay-offs due to contraction in demand and production. In the longer run, increasing productivity per man-hour has let the demand for labor shrink because the expansion of production has proved insufficient to provide adequate compensation for the productivity effect, as it had done beforehand. In the Third World, with its long-standing problems of underemployment, the crisis of economic growth has destroyed the hopes for a continuous absorption of the labor resources and has actually made the situation deteriorate considerably. To meet the challenge of unemployment, the Western nations may have two broad strategic options: (1) regaining high economic growth rates, and (2) adjusting their labor markets to slow growth by slowing down the growth of average productivity per man-hour and by reducing the supply of man-hours. The Third World has only one chance: rapid growth, even though this by itself does not generate a solution to mass unemployment. In any country, the question of what can be done about unemployment demands answers to the question of what can be done about economic growth. It is the anatomy of the worldwide economic crisis where the inquiry into the transnational dimensions of unemployment must start.

To attribute a global character to the crisis of economic growth and to the ensuing problem of unemployment can imply different notions of the world economy and the place of national economies within it. Generally accepted is the view that economic developments in some countries have effects throughout the world economy and that their reactions in other countries likewise are fed back into the international system. In this way, healthy economies are affected by stagnant tendencies elsewhere, because they are part of a larger world economy. The appropriate analogy would be a crew sitting in a rowboat. Everybody advances more slowly if one member of the crew becomes tired. It may even be that the other members then also drop out because they cannot support the additional strain caused by the first dropout. Of course, in the world economy, interdependence is not symmetrical. Some economies are more dependent than others on the world market and some affect more than others the destiny of the world economy. The notion of dominant economies refers to this symmetry. One can go back once more to our analogy and think of the national economies as crew members of different strength and, therefore, with different impact on the boat's speed. But the analogy does not catch a crucial aspect of asymmetrical economic interdependence. One would have to say that some crew members are sitting more in the common boat than others. What matters is the different ability to generate and maintain national economic growth—leading eventually to national full employment—regardless of economic growth elsewhere. This ability is not just a function of strength and relative weight in the international economy but one of nonintegration into the world economy—in terms of our picture, the availability of one's own little rowboat.

The more we are inclined to consider the world economy, or at least the capitalist world economy, as one integrated system, the less independent growth-generating ability we can attrib-

ute to the single nation-state. The most we can concede, then, to the effectiveness of national growth policies resembles the impact of a strong crew member's determined efforts on the performance of the rest of the crew. The so-called locomotive theory, which has been playing a role in international economic diplomacy in the last decade, argues in this direction, even though the image of an active locomotive and passive railroad cars overstresses the difference between the various countries' potential contributions to global economic growth. But it is quite possible that no single crew member is strong enough to get the common boat moving fast again and that any attempt to do so only ends up exhausting its initiator if the other crew members do not increase their efforts as well. It seems that in this case only a coordinated attempt can be successful.[1]

However, applying this idea to the reacceleration of worldwide economic growth presupposes that a recipe for making the economies move fast again is indeed available, that it is only the ingredient of international coordination or of agreement among national governments that is still missing. Perhaps it is more appropriate to think of the crew members rowing in the global economy boat not in terms of nation-states but in terms of economic sectors: the world automobile industry, the world electronics industry, the world steel industry, various national construction industries, and so forth. Then the question is, Who can do what to make these eco-

1. For a discussion of the locomotive theory, see Kurt W. Rothschild, "The Neglect of Employment in the International Economic Order," this issue of *The Annals* of the American Academy of Political and Social Science.

nomic sectors grow faster again? Who are the ones who must coordinate whose actions? Is it national governments that can meaningfully agree upon something that accelerates permanently the expansion of production in sufficient economic sectors? Agree on what? The answers obviously depend on the nature of the economic growth process in an integrated market system and on the causes of its slowdown, which brings us back to our earlier question.

The notion of global economic integration or interdependence elevates to the international level the problem that otherwise would arise on the national level. The difference is that the distinction between national and external factors becomes rather irrelevant, at least as a starting point. The attempt to locate the origins of the crisis aims primarily at attributes of the global economic system as a whole rather than at attributes of specific countries, even though it does not exclude the latter a priori either. It is similar to a diagnosis of an infectious fever: the search for the causing microbe does not focus on certain parts of the body, such as the left upper arm or the lower jaw.

But, of course, all these preliminary thoughts can only open our eyes to diagnostic possibilities that might escape our attention if we focus too narrowly on the national economy. As Lars Anell emphasizes in his article in this issue of The Annals, our understanding of the worldwide economic crisis is still very limited. We might suspect that it is a virus that affects the international system as a whole rather than certain parts of it. But maybe we have not yet discovered the virus and we are very uncertain about how it works. Before we review briefly the contributions of this volume to the search for the virus of

economic stagnation, a few words are in order on the structure of the ongoing discussion.

The frequently made distinction between explanations that emphasize the insufficiency of demand and others that stress the deficiencies on the supply side of the market economy[2] appears less important to us than another one. There are those who attribute the end of the postwar period of high growth rates and full employment to maladjustments or disturbances that are essentially of an accidental nature and that can be compensated for by appropriate policies. The neglect of inflation since the end of the 1960s, the overshooting policy reactions since the late 1970s, the escapades of the price of oil, and the malcoordination of the international economy since the breakdown of the Bretton Woods system would be such correctable factors. Among the contributions to this Annals volume, the one by Wilhelm Hankel reflects perhaps most clearly this approach. Kurt Rothschild's and Wolfgang Hager's articles contain essential elements of it.

But there are other approaches to explain the crisis that focus on more profound evolutionary changes. Their common paradigm is that of a long-term, cumulative process in the course of which the fundament of favorable conditions on which the long postwar boom rested is eroded. Among these more pessimistic approaches, a sociologically inclined school has gained a certain prominence. It registers a progressive societal sclerosis all over the West that affects the central ingredients

2. On this issue, see Wolfgang Hager, "The Neomercantilist Constraint," this issue of The Annals of the American Academy of Political and Social Science.

of sustained economic growth—namely, entrepreneurial investment initiatives and the steering function of the market. Increased emphasis on economic security, unwillingness to adjust to changing conditions, concern with the distribution—rather than the creation—of wealth are said to be corollary aspects of this sclerosis.[3]

The theme is echoed in part by theories that stress the cyclical nature of long-term growth periods like the period comprising the first two postwar decades. They see at the beginning of such a long-lasting—albeit not completely uninterrupted—prosperous phase a syndrome of favorable social, political, technological, and economic conditions that at first reinforce each other. But they also have their own evolutionary dynamics. So, as time passes, the originally mutually supporting aspects of the syndrome contradict each other more and more. The economic machine, so to speak, runs less and less smoothly and becomes increasingly vulnerable to external disturbances. According to this way of looking at the crisis, which is exemplified by Elmar Altvater's contribution, it is not sufficient to correct one or another imbalance, like excessive wage increases, too stringent monetary targets, or chaotic exchange rate fluctuations. What is needed is rather the formation of a new syndrome of mutually reinforcing favorable conditions. To promote this formation process would then be the true challenge of unemployment.

If our suspicion, mentioned earlier, that we live today in a highly integrated

global economy is true, the desired new dynamic of accumulation can only be a global one. And the new growth-conducive set of conditions could only be established on a global level. The right sort of international economic relations, adjusted to the social and political dynamics of the nation-states, would have to be a vital part of the set.

The notion of a high-growth syndrome implies that it is historically specific, responding to the technological, political, and cultural givens of the historical moment. It is not a question of restoring timeless principles of economic order, like some of the supply-side theoreticians seem to insinuate. For it is precisely the divergent evolution of the various spheres of reality that leads to increasing maladjustment and transforms the growth syndrome into a crisis syndrome. Seen from such a historical perspective, the central intellectual challenge would not be to find the crisis virus that affects the economic organism, but to arrive at an adequate understanding of the new historical situation with its specific constraints and its specific possibilities. It is almost needless to repeat our suspicion, that essential features of this new situation are to be looked for in the international and transnational sphere.

In our short discourse we have used various metaphors that correspond to different steps in the intellectual globalization of the employment problem: interdependence of national growth rates, integrated dynamic of global accumulation, complexity and historical evolution of the conditions of accumulation. This sequence of conceptual steps denotes a possibility rather than a logical necessity. Obviously, not every student of the global employment problem is willing to follow it. But it provides the

3. This aspect is considered in Lars Anell, "The Breakdown of the Postwar Boom," this issue of *The Annals* of the American Academy of Political and Social Science; Manfred Wegner, "Creating New Jobs in the Service Sector," ibid.

editors of this volume with a device to order the various contributions as far as the first part of the challenge is concerned, namely, the recuperation of rapid economic growth.

ARTICLES IN THIS VOLUME

The first two articles in this volume adopt the perspective of an integrated capitalist world economy that is as a whole confronted with growth-reducing circumstances. Lars Anell sees them to some degree as the result of a normalization process that occurred when the reservoir of extraordinarily favorable circumstances that had sustained the long postwar boom was depleted. Emphasizing that this whole process is still not too well understood, he lists a number of factors—mostly demand-side factors—that once had facilitated rapid growth but could not do so forever. As new growth engines need to replace the old, worn-out ones, social rigidities are increasingly felt that may have been building up during the phase of prosperity. Even though Anell makes clear that a lot more could be done about stimulating growth, his main thrust of policy recommendations goes in the direction of making full employment more compatible with the generally slower pace of economic growth.

Elmar Altvater adopts very decidedly the point of view of one integrated capitalist world economy, which is in crisis. Trying to explain the persistence of this crisis, which, according to him, has its origin in the decline of profits, he points to a crucial vicious circle: the tremendous expansion of purely financial investment and debt, initially caused by the dearth of real investment opportunities, continually reinforces the impediments to the recuperation of real invest-

ment and, thus, of economic growth. The network of international financial relations with its structure of vested interests—interests of transnational agents and of national governments—will have to be somehow undone if renewed priority is to be given to growth and employment.

The theme of wrong priorities being embedded in the system of international economic relations is also brought up by Kurt Rothschild. He points out that the extent of worldwide economic interdependence is given inadequate recognition in the rules that govern international economic relations. As a consequence, growth and employment goals are subordinated and often sacrificed to the concern for balanced foreign accounts, because the latter defines an international obligation whereas the former are still—but wrongly—considered a national affair. To use once more our first metaphor, the fellows in the rowboat are very strict about not getting entangled, because—after all—they sit very close to each other; but they forget about moving the common boat forward. Rothschild's obvious solution is: either allow those who want to move faster to use their own private boat or, better, subject the whole crew to the discipline of fast common motion—or at least create a commitment to the advancement of the common boat.

For Rothschild it is the asymmetry of international regulation that impedes effective full-employment policies. Wilhelm Hankel, in turn, emphasizes the deficit of international regulation in the monetary sphere, which for him is responsible for the emergence of the growth-paralyzing debt crisis. In this aspect he agrees with Elmar Altvater, without subscribing, however, to the causal notion of insufficient real profits. For

Hankel the crucial point is that policy instruments that on the national level have proved rather effective in keeping the crisis dynamics, whatever their origin, under control are simply not being used on the global level. The problem is not the disease as such but the fact that the vaccine that is known and available is not applied, because nobody is in charge of doing so. Hankel pleads, in addition, for policies that would increase the employment-generating capacity of the growth rates—albeit limited ones— that can realistically be expected. We shall come back to this part of the issue.

A very different mechanism by which international considerations impede the pursuit of economic growth and full employment is identified by Wolfgang Hager. For him, it is the absolute priority attributed nowadays in most industrialized countries to international competitiveness that proves incompatible with a deliberate stimulation of demand. As Hager points out, the measures adopted by a country to improve its chances in the high-technology race have a strong austerity bias and, in addition, promote the replacement of human labor by sophisticated capital equipment. Only a certain liberation from the dictate of international competitiveness can, according to Hager, restore full employment in the Western countries.

Hager's thesis is theoretically underpinned by Alfred Pfaller, who reconsiders the wealth of nations within a hierarchically structured global economy. A decisive element in his line of reasoning is that the wealth-creating productive apparatus of a nation is not just an outcome of national hard work, saving, investment, innovation, and the like, but also the result of a country's position in the global market. Spatial concentration of the world's productive

potential together with spatial access barriers make for positive and negative income privileges of national populations. Since the national economic interest is closely associated with such privileges, the nation-states are compelled to make considerations of market creation secondary when the privileged market positions are at stake. This is precisely the case with the ongoing technological revolution. It triggers the effect Hager observes and, thus, also brings to an end the whole syndrome of the stability-based and mass-consumption-based postwar boom. Pfaller's analysis also attributes crucial importance to the way the labor surplus of the world's less developed regions becomes incorporated into the global market, potentially threatening—as old access barriers fall—the economic privileges of the industrialized countries' work force.

This whole complex of global surplus labor and its significance for the traditional full-employment regions is the topic of the volume's second section. Hilde Wander analyzes the demographic background of the problem. She makes abundantly clear that "major employment problems are still to come," even if in major parts of the world people's generative behavior should be rapidly adjusted to the conditions of a new demographic equilibrium. At the same time she emphasizes the interconnection of relative economic stagnation and demographic dynamics and pleads for a disruption of the vicious circle by establishing comprehensive patterns of decentralized growth and meaningful personal advancement on the communal level—a program that requires, we would like to add, free space for the development of local production for local needs.

That in reality economic dynamics in less developed countries work almost always in the opposite direction is the message of Guy Standing's contribution. He analyzes various "development strategies" that have been pursued so far and concludes that with the exception of East Asia's rather exclusive export-oriented industrialization they all exacerbate the problem of unemployment. Subjecting the very concept of unemployment to a critical examination, Standing defends his findings against the contradictory view of the World Bank and others.

Peter Gray's contribution, like those of Hartmut Elsenhans and Alfred Pfaller, deals with the way Southern unemployment communicates with the Northern labor markets. Unlike the other two, he focuses on the adjustment problems caused for the industrial countries by the increasing industrial competitiveness of low-wage countries. According to Gray, these problems arise because (1) Southern imports might not right away compensate every Northern trade partner's loss of business and jobs to the new low-wage competitors; (2) those Northern industries that grow in response to increasing Southern demand are less labor-intensive than the ones that shrink due to Southern competition—that is, there is a jump in average Northern productivity that in the absence of corresponding adjustments causes technological unemployment; (3) there are serious supply rigidities that impede the compensating expansion of competitive industries; and (4) part of the labor force simply is not suited for the new growth industries. All these deficiencies in the various markets'—most of all the Northern labor market's—adjustment flexibility can cause considerable unemployment in the short and medium term. But in the long run the problems analyzed by Gray would tend to disappear.

This is not the case with the problem identified by Hartmut Elsenhans. Like Pfaller he points to the danger of an uncompensated net replacement of Northern high-wage by Southern low-wage labor and the concomitant export of Southern mass unemployment to the Northern labor markets. But for him this does not just mean that growth that was once North-bound dissipates to the Southern periphery of the world economy. Elsenhans comes to the conclusion that global economic growth is jeopardized because the worldwide abundance of labor uncouples wages from the development of labor productivity and thus causes a systematic shortage of demand. Accordingly to his analysis, improving the flexibility of adjustment in the North will do nothing to solve the problem. What is needed is to absorb the Southern surplus labor through autonomous accumulation processes in the South and thus to prevent Southern labor abundance from communicating with the Northern labor markets. By sketching out the main lines of the appropriate development strategy—which echoes several of Hilde Wander's proposals—Elsenhans also suggests an answer to the question raised by Standing's account of strategy failures.

Elsenhans's basic idea of restoring autonomous accumulation processes on a less than global level is also central to the somewhat different problems addressed by Hager and in part by Pfaller. This idea is linked—albeit in different ways—to another central idea: to put politics in control of markets again. For Hager it is most clearly a matter of keeping the economic dynamic within the reach of enforceable political priorities—that is, in the reach of the nation-state—and of curbing correspondingly the process of globalization. Gray recommends, more hesitatingly, a shock-absorbing national resistance to a process that in essence should—and could—not be stopped. Rothschild and Hankel—and less clearly, also Alvater—go in the other direction; they plead for extending the reach of politics beyond the nation-state into the global sphere and for thus imposing the socially desirable priorities again on the internationalized economy. For Pfaller it would not only be the control of politics over markets that matters but also the adjustment of the nationally fractured political dynamics of priority setting to the new supranational common interest as it is being defined by the increasing transnationalization of the economy; that is, the economic policy would have to be denationalized, too.

Not all the contributions to this volume treat higher economic growth rates as a precondition for full employment and discuss ways of restoring this precondition. Several authors address the question of how the creation of employment can be adjusted to the context of generally slower growth. Since this perspective takes the demand function for labor by and large as given, it must focus on the supply side of the labor market. The problem returns, thus, to the national or even more local level. The two basic approaches are to (1) make labor cheaper to potential employers, and (2) reduce the supply of labor.

The first one is elaborated by Wilhelm Hankel and by Manfred Wegner. Lars Anell also emphasizes its importance. Wegner attributes the creation of a great number of new jobs in the American service sector during a period of rather moderate economic growth predominantly to the flexibility in the labor-supply conditions, including wages, working hours, length of employment contracts, and others. Whereas this approach burdens the costs of adjustment on the job seekers, Hankel and Anell favor changes in tax regimes that increase labor's competitiveness vis-à-vis capital without reducing the worker's real income. In addition, Hankel would relieve restrictions that declare certain forms of work as illegal.

Both Hankel's and Wegner's approaches amount to keeping average labor productivity within the limits set by economic growth. In part, this means renouncing possible benefits of labor-saving technical progress, which is not the case in the approach recommended by Louis Emmerij. He presents a most comprehensive scheme of bringing the demand for jobs in line with their supply. In Emmerij's own words, it "amounts to profound changes in the social and cultural domains of society with a view to achieving a better balance between remunerative work and other aspects of human life." Central ideas are a more flexible sequence of periods devoted to working, leisure, and education during a person's lifetime and the uncoupling of income flow and traditionally defined work. It should be noted, however, that such national schemes of reducing the supply of job-seeking labor presuppose that the problem of industrial relocation to labor-abundant countries is somehow under control.

The policy proposals presented by Emmerij, Hankel, Wegner, Elsenhans, and, less elaborately, by others can all be discussed as to their respective merits and flaws on a technocratic level: would they indeed have the effect attributed to them by their advocates? At what costs? The second question implies that the challenge is not only an intellectual one of finding out causes and devising remedies, but that choices might have to be made in favor of employment at the expense of other goals. To meet the challenge of unemployment means both to find solutions and to impose them. As we mentioned earlier, imposing solutions can in part be a matter of extending the reach of politics into the economic sphere. But it is more than that. It requires the political will to take the necessary steps and it requires that those who want to take them can overcome the resistance of those who do not want to bear the costs.

In a way, the central message of Rothschild's contribution—echoed also in Hankel's article—is that the concern for employment has been absent in the regulation of international economic relations. Thus the decisive step toward a solution would be that governments introduce full employment as a priority consideration into international economic relations and reshape the rules accordingly.

That much can be done, regardless of worldwide economic difficulties, for full employment in each industrialized country if political priority is given to it is shown by Manfred Schmidt. His comparison of 15 countries of the Organization for Economic Cooperation and Development shows significant differences in unemployment that can only be explained by differences in political aspects. His conclusion—simplified here—is that those countries where political processes produced a "willingness to pursue a policy of real full employment" also achieved their goal. Rather than a matter of economic growth, it becomes one of distributing the costs of economic adversity.

This provides the background for the final article, by Bertram Gross, which deals with the problem of how to make full employment an effective political priority on a worldwide scale. Echoing a central theme of Standing's article, Gross maintains that the prevailing response to mass unemployment is to play it down and to define it away to the point where so-called natural—and hence somehow not problematic—unemployment in reality means the maximum rate of unemployment that is politically tolerable. Gainful employment would have to be considered an inalienable right of every adult person, if adequate and imaginative means—see Emmerij's article!—were to be devised to deal with economic adversity rather than blaming it for its supposedly unavoidable social costs. It would be essential to revitalize in the United Nations the commitment to this basic right in order to bring about a global response to the challenge of unemployment.

ANNALS, *AAPSS*, **492**, July 1987

The Breakdown of the Postwar Boom

By LARS ANELL

ABSTRACT: Mass unemployment has returned to Europe, and we know precious little about its causes and effective remedies. There is, however, a clear connection with the breakdown of the postwar boom. In the 1970s a long period of rapid stable growth abruptly gave way to sluggish, unstable growth and financial insecurity. The general consensus among economists is that classical unemployment increased rapidly during the 1970s. There are, however, manifest problems on the demand side. The international economic system is intrinsically geared toward contraction. The classical remedy—that is, lower real wages—could work in theory. In practice, it is too painful and wasteful to be politically feasible. The obvious measures are lower payroll taxes and social service charges in order to reduce labor costs without reducing wages; internationally coordinated demand management; and more employment-focused priorities.

Lars Anell graduated from the Stockholm School of Economics and from the University of Stockholm in 1966 and joined the Treasury. During most of the 1970s he was head of the department for planning and research in the Foreign Office. In 1978-79 he was a research fellow with the Secretariat for Future Studies before becoming director general of the Swedish Agency for Research Cooperation and Developing Countries. In 1983 he joined the Prime Minister's Office and was appointed Swedish ambassador to the United Nations Organization in Geneva in 1986.

TWO things are really striking about the present unemployment in Western Europe. The first is that so many countries have slipped into mass unemployment without serious political—or even electoral—consequences. The second is the inadequacy of our knowledge of causes and remedies. The only real improvement as compared with the interwar years is that we are now more concerned about unemployment, and professional economists devote a lot of effort to both empirical and theoretical research.[1]

In view of this state of affairs, we must be modest about what can be achieved in a brief article. Thus there will be no attempt here to present an outline of a theory to explain high unemployment. The approach will be much more pedestrian. We will try to indicate some factors that obviously contribute to increased unemployment. The aim is to point out a selected number of policy measures that should promote employment in the long run. We shall not argue that these measures together are sufficient to achieve full employment, but simply that they will promote a shift in the right direction. And that is better than to accept high unemployment and shut one's eyes to even the most obvious causes.

THREE TYPES OF UNEMPLOYMENT

In accordance with what is now almost common practice we shall distinguish between classical, Keynesian, and frictional unemployment.

Classical unemployment is caused by wages that are too high. Firms refrain from hiring available labor since the additional costs thus generated will exceed the extra revenue. It is usually asserted that this type of unemployment is voluntary in the sense that the unemployed choose to be so instead of offering their services at a lower price. The assumption behind this notion is that everybody could be gainfully employed if only they were ready to accept the wage rate that would clear the market. Thus another way of explaining classical unemployment is to say that some people prefer leisure to the wages actually offered.

In this classical world there are very strong forces at work to maintain full employment equilibrium and market clearing. The process that is supposed to reestablish full employment could proceed something like this. An excess supply of labor exerts a downward pressure on wages. Since wages constitute costs—as a matter of fact, the overwhelming part of variable costs in the short run—there will also be a fall in prices for goods and services in a competitive economy. However, the fall in the price level will be less than proportionate to the reduction of the wage level. Now the real value of money has increased and the rate of interest will fall. Investments will increase and cause a higher demand for labor. It is worth noting that Keynesian economists would not necessarily object to this on theoretical grounds, but they would rule it out as a practical possibility. Nominal wages

---

1. According to Mark Blaug, "The striking characteristic of British economics in the 1920's was the lack of concern over unemployment and the failure to realize its extent." Blaug, *Economic Theory in Retrospect* (Homewood, IL: Richard D. Irwin, 1968), p. 661. Guy Routh points out that very few articles about employment were published in academic journals in the thirties. Routh,

The Origin of Economic Ideas (New York: Vintage Books, 1977), pp. 266-67.

TABLE 1

NUMBERS OF UNEMPLOYED PERSONS IN THE ORGANIZATION FOR ECONOMIC
COOPERATION AND DEVELOPMENT (OECD) AREA (Thousands)

	1970	1975	1980	1982	1983
Australia	91	302	402	486	693
Austria	42	53	58	115	135
Belgium	69	168	311	465	514*
Canada	476	690	867	1,314	1,448
Denmark	17	121	164	290	312*
Finland	41	51	114	149	156
France	510	902	1,452	1,863	1,864
Germany	149	1,074	889	1,833	2,258
Greece	138	99	132	215	290*
Iceland	1	0	0	1	1
Ireland	65	73	76	137	180
Italy	1,111	1,230	1,698	2,068	2,278
Japan	590	1,000	1,140	1,360	1,560
Luxembourg	0	0	1	2	2
Netherlands†	45	260	326	655	801*
New Zealand	1	3	29	52	76*
Norway	12	40	33	52	67
Portugal	—	222	330	316	388*
Spain	329	581	1,638	2,260	2,461
Sweden	59	67	86	137	151
Switzerland	0	10	6	13	26
Turkey‡	1,792	2,120	2,651	3,279	3,634*
United Kingdom	555	838	1,513	2,770	2,984
United States	4,093	7,929	7,637	10,678	10,717
North America	4,569	8,619	8,502	11,992	12,165
OECD Europe	4,931	7,910	11,478	16,620*	18,502*
Total OECD	10,186	17,834	21,553	30,510*	32,996*

SOURCE: Organization for Economic Cooperation and Development, Paris. Reprinted from the
OECD Observer, no. 130 (Sept. 1984).

*Secretariat estimates.

†Data from 1975 onward are not consistent with those of earlier years.

‡Including estimates for unemployment in agriculture.

are too rigid to fall even if there is an excess supply, and investors are normally too unresponsive to small changes in the rate of interest in a depression.[2]

Another classical possibility, which would work even with sticky wages, is to assume that when demand falls in the commodity market, money is diverted

2. Keynes did not rule out the possibility of reducing nominal wages, but he did not believe that flexible wages would be "capable of maintaining a state of continuous full employment." J. M. Keynes, *The General Theory of Employment, Interest and Money* (New York: Harcourt, Brace & World, 1936), p. 267. It is worth pointing out here that it is logically possible to believe that

market forces unaided by any "visible hand" would eventually bring back full employment equilibrium but still opt for government intervention because the automatic adjustment process, when it takes place in the real world, is too wasteful and painful. See, for instance, Don Patinkin, *Money, Interest and Prices*, 2nd ed. (New York: Harper & Row, 1965), pp. 339-40.

to the bond market, thereby bringing down the rate of interest. And again investors will see the silver lining.

Keynes, however, refuted emphatically the whole idea that the free-market economy on its own could be relied upon to provide full employment. Even if the government pursued an active monetary policy, interest inelasticity and expectations effects would prevent automatic market forces from reestablishing a full employment equilibrium. Interest, in Keynes's basic view, would not come down and provide incentives strong enough to start an investment boom. And even if this could happen, as a result of the so-called real-balance effect, it would be of interest only "in our *theoretical* analysis; it is too weak, and in some cases (due to adverse expectations) too perverse, to fulfill a significant role in our policy considerations."[3]

Keynesian unemployment is mainly due to lack of aggregate demand that is caused by the unwillingness of the investors to use all available resources.[4] In the closed economy analyzed by Keynes, the situation is stable as long as the income level and the future expectations of investors are given. In the real world of small, open, free-trading nations, one could, of course, imagine that external shocks could set in motion a process toward full employment. But it is just as likely that outside forces would aggravate the situation.

3. Don Patinkin, quoted in Blaug, *Economic Theory in Retrospect*, p. 652.

4. There is a lot of disagreement about what actually caused an unemployment equilibrium in Keynes's theory. See Blaug, *Economic Theory in Retrospect*, pp. 646 ff. There is, however, no doubt that the expectations of investors formed a crucial part of his theory. "The weakness of the inducement to invest has been at all times the key to the economic problem." Keynes, *General Theory*, p. 348.

Frictional unemployment will always exist in an economy where structural adjustment is taking place and where consumer preferences are changing. The magnitude should be dependent on a number of economic, social, and cultural factors such as the level of unemployment benefits, work ethic, mobility of the labor force, post-material values, and skill differentials between the jobs being phased out and the new ones created.

THE BREAKDOWN OF THE POSTWAR BOOM

In historical perspective the period from the late 1940s until the first oil crisis, in 1973-74, will be regarded as one long, uninterrupted boom in the industrialized countries.[5] Total production grew at an unprecedented rate and the expansion was extraordinarily steady. If one looks at individual countries, there are a few examples of radical shifts from one year to another. The overall picture, however, was characterized by an even and steady expansion with mild undulations around a stable long-term trend. This was particularly true for the European countries of the Organization for Economic Cooperation and Development (OECD) and above all during a period from the end of the fifties till the early seventies.

Also, international trade expanded at a rapid, stable rate. The volume of world export grew by around 8 percent annually between 1955 and 1973. The stability was further emphasized by the system

5. This section relies heavily on Lars Anell, *Recession, the Western Countries and the Changing World Order* (London: Frances Pinter, 1981). Cf. also Lars Anell and Birgitta Nygren, *The Developing Countries and the World Economic Order* (London: Frances Pinter, 1980).

TABLE 2
ECONOMIC DEVELOPMENT IN OECD COUNTRIES, 1950-82
(Annual Percentage Change)

	1950-73	1974-82
Gross domestic product	5	2
Exports	9	4
Inflation	3	9

of fixed exchange rates and the insignificant rate of inflation.

Expansion and stability were mutually reinforcing. A steady, easily predicted increase of real resources made it easy to solve distributional problems and maintain a consensus about the social order. Business was good and the welfare state was gradually being established. New employment was created at the same pace at which old jobs were phased out. This secure business environment, where the future could be described by extrapolating existing trends, was extremely conducive to long-term investments. My proposition is that this beneficent circle was sustained by a unique combination of economic and political factors. They have all been considerably weakened or even reversed.

Strong demand in Western Europe was sustained, first, by the reconstruction program after the war and then by the consumer society. A vast range of goods previously reserved for the privileged few became available to lower-middle- and working-class people mainly due to industrial mass production. Residential building expanded to meet the need for reconstruction and higher housing standards. An increased flow of consumer capital goods turned the homes into small factories. This was also the period when the tremendous expansion of motoring transformed physical infrastructure as well as lifestyles in Western Europe. During the period 1953-65 the number of cars quad-

rupled in Belgium, Sweden, and France. Car ownership among the Dutch multiplied sixfold, that of the Germans eightfold, and in Italy the number of private cars multiplied ninefold.

Since the late 1960s—that is, well before the first oil crisis—it has been evident that demand for housing, cars, and traditional consumer capital goods has slackened and in some cases decreased.

Second, there were a number of reasons why production could keep pace quite easily with the rapidly increasing demand in this period. Modest investments to remove bottlenecks and mend missing links in war-damaged infrastructure and production systems paid off very well. European industry was able to copy the superior technology already developed and tested on the other side of the Atlantic. Millions of people were easily persuaded to leave low productivity in agriculture for higher productivity and better pay in expanding industry. Something like 10 million people made this change in Western Europe between 1963 and 1973.

This structural transformation of the economies and rationalization of industry was greatly facilitated by the fact that full employment was almost taken for granted. New jobs were continuously created to replace those that disappeared.

In all these respects significant changes have taken place. For one thing, the gains from the agriculture-to-industry switch have been exhausted and, in fact, reversed. Now industrial employment is decreasing, relatively, everywhere and in some cases also absolutely, while the low-productivity service sector is increasing together with do-it-yourself-work of very low productivity. Also, the simple source of technological improvement—to copy an existing technologically superior economy—has largely dried up. The technological gap between American and European industry has been closed. Finally, the climate for industrial restructuring and economic adjustment has worsened. Unions and people are not ready to see old jobs phased out when the new ones are not in sight.

Third, the long postwar boom took place within the commonly accepted paradigm of Keynesian macroeconomic policies. This is neither to say that the stable expansion was caused by a sophisticated set of policies nor that the theory was necessarily right. Unlike Keynes, I do not believe we are all victims of some defunct theory. The driving forces behind the postwar boom were in fact strong enough to withstand any theory. The important point was that governments until the late sixties believed that they had the instruments to cope with inflation and unemployment and that almost all Western European governments used the same frame of reference to analyze common problems. This greatly facilitated international cooperation.

Fourth, the welfare state in Western Europe was created in the first two postwar decades. The major reasons were the increased strength of organized labor and the greatly strengthened influence of egalitarian values. Keynesianism also helped to pave the way in the sense that it gave scientific legitimacy for a more active role for the government. On average, government final consumption expenditure in European OECD countries increased from 13.5 percent of gross domestic product in 1960 to 18 percent in 1975. Total government outlays increased even more, from 31 percent in 1960 to 44 percent in 1975. No doubt this development of the welfare state helped to sustain demand and full employment during the period concerned.

As a consequence of recession and instability in the seventies, most Western European governments tried to curb public sector growth. The others were faced with huge financial deficits. It is quite clear that the public sector, as a share of gross domestic product, will not continue to increase at the same pace as in the fifties and sixties. Only on the basis of a strong, stable expansion of the whole economy will it be possible to continue to develop the welfare state.

A fifth and final important aspect of this unique period was that the world economy was managed from one central institution, the administration in Washington. The international economic order that was established was an American blueprint that had been drafted already, during the war. The United States became the world's banker, supplying credits and loans to war-torn Europe, and the monetary system was more an extension of the Federal Reserve than a creature of the International Monetary Fund.

But this old order is now crumbling. The United States is no longer able—perhaps not even willing—to play a predominant role. The world is multilateral—and much more difficult to manage.

The crisis during the 1970s can be interpreted both as a cyclical and as a structural phenomenon. My own understanding is roughly this. The sudden oil shock coincided with and intensified a number of structural problems that had long been on their way to the surface.

Structural adjustment always hurts— and those that are most affected are seldom reasonably compensated even if the whole economy benefits in the end. Thus there is always some resistance to structural change. During the prolonged and stable boom, governments were provided with ample resources to subsidize away any potential resistance to reorganization. The regional policies that emerged during the 1960s were both an expression of new values and a new name for government subsidies to ailing industries. In most OECD countries, state subsidies, as a share of gross domestic product, increased from the middle of the 1960s. Mobility in the labor market decreased for both demand and supply reasons. These tendencies—which undermined the expansive forces and diminished the automatic adjustment capacity of the economies—slowly increased in strength throughout the sixties.

At the same time, demand gradually fell off for a range of important consumer capital goods. This did not only mean that the demand pressure in general was subdued. Of equal importance was that it created a growing uncertainty as to what products would be demanded in the future. On the productivity side, the simple and easy methods had been exhausted. There was no longer a superior North American industry to copy. Instead the OECD countries were threatened from behind by a number of new industrial countries in Asia and Latin America. The gains derived from people moving out of agriculture into industry were reversed.

As early as the end of the 1960s a gap arose between potential and actual output. Not even during the intensive and synchronized boom that preceded the first oil crisis was this gap closed. Part of the productive capacity that was kept

alive with state subsidies was redundant even during the peak of the business cycle.

We can thus see that the economic order—both national and international— was already under severe stress when the first oil crisis occurred in 1973-74. The principal effect was to make at once visible and acute all the structural problems that could no longer be kept back. For instance, after the quadrupling of the oil price in 1973, as much as a quarter of the world's tanker and bulk tonnage became redundant overnight. The already ailing shipping industry was further weakened. Shipyards were entirely deprived of new orders and reduced their purchases of steel; thus the effects were extended to the mining industry.

In a wider sense, the oil crisis generated, throughout the industrialized world, an uncertainty that indirectly affected every single major investment decision. The old beneficent circle, forged by equal portions of growth and stability, turned into its opposite. Since 1973 the growth rate in Western Europe has been more than halved, and there is a genuine uncertainty even about the short-term future.

THE GROWTH OF UNEMPLOYMENT

The most troublesome legacy of the crisis during the 1970s is an extensive unemployment. The slump of 1974-75 caused the number of unemployed people in the OECD countries to rise from 8-9 million to over 15 million people. At the beginning of 1977, the International Monetary Fund estimated that 16.3 million people—about 5.5 percent of the labor force—were out of work in the industrialized world. By 1980 the rate of unemployment had increased to 6.0 percent. Now the total number of unemployed amounts to 33 million in OECD countries, of which 18.5 million are out of work in European OECD countries.

Many of the unemployed, those with little or no education or previous work experience, seem to be permanently rejected or shut out from the labor market. In at least eight OECD countries—Australia, Belgium, France, the Federal Republic of Germany (FRG), Ireland, the Netherlands, Spain, and the United Kingdom—more than half of those unemployed in 1983 had been out of work for more than 6 months. In six countries—Belgium, France, Ireland, the Netherlands, Spain, and the United Kingdom—roughly one-third or more had been unemployed for 12 months or more.

Unfortunately, it is not possible to be very precise about what kind of unemployment has increased most. The prevailing view seems to be that the substantial increase of unemployment in the 1970s was largely classical, that is, resulting from real wages above the full employment equilibrium. Jeffrey Sachs has pointed out that "real wages in the late 1960s grew faster than productivity"[6] and "the slowdown in the 1970's was preceded by a dramatic rise in real wages and a shift in income distribution toward labor in most large economies."[7] M. Allais asserts that classical unemployment started to emerge in France in the late 1960s after having been negative during the earlier postwar period. Now classical unemployment in France, according to Allais, is of the same magnitude as its Keynesian counterpart.[8]

I have no data to question the con-

sensus on the importance of classical unemployment. Some comments are in order, however. It seems quite clear that the lack of internationally coordinated demand management has aggravated the situation. Immediately after the first oil shock, which represented an externally imposed value-added tax of about 2 percent, some major OECD countries shifted their whole attention to inflation. Many other governments tried to pursue more expansionary policies to sustain employment. This latter policy was, however, doomed from the start when their major international competitors and export markets contracted their economies. The distribution of the oil deficit was extremely uneven. In 1975 the United States and the FRG had a combined surplus of their current accounts of about $22.5 billion while Japan and France were in balance. The rest of the OECD countries showed a total deficit of about $40 billion. Aggregate demand fell both because some countries chose to pursue contractional policies and because the lack of international coordination forced also the so-called progressives into line when they were unable to finance their internal and external deficits. Overall, the volume of industrial output in the OECD countries diminished by 10 percent from July 1974 to April 1975 and the volume of intra-OECD trade fell by 13 percent.

As a consequence of these developments, we now have a strong built-in bias toward contraction in the world economy. In all finance ministries and trade union headquarters there are vivid memories of double-digit inflation. All countries have realized that demand stimulus in isolation is a no-win strategy not feasible even in a country like France.

Another Keynesian aspect of the present problems is that increased uncer-

---

6. Jeffrey Sachs, "Wages, Profits and Macroeconomic Adjustment: A Comparative Study," *Brookings Papers on Economic Activity*, 2:269 (1979).

7. Ibid., p. 311.

8. M. Allais, *Rapport d'activité scientifique* (Paris: Centre d'analyse économique, 1978; 1980).

TABLE 3
LONG-TERM UNEMPLOYMENT IN SELECTED OECD COUNTRIES
(As Percentage of Total Unemployment)

	1979		1981		1983	
	6 months and over	12 months and over	6 months and over	12 months and over	6 months and over	12 months and over
Australia	38.0	18.1	39.0	21.1	52.8	27.6
Austria	19.4	8.6	16.1	6.5	25.8	9.0
Belgium	74.9	58.0	72.5	52.4	77.9	62.8
Canada	15.6	3.5	16.1	4.2	28.0	9.5
Finland	41.5	19.3	34.8	12.5	38.3	14.6
France	55.1	30.3	55.8	32.5	67.3	42.6
Germany	39.9	19.9	38.1	16.2	54.1	28.5
Ireland	47.9	31.8	48.9	30.5	50.9	31.0
Japan	38.1	17.2	30.3	13.4	n.a.*	n.a.
Netherlands	49.3	27.1	48.7	22.0	69.6	43.7
Norway	7.9	3.0	15.0	3.0	17.9	7.0
Spain	51.6	27.5	66.8	43.6	71.3	53.8
Sweden	19.6	6.8	18.0	6.0	24.9	10.1
United Kingdom	39.7	24.5	45.7	21.6	57.8	36.2
United States	8.8	4.2	14.0	6.6	23.9	13.3

SOURCE: Organization for Economic Cooperation and Development. Reprinted from the OECD Observer, no. 130 (Sept. 1984).
NOTE: Measures of long-term unemployment are particularly uncertain, and international comparisons are difficult since the type of sources used varies from country to country. Data for Australia, Canada, France, Japan, Norway, Spain, Sweden, and the United States are from household surveys while data for the remaining countries are based on registration records maintained by employment offices. In the case of France, Norway, and Spain, persons for whom no duration of unemployment was specified are excluded from total unemployment. Measurement is at different times of year in different countries.
*n.a. = not available.

tainty about the future has dulled the animal spirits. The first oil crisis had a severe and negative impact on the expectations of investors. In general, companies have shortened their horizons and opted for rationalization of existing plants and processes instead of creating new capacity.

It is also important to note that even if the problem is classical, it does not prescribe lower real wages as the major or only remedy. Demand expansion will also affect classical unemployment. The final result depends on how wages, prices, productivity trends, expectations, and animal spirits respond to a demand

stimulus.[9] As already pointed out, it is evident that such factors as economic and political instability—in particular, the uncertainty surrounding exchange rates and energy prices—rigidities on the supply side, and a built-in bias toward contraction are increasingly important. An international economic environment more conducive to long-term growth and stability would affect also a classical problem. It seems clear,

9. It is enough to recall that a higher level of aggregate demand may cause inflation. This was, of course, the only realistic way Keynes could imagine to lower real wages quickly. Today, however, increased inflation is hardly a proper solution to our employment problem.

for instance, as Sachs has pointed out in a later study, that the jump in unemployment after the second oil crisis was caused by unnecessarily tight monetary policies. Thus it is not improbable that classical unemployment in the 1970s, caused by a profit squeeze and too high real wages, was aggravated in the 1980s by contractional economic policies.[10]

There may be important differences between various markets. This is quite clear in the case of demand for labor from firms and households. Labor costs for the firm are tax deductible. Possibilities to reduce labor costs by increasing productivity are often adequate in industry. Households purchasing services for car repair, house maintenance, and entertainment pay with their after-tax income. Thus both increased nominal wages and higher taxes, including payroll taxes and social security charges, increase the cost of services. Furthermore, productivity in this field has been lagging. The cost of one hour's service work paid with an individual's income after taxes is probably the most significant relative change of prices in the welfare states. It is evident that expenditure for this type of service is declining as a share of household budgets.[11] Instead people are buying consumer capital goods and do-it-yourself equipment to perform services for themselves.

Finally it should be remembered that Keynesian policies are based on two crucial assumptions. First, there should be a general underutilization of capacity as distinct from productive resources that are redundant for structural rea-sons. Second, the supply side of the economy must have a reasonable flexibility. There must be a capacity for automatic adjustment, and the labor force must be willing to accept structural transformation and mobility. In these respects the economies in Western Europe have become more rigid partly as a result of deliberate choice and partly because of protective measures. Whether the extra unemployment caused by institutional rigidities should be called Keynesian, classical, or frictional unemployment is a moot question.

Frictional unemployment has certainly increased, and sometimes for very good reasons. Unemployment benefits have reached a level that makes it financially possible to extend the search period. There are a wide range of opportunities for education and vocational training as alternatives to employment. The mobility in the labor market has decreased mainly as a result of the fact that more and more families own their own dwellings and have two breadwinners. The financial incentives to move have decreased in value in relation to the social and economic costs of doing it. In some countries pension schemes decrease labor market mobility.

A more important and serious reason for increased frictional unemployment is that the gap between skill requirements for the disappearing jobs and those for the new ones created may have widened a great deal. People who left agriculture in the fifties or the textile industry in the sixties for the manufacturing and engineering industry could, after some on-the-job training, master the skills required. Today there is a considerable gap between the training and experience of the unemployed and the requirements for the attractive positions in the information-processing indus-

10. Jeffrey Sachs, "Real Wages and Unemployment in the OECD Countries," *Brookings Papers on Economic Activity,* vol. 1 (1983).

11. Jonathan Gershuny, *After Industrial Society: The Emerging Self-Service Economy* (London: Macmillan, 1978).

try.[12] Fewer of the unemployed can master the new skills required, and those who can need longer training to do so.

SOME OBVIOUS AND SOME NOT SO OBVIOUS MEASURES

It is sometimes asserted that Keynes said, or even proved, that employment would not increase even if real wages fell. The reason was that wages constitute income that is the basis for aggregate demand, which has a decisive influence on national income. Thus lower wages would mean lower aggregate demand and a new equilibrium below full-capacity utilization.

This could, however, only be true if wages and all other prices fell by exactly the same proportion. Then the relation between labor costs and all other costs would be unchanged and investors would have no extra inducement to hire more people. However, wages are only part of the production costs even in the short run, and due to inertia even this partial effect would need time to work its way through the system. Furthermore, many OECD countries sell 20 to 30 percent of their total production abroad to consumers that are totally unaffected by a domestic wage cut. In this sense, a reduction of nominal wages is equivalent to a devaluation but without the inflationary effect caused by a lower exchange rate.

Thus the argument against a reduction of wages or wider wage differentials cannot simply be that it does not work. To some extent it would work, in particular in the long run. My own counter-

argument is that we would not like the kind of society that would emerge—or, rather, reemerge—if the floor of the wage structure was considerably lowered and a significant minority were forced to live at subsistence levels. Once again the old class society would be visible because, as all evidence indicates, a reduction of wages would have to be drastic in order to produce a significant employment effect.[13] It is also evident that even if wages and prices were fairly flexible, the natural dynamic process of the classical economy would need considerable time to move the system back to full employment equilibrium. There are important lags that can hardly be removed, as Patinkin has pointed out. "They are the rigidities of sovereign consumers and investors unwilling to modify their expenditure habits on short notice."[14]

A much more sensible approach would be to lower labor costs without reducing wage levels. This can, of course, be achieved if payroll taxes and other social security charges were reduced by shifting the tax burden to, for instance, corporate wealth, energy consumption, raw materials, foreign trade, and commodity production. A reduction of the payroll tax would have a full immediate effect on labor costs while aggregate demand would be unaffected. The shift of the tax burden would help to make capital relatively more expensive in relation to labor. On the whole, all OECD countries have pursued economic policies that have made labor more and more expensive and capital cheaper and cheaper. This may have been sensible during the prolonged boom, when full

12. Christopher Freeman, "Capital Shortage, Technology and Unemployment" (Paper delivered at the seminar "Technical Change and Employment," Alborg Institute of Production, Alborg, Denmark, 27-28 Apr. 1984).

13. Blaug, *Economic Theory in Retrospect*, p. 651.
14. Patinkin, *Money, Interest and Prices*, p. 342.

employment was taken for granted. With 33 million people out of work, it is long overdue to reconsider that strategy.

After all, there is a very simple and universally valid rule saying that if you want less of something, tax it, and if you want more of it, subsidize it. At present, nothing is taxed as heavily as personal income flows and wages—and the result is that the whole system is geared to reduce labor input.

The labor force has become less mobile for several reasons. To some extent it may be a result of deliberate decisions. Many people see a trade-off between material gains in the cities and a better quality of life in smaller communities. One problem is, however, that even the financial scales have been tilted against mobility. Wage rates and all government-financed benefits are more or less the same all over the country. But a lot of things are substantially less expensive in the countryside. Thus the cost of housing is radically different between larger towns and cities on the one hand and smaller communities on the other. There are also considerable opportunities outside the urban conglomerations to take advantage of the informal sector and avoid forced consumption of services. Thus at the same time that people have become more and more tied to the place where they have settled down, the material incentives to move have weakened. To put it another way, those who would be willing to move do not receive rewards in proportion to the services they render to society.

Another type of rigidity is caused by the increasing role played by small interest organizations, more and more concerned about the benefits they can extract exclusively for their own members and less and less troubled by the effects on the community as a whole. Many of these organizations—and they are both producer associations and trade unions—have obtained monopoly rights to perform a certain function that sometimes give them undue influence on public decisions. Above all, they will have a very strong position to prevent changes.[15] The French truck owners' strike early in 1984, which held a whole nation at ransom, comes to mind. Another effect of this kind of institutional rigidity is almost certainly that the rate of inflation increases.

Thus improved rewards for those who are willing to move and determined efforts to reduce institutional rigidities will have two effects; they will release the inherent growth potential and help contain inflation.

Education and vocational training in order to meet the demand in the new labor market are among the obvious measures. The overwhelming majority of those who have been out of work for a long period have very poor education and limited or no work experience. Programs that make it compulsory to hire young people for certain periods in order to give them experience of working life may well give handsome social returns. Furthermore, it seems possible to define broadly the kinds of skills that need to be upgraded. According to Freeman,

A new technological paradigm began to emerge in the 1960's and to penetrate most industries and services in the 1970's. This paradigm is based on a combination of microelectronics, computerization (microprocessors in the 1970's), tele-communica-

15. Mancur Olson, *The Rise and Decline of Nations: Economic Growth, Stagflation and Social Rigidities* (New Haven, CT: Yale University Press, 1982); Samuel Beer, *Britain against Itself: The Political Contradictions of Collectivism* (London: Faber and Faber, 1982).

tions technology and information technology and may be loosely described as the information revolution.[16]

Another way to help young people enter the labor market is to make the provisions for early retirement more attractive. Many people would like to shorten their working life if only they could afford it. All evidence suggests that increased retirement from the labor market has much more significant employment effects than shorter working weeks. And the economic calculus may be quite feasible when savings in the form of reduced expenditure for employment benefits are deducted from increased outlays for pensions.

It is often asserted that the crises of the 1970s also meant the final demise of Keynesian economics. However, it is a bit difficult to judge whether stagflation was caused by overly ambitious Keynesian policies or by structural and institutional rigidities and governments that could cope with strong interest organizations only by letting inflation scale down their excessive claims. Another problem is that the Keynesian strategy assumed a closed economy. But the long and stable postwar boom meant, among other things, that the world economy rapidly became more integrated. In particular, trade in manufactured goods and capital flows between OECD countries increased rapidly. This meant that demand management policies became increasingly interdependent. Expansionary policies in one country would weaken its competitive position vis-à-vis countries that undertook contractional measures. Countries trying to achieve full employment through old-fashioned Keynesian policies were thus likely to be

faced with external deficits that would force them to abandon their ambitious aim.

The solution that has been proposed is global demand management[17]—an effort to coordinate economic policies in at least the major industrial countries. The problem is, of course, to achieve a recovery and increased employment without increased inflation. One of many prerequisites for global Keynesianism seems, therefore, to be that all participating countries succeed in bringing inflation firmly under control.

A final measure in order once again to achieve full employment would be to reorganize political priorities. Unfortunately, there are perfectly simple reasons why mass unemployment has reappeared without causing major social unrest. Most of the unemployed people belong to politically weak, marginal groups like immigrants, women, young people with no previous work experience, and people with low skills and little education. Fritz W. Scharpf gives the following description of the situation in the FRG:

In all modern societies, the relative size of groups entirely outside of the labor market or in highly secure jobs is increasing. In West Germany, for instance, even after ten years of mass unemployment, about two thirds of all wage earners have never been personally affected by unemployment at all. And, paradoxically, the fear of unemployment may lose its political salience as the economic crisis continues, because those who have not yet lost their jobs will have powerful psychological motives to develop explanations and justifications for their immunity. Thus, unemployment is for the great majority of

16. Freeman, "Capital Shortage, Technology and Unemployment."

17. *Promoting World Recovery* (Washington, DC: Institute for International Economics, 1982); Helmut Schmidt, "The World Economy at Stake," *Economist,* 26 Feb. 1983.

voters an "altruistic" political issue, rather than a problem which they see as affecting directly their own, "egoistic" economic interests. . . . There is, in other words, no compelling reason of economic self-interest that would prevent the formation of relatively stable majorities from the "raw material" of all those voters who are not, and do not expect to be, affected by unemployment. Furthermore, once mass unemployment continues year after year, it tends to be defined more and more as a problem which no government would be capable of eliminating.[18]

Thus it is probably not enough for social democratic parties to place the employment issue at the top of the political agenda. We must also convince the majority of the voters with secure jobs that there are effective and feasible ways to achieve full employment.[19]

18. Fritz W. Scharpf, "The Economic and Political Basis for Full Employment," in *Eco-*

nomics and Values, ed. Lennert Arvedsson et al. (Stockholm: Almqvist & Wiksell International, 1986).

19. According to the polls in Britain, an overwhelming majority of the voters thought Labor cared about unemployment but only a minority thought they would be able to do anything about it.

The Crisis of the World Finance System

By ELMAR ALTVATER

ABSTRACT: Unemployment has become a structural feature in all industrialized countries because a worldwide decline in the profit rate has reduced the speed of economic growth. This decline has been due mainly to the decreasing productivity of capital in the course of ever increasing capital intensity of production. The crisis is perpetuated by two additional factors: (1) the decay of the order-maintaining capability of the United States; and (2) the expansion of uncontrolled international credit, as funds were diverted from relatively unprofitable real investment to profitable financial investment. The need to service the debt, which was thus accumulated, keeps up the demand for fresh credits and prevents interest rates from becoming low enough not to discourage real investment. To overcome the crisis, debt would have to be written off, which in turn requires some form of consensus on how to distribute the resulting losses.

Elmar Altvater studied economics and sociology at the University of Munich and wrote his doctoral thesis on social production and economic rationality—the problems of external effects in a centrally planned economy (1968). Since 1970 he has been professor of political economy at the Free University of Berlin. His publications have dealt with crisis and accumulation theory, economic strategies in advanced countries, world market tendencies, the debt problem, and regional development in Amazonia; he is coeditor of the quarterly Prokla.

A distinction is traditionally made between the propensity to invest and investment potential. In Keynesian terminology the propensity to invest is dependent upon the marginal return on capital, or, using Marxist concepts, the rate of profit. As persistently noted by Hyman Minsky,[1] the investment process is fundamentally unstable because of the uncertainty, implicit in the marginal profitability of capital, when it comes to linking the past, or existing capital stock, the present, or alternative uses of liquid assets, and the future, or sales expectations.

This raises a number of doubts about the employment-creating effects of investment. First of all, there is the long-term decline of the investment quota measured against gross domestic product.[2] Second, the share of replacement investment—equaling depreciation—in gross capital investment increases with increasing capital stock. The weight of the capital stock—the burden of the past—becomes greater and thus reduces the rate of accumulation, or net fixed investment (I) in relation to capital stock (K). If capital intensity increases at the same time owing to technological change, there must be a negative effect on employment, unless policy measures, such as some form of reduction in the length of the working week, are taken.

Third, the share of profits going into net investment is declining in all industrialized countries. This is true regardless of whether one takes total revenue from business activity and capital or the net surplus on company accounts as an indicator. While the share has shown cyclical changes, the trend over the past ten years has been clearly negative. Peaks in the curve, which occur at the end of economic upswings, when planned investment projects continue to go ahead while profits are already on the decline, were lower at the end of the 1970s and the beginning of the 1980s than at the beginning of the 1970s. There has also been a downward trend in troughs in the curve that have occurred at the end of crisis periods, when profits increase before investment gets under way. This trend is particularly pronounced in the United States and Britain, where only about 10 percent of corporate profits went into net fixed investment. But even in Japan, where the propensity to invest has been comparatively high, one can identify a negative trend.

Fourth, there has also been a change in the character of investment. Since the beginning of the period of stagnation, investment in rationalization has outweighed investment in expansion. Consequently, those investment projects that do still go ahead tend to reduce employment rather than create new jobs. This appears to be the corporate answer to the stagnation of the markets. When high rates of growth of sales are no longer possible, efforts are made to increase productivity and thus profitability by reducing costs. Following a long period of sustained economic growth generated by product innova-

1. Hyman P. Minsky, "Financial Markets and Economic Instability, 1965-1980," *Nebraska Journal of Economics and Business*, 20(4) (1981); idem, *Monetary Policies and the International Financial Environment*, Working Paper Series (St. Louis, MO: Washington University, 1983).

2. The gross investment quota of the seven largest countries of the Organization for Economic Cooperation and Development (OECD)— the United States, Japan, Germany, France, Britain, Italy, and Canada—averaged just under 21 percent between 1963 and 1968 and climbed to a peak of 23 percent in 1973, only to fall to 20 percent by 1983. This trend can be observed in all OECD countries. See *OECD Economic Outlook*, no. 37, p. 158 (June 1985).

tion, process innovation has now become more important. While process innovation can be capital saving, its main characteristic is that it is labor saving. Labor is released for which no alternative employment opportunities exist because of the lack of investment in increased capacity. In the absence of compensating employment policies, mass and long-term unemployment is the inevitable consequence.

In essence, therefore, the process of real accumulation has come to a halt due to the low propensity to invest. The result is that employment has fallen—and unemployment has become a structural feature—in all industrialized countries, albeit to significantly different degrees. One can, therefore, also speak of an uncoupling of growth and employment, which has led to the demise of the full employment economy. The question that remains to be answered is why the investment trends have been fundamentally the same in a range of countries, despite differences that certain analysts like to attribute to the different degrees of corporatist and market regulations.[3]

THE LIMITS OF THE POSTWAR GROWTH MODEL

When all countries show similar signs of crisis, then the system of world capitalism is in crisis. The object of study then is no longer the individual country in comparison with others, but the capitalist world economy itself. What is at the core of this trend toward inter-

national crises? If profitability were adversely affected in only one country, one could clearly find fault with the functioning of the process of capital accumulation in that country. But when this happens in all the national economies, then the system clearly is not functioning properly. For the purposes of this article, an effective system shall be defined as consisting of a number of elements: (1) the global diffusion of an efficient accumulation, or growth, model; (2) an economic policy on the part of the hegemonic power, the United States, that enables all the countries participating in the system to benefit from a positive-sum game; and (3) the securing of the flow of money and capital by international monetary institutions.

Diffusion of an efficient accumulation, or growth, model

The postwar growth model could be called Fordist, because it was based on a particular rationality of production.[4] In this, work was structured according to the rules of the scientific organization of labor developed by Taylor. The production process followed the principles of mass production and mass marketing implemented by Ford. Finally, the economy as a whole was regulated thanks to the principles worked out by Keynes—

---

3. See Göran Therborn, *Arbeitslosigkeit: Strategien und Politikansätze in den OECD-Ländern* (Hamburg: VSA, 1985); Manfred Schmidt, "Arbeitslosigkeit und Vollbeschäfigung; Ein internationaler Vergleich," *Leviathan*, 11(4): 451-73 (1983).

4. See inter alia in a now-large volume of literature, Michel Aglietta, *A Theory of Capitalist Regulation: The US Experience* (London: New Left Books, 1979); Alain Lipietz, "Towards Global Fordism?" *New Left Review*, vol. 132 (Mar.-Apr. 1982); Mike Davis, *Prisoners of the American Dream: Politics and Economy in the History of the U.S. Working Class* (London: Verso, 1986); Jacques Mazier, "Growth and Crisis—a Marxist Interpretation," in *The European Economy*, ed. Andrea Bolth (Oxford: Oxford University Press, 1982), pp. 38-41.

and others!—to control the general direction of the economy and sustain effective demand. The form of regulation—growth model or specific historical form of reproduction[5]—created by these ingredients had its beginnings in the 1920s in the United States and in the "recasting of bourgeois Europe"[6] after World War I. It was not, however, until after World War II that its full potency was released with the result that the system experienced a period of sustained dynamic economic growth unique in the history of the capitalist world. This growth began in the United States and spread first to Western Europe. It drew Japan in its train but with a certain delay, and at the beginning of the 1970s it even looked as if a number of newly industrializing countries (NICs) in Southeast Asia and Latin America might import the Fordist model into the periphery of the capitalist world system.

The mechanism that spread this growth model was the same as that which brought about the internationalization of capital after World War II. The Bretton Woods international monetary system, followed by the General Agreement on Tariffs and Trade and generous U.S. assistance in the form of the Marshall Plan for a Western Europe hard-hit by war did in fact establish the

institutional framework for the internationalization of the flow of goods, money, and capital. As the process of internationalization advanced, it led to more uniform patterns of consumption and living conditions, but also to more uniformity in the political regulation of social conflicts.

The hegemonic position of the United States was reflected in a permanent trade surplus achieved by virtue of U.S. technological superiority. This situation endured until 1971, when the Nixon administration ended the gold convertibility of the dollar and thus brought the Bretton Woods system to an inglorious end. The 1960s also saw the internationalization of production as well as capital. After barriers to currency convertibility fell in 1959 there was a flood of direct investment, mainly from the United States. During this period Latin America was relegated to number two as a destination for U.S. direct investment, being replaced by Europe.[7] The direct investment in Europe was, however, mainly in productive industry, whereas in Latin America and elsewhere in the so-called periphery it was mainly in the extraction of primary and raw materials. The consequences of this for the international growth model were clearly twofold.

First, new investment locations and thus growth areas were created. This in turn resulted in high rates of economic growth in almost all countries and an expansion of world trade that far

5. These terms are often treated as synonyms although they stem from different theoretical tracts. I prefer the term "form" because this not only covers the specific epoch in which the growth model or reproduction model is effective but also the period of transformation to a new form of capitalistic reproduction and regulation. See Elmar Altvater, "Bruch und Formwandel eines Entwicklungsmodells," *Überproduktion, Unterkonsumption, Depression,* ed. Jürgen Hoffmann (Hamburg: VSA, 1983), pp. 217-52.

6. Charles W. Maier, *Recasting Bourgeois Europe* (Princeton, NJ: Princeton University Press, 1975).

7. U.S. direct investment in 1950 was US$1.7 billion in Europe and US$4.6 billion in Latin America. In 1960 the respective figures were $6.7 billion in Europe and $9.3 billion in Latin America, but by 1968 they were $19.4 billion in Europe and $13 billion in Latin America. Statistisches Bundesamt, *Statistisches Jahrbuch 1970* (Stuttgart: Kohlhammer, 1970), p. 143.

exceeded the rate of growth in gross national product during the 1960s. Second, there was a diffusion of technological know-how, and the Fordist regulation model also became established in Europe. The United States thus progressively lost its competitive lead as well as the economic basis for its hegemonic position. This was reflected in the turbulence in currency markets, which began in the 1960s, and the decline in the U.S. dollar, the international currency, which no political measures seemed able to halt.

There is a third aspect to this process. The diffusion of the growth model also meant the diffusion of sources of imminent crisis. As long as the conditions of national growth differed, there were also asynchronous economic cycles. This situation had the advantage that economic recession in one country could be relatively quickly overcome by means of the price mechanism stimulating increased export demand.

More important, however, than the synchronization of the crisis cycle has been the general decline in profitability in all the centers of capitalism. Productivity growth was achieved by overproportional increases in capital intensity with the result that there was a decline in the productivity of capital. In addition, the success of trade unionism, such as in the Federal Republic of Germany, or militant labor action, such as in France, Italy, and Great Britain, squeezed profits[8] so that there was also a temporary reduction in the profit quota. But the negative trend in the productivity of capital has obviously been decisive for the fall in the rate of profits.[9] Figures

from the Organization of Economic Cooperation and Development show a clear negative trend in gross profits in almost all countries during the 1960s and 1970s.[10]

This falling trend in the rate of profits merely reflects the limits of the growth model, which have become increasingly apparent since the middle of the 1970s. The mechanism regulating this model neither can provide enough jobs for those seeking work nor control the flow of international trade and capital. As already described, the fall in profitability has a negative effect on investment. Although it is impossible to give one specific rate of profit at which there would still be investment or at which production and investment would begin to be reduced, it is possible to indicate three systemic barriers to investment under conditions of declining profitability.

The first is the point at which the return on investment is estimated to be below previously achieved levels of profitability. Such a comparison over time will clearly have scarcely any consequences for investment behavior as long as there is competition on world markets. Companies would be forced to invest in new technology and marketing in order to keep up with international

---

8. Andrew Glyn and Bob Sutcliffe, *British Capitalism, Workers and the Profits Squeeze* (Harmondsworth: Penguin Books, 1972).

9. "The secular decline in profits . . . has been

faster than in shares, and, as with profit shares, more marked in manufacturing than in broader sectors of the economy. . . .Decelerating or falling capital productivity is the main factor behind these trend declines." *OECD Economic Outlook*, no. 36, p. 64 (Dec. 1984).

10. Ibid. Figures given in this source show that during the 1960s and 1970s in all countries studied there was a negative trend in the rate of gross profits in manufacturing industry, with the exception of Italy and Norway, where the trend was slightly positive. The strongest negative trends were in Great Britain (-5.3), Sweden (-5.2), and Japan (-4.9).

competition and avoid falling hopelessly behind and thus disappearing from the market. A second more significant barrier is when the general rate of return on capital investment declines due to additional investment-increasing capacity, which in turn increases supply with the result that prices fall. It is possible for investors to get around this barrier when interest rates are relatively low by borrowing in order to sustain levels of return on capital—the leverage effect. It was because of such a leverage effect that the general decline in the return on capital did not have a negative effect on investment activity in the large capitalist countries such as the United States, Japan, France, the United Kingdom, and the Federal Republic of Germany as early as the 1960s.[11]

A third barrier therefore occurs when the rate of return on capital investment is close to, or even below, the monetary interest rate. It may then be more lucrative to put funds that could have been invested in real, productive investment into the money markets. More important, the leverage effect becomes negative

11. In the case of the Federal Republic of Germany, the Bundesbank noted that the share of capital reserves in net trading balances of all companies fell from 30 percent in the 1960s to 18 percent in 1983. "This brought the so-called 'leverage effect' into play. As long as borrowed capital earned more than the interest rate, this meant that every increase in debt resulted in more profit and greater return on investment in relation to capital reserves." Deutsche Bundesbank, "Rentabilität, Finanzkraft und Liquidität der Unternehmen," *Monatsberichte*, p. 30 (Aug. 1985). See also Philip Armstrong, Andrew Glyn, and John Harrison, *Capitalism since World War II* (London: Fontana Papers, 1984), p. 265: "The expansion of credit helped to maintain the return on shareholders' investment. Even though investment earned less overall, by financing an increasing proportion through borrowing at declining real interest rates, capitalists helped maintain the profitability of shareholders' funds."

when the interest paid on borrowed capital reduces the overall profitability of capital if borrowed capital accounts for a large share of total capital.[12] This had a fundamental effect on the substance of companies staggering under the burden of borrowed capital and demanded significant consolidation during the 1970s.

U.S. hegemony

In order to hold its position without being consistently challenged, the hegemon must sustain a global economic system from which all the participating countries, companies, and social organizations can benefit. In other words, it must be a positive-sum game. To put it very simply, the hegemon must ensure that the global social product grows, because under such conditions everyone is likely to be able to benefit from the system. This must be done despite cyclical fluctuations. Otherwise the specific hegemonic form of the global system is endangered, as is the hegemon itself.

It is by no means certain that the hegemon will succeed in securing such a pax hegemonica that benefits all and the continued existence of which is thus in the interests of all participants. One can on the contrary identify a type of hegemonic cycle beginning with the rise of the hegemonic power, continuing through its delegitimization, and finally ending with the erosion of the instrumental means by which the hegemon controls the system.[13] One can also describe this

12. "If there are losses the cushion against risk in the form of capital reserves is eaten into faster the higher the share of borrowed capital in total capital employed." Deutsche Bundesbank, "Rentabilität, Finanzkraft und Liquidität der Unternehmen," p. 32.
13. George Modelski, "Long Cycles of World Leadership," in *Contending Approaches to World*

process using form-theoretical terms. In order to maintain the historical form of the hegemony, the hegemonic power must be able to fulfill a number of functions and thus control the system. Functions are carried out by institutions using specific media such as law, power, and money but also drawing on consensus-forming appeals for ideological solidarity.

The delegitimization of a hegemonic power usually comes about as a result of the tide of history's exposing the deficiencies of existing institutions and the eventual failure of appeals for ideological support.[14] The instruments are eroded by the decline of legal and political authority as well as the collapse of the hegemon's currency as an international currency.

The hegemonic cycle, described here in very general terms, took place during the period of the Pax Americana. The institutions lost legitimacy, and the world awoke from the American dream. Above all, the daily adjustments of the dollar on currency markets were a constant reminder of how the dollar no longer provided the instrumental means of exercising hegemonic power by virtue of its being a global currency.

Three things happened in the second half of the 1970s that illustrate how the instrumental means of exercising the U.S. hegemony were being eroded. First, there was the attempt, in the shape of the Trilateral Commission, to spread the

burden of the regulation of the hegemonic system on a number of shoulders. This not only showed that the United States was no longer able to carry the burden of regulation alone, but that Western Europe and Japan, either together or individually, were not yet able to provide the institutions or instruments with which the hegemony could have been sustained. Not surprisingly, therefore, this attempt at trilateralism failed. Second, the dollar was increasingly replaced as a reserve, trading, and intervention currency by other currencies. This was the case even though the dollar, despite abdicating its systemic role as a fixed reference currency with respect to gold in the years 1971-73, remains the most important currency. Third, the European Monetary System was created in March 1979. This must be interpreted as a European or regional response to the erosion of the dollar as a global currency.

In this respect it is important to note that, in contrast to the decline of British hegemony between the two world wars, there is currently no power—like the United States sixty years ago—that is a serious contender for the role of hegemon. "The crisis exists precisely because the old is dying but there is nothing new to replace it," Antonio Gramsci has said. The crisis may therefore continue until a new form of political control is found.

Money and capital flows

The third component of the growth model is money and capital flows. First of all, it is necessary to recall that the internationalization of goods and productive capital, which began in the 1960s and accelerated during the 1970s, was complemented by the internationaliza-

---

System Analysis, ed. William R. Thompson (Newbury Park, CA: Sage, 1983).

14. Joanne Gowa, using hegemony theory, has presented a case study of an attempt at the institutional reorganization of the International Monetary Fund with substitution accounts. See Joanne Gowa, "Hegemons, IOs, and Markets: The Case of the Substitution Account," *International Organisation*, 38(4):661-83 (Autumn 1984).

tion of credit. Indeed, it is only possible to speak of the existence of a genuine world market when all forms of capital, including goods, means of production, and money, have been internationalized and the corresponding institutional forms have been developed. This market then works as an instrument of private interest and against the efforts to retain political control of the system, because a system of fixed exchange rates cannot resist the pressures of value and capital valorization. Given the growth in importance of international financial centers—free banking zones—during the 1960s, and the immense sums of international liquidity recycled[15] by such institutions, the collapse of the system of fixed exchange rates at the beginning of the 1970s was inevitable.

The logic this system obeys is clearly totally different from that of the political control of international money that was the legacy of the Bretton Woods system.[16] It is simply based on maximization of profits by banking capital exploiting differences in interest rates, divergent risks, and changes in exchange rates. In such circumstances, international capital assumes a kind of single corporate identity that sees real productive investment as, at best, just one of many forms of investment.

This does not, of course, mean the end of the dollar as an international currency. More than three-quarters of all contracts are still negotiated in dollars, so that the currency along with the U.S. banking system assumes a new importance. The dollar is, however, no

longer an instrument with which political authorities can influence world markets, but rather the vehicle of private interests operating on international financial markets.[17] These private interests still need a clearing system, and as most international monetary and capital business is conducted in dollars, it is the U.S. banking system that offers such a service. In other words, the dollar changed during the 1970s, from a world currency that facilitated political regulation of markets to a medium for private capital deposits.

THE INTEREST TRAP OF CATCH-UP INDUSTRIALIZATION AND THE DEBT CRISIS

These developments show that the decline in the propensity to invest by no means meant that there was a reduction in investment possibilities. On the contrary, profits continued to grow strongly, especially for large companies, not least because of pricing policies, such as administered pricing, that one would not normally expect during a recession. Only a small percentage of these funds were, however, reinvested; the rest increased bank liquidity with the result that international interest rates fell during the years of crisis following 1974. In the second half of the 1970s there were even negative real interest rates, except in the Federal Republic of Ger-

15. Compare here the analysis of Alexander Schubert, *Die internationale Schuldenkrise* (Frankfurt: Suhrkamp, 1985).

16. Salvatore Biasco, *L'inflazione nei paesi capitalistici industrializzati* (Milan: Fetrinelli, 1979), pp. 43-55.

17. However, it must be emphasized here that in the Bretton Woods system also the dollar was never just a technical means of monetary circulation controlled by the U.S. government. As soon as it left the United States, it functioned as capital, apart from the grants and public aid. This is a general problem of state intervention in the capitalist societies. As an important means of regulation, money is not only money but also monetary capital that assumes a value and therefore follows a logic other than that of public control.

many and Japan, because of the high and sometimes rising rates of inflation.[18] As no investor can anticipate whether or not he or she will be able to pass on inflation in price increases, the comparison of rates of interest and inflation is of limited significance. Nevertheless, low or even negative real interest rates are an indication of unused loan capital, which the banks in their role as financial intermediaries can provide to borrowers. However, when such interest rates do not stimulate investment, the expectations of future real returns on productive investment will be even lower. In such a situation, interest rates lose their effectiveness as a policy instrument because they cannot fall as low as company expectations about the rate of return on investment clearly can.

This opens up an interest-rate trap, into which fall a number of borrowers who have previously played a less important role in international money and capital markets. This insufficient absorption of liquid assets by the corporate sector led to increasing public debt in the industrialized countries, but also to a growing indebtedness of companies and public institutions in the NICs,

which hoped to speed the process of industrialization by drawing on external savings. This heralded a new phase in the post-World War II hegemonic cycle, that of indebted industrialization.

A double-bind situation was created in which, no matter what happened, the international economic system would have been unable to cope with pressures. If the new competitors were successful in their strategy of industrialization based on debt, the system would have been unable to withstand the pressures of increased competition. If the strategy failed, however, the existing structures would have been equally incapable of salvaging the inevitably shaky credit relations with these countries. In fact, of course, the system was exposed to both pressures. Not only were some East Asian NICs very successful in industrializing, which along with other factors provoked virulent protectionist tendencies in the world economy; but the Latin American NICs ran into a debt crisis because they could not service their dollar debts through domestic production.

The reasons why countries fail in debt-financed industrialization are numerous and cannot be fully covered here.[19] Whatever the reasons for failure, the debts represent a major defeat for the countries concerned, and a fateful warning for the capitalist world economy as a whole, that the Fordist model of industrialization is limited. In effect, they mean that not all the regions of the capitalist world economy can catch up industrially as long as they are subject to the existing monetary regime.

The transnational banks also have problems. During the first phase of the crisis in the 1970s they were able to

18. Short-term average real interest rates have moved as follows in the seven major OECD countries, which are the United States, Canada, Japan, France, the Federal Republic of Germany, Italy, and Britain; 1976: -0.3 percent; 1977: -0.6 percent; 1978: -0.3 percent; 1979: 1.2 percent; 1980: 2.4 percent; 1981: 4.2 percent; 1982: 4.0 percent. The international average is made up of the average rates of interest in each country weighted, for the year concerned, in relation to the dollar by the gross domestic product over the previous three years. See International Monetary Fund, *World Economic Outlook*, Occasional Paper 71 (Washington, DC: International Monetary Fund, 1983), p. 227; see also Oliver J. Blanchard and Lawrence H. Summers, "Perspectives on High World Real Interest Rates," *Brookings Paper on Economic Activity*, 2:276-87 (1984).

19. Schubert, *Die internationale Schulden-krise*, pt. 2.

provide cheap credit because they were taking inflows of low-interest capital. As this credit business expanded, thanks in part to the active encouragement of the banks, they became dependent upon a continuous inflow of liquid funds, which they needed in order to cover other commitments in their portfolios. Such borrowing, therefore, became an unpleasant necessity when debtors could not meet their obligations. The main problem for debtors was in meeting interest payments rather than repayments of principal. If interest payments are not made punctually the banks themselves need refinancing. In order to remain solvent and retain confidence, the banks must, however, continue to pay their own interest on time. This means they must either draw on reserves or obtain short-term funds on the interbank markets. Consequently the demand for liquidity grows, which pushes up interest rates unless there is an equivalent growth in the money supply. This trend is further strengthened by the fact that borrowers will also seek short-term credit in order to remain solvent or solve short-term liquidity problems. Interest rates must therefore inevitably rise whenever borrowers cannot get the funds they need for whatever reason. In other words, interest rates would have risen even if the Federal Reserve System had not pursued a tight money-supply policy from the end of 1979 on.

The countries that borrowed during the 1970s all faced liquidity or insolvency crises at the beginning of the 1980s, with the result that the transnational banking system saw itself confronted with requests for rescheduling totaling $37.9 billion in 1982 and $60 billion in 1983.[20] But why did this happen? Looking at the International Monetary Fund's programs produced during rescheduling negotiations, one would think the difficulties were entirely due to the mistaken economic policies pursued by the debtor countries, which meant that these were unable to raise enough money to service their debts. This rather too comfortable view takes no account of the fact, mentioned before, that the cause of the debt crisis is to be found in the crisis of the capitalist world economy and cannot therefore be solved by national measures of the debtor countries alone.

From the very outset there was an inherent contradiction in the growth of indebtedness. Inevitably, therefore, the problems became more acute as the growth and investment weakened in the wake of declining expectations about the rate of return on capital. To begin with, it was thought that growth in the NICs could be stimulated by recycling part of the industrialized countries' savings. But this view underestimated the difficulties of servicing the debt, even when the credits were used productively and investment projects were viable. Insufficient account was taken of the fact that earnings in national currencies still had to be transferred in the contract currency, which was mostly the dollar. The transfer-problem debate at the end of the 1920s showed that, with a certain combination of export and import elasticities in the debtor and creditor countries, a transfer profit can result even for the debtor country.[21] As

20. See E. Brau et al., "Recent Multilateral Debt Restructurings with Official and Bank Creditors," Occasional Paper 25 (Washington, DC: International Monetary Fund, 1983); Ernst Löscher, Souveräne Risiken und internationale Verschundung (Vienna: Manzsche Verlags und Universitätsbuchhandlung, 1983), pp. 54-67.

21. On the transfer question in the late 1920s, see John Maynard Keynes, "The German Transfer

is brutally and clearly demonstrated by the current debt problem, however, it is almost impossible to bring about such a transfer, given the structure of the world economy in the 1980s. If debtor countries have to achieve a net export of capital to cover interest charges or make repayments of principal, they must produce an equivalent surplus in trade and services. This, however, is only possible if the creditor countries are prepared to accept equivalent deficits.

In an expanding world economy this would not present a problem; creditor-country exports could still expand even though there would be a trade deficit. A reversal of the deficit-surplus positions of the creditor and debtor countries would not produce significant problems. All that would be needed would be for exports of the debtor countries to grow faster than those of the creditor countries. An absolute growth in creditor-country exports would in no way be excluded. It is, however, different when countries are competing strongly for larger shares of stagnating world markets. Under such conditions, it is then very difficult to see how debt can be serviced by achieving trade surpluses in excess of the deficit on capital accounts. As a result, currencies have tended to be devalued. But devaluation in such circumstances is unlikely to have a positive effect on exports for two reasons.

First, devaluation increases the costs of imports. Second, the volume of exports needed to match debt-service requirements grows in real terms as the currency devalues. This reduces the supply of goods on domestic markets, including goods needed for investment.

As the experience of all debtor countries shows, these factors combine to produce galloping inflation that destroys the national currency, which in turn results in the disintegration of social structures. Indebted industrialization, therefore, leads to inflation and social decline.[22] Indeed, because investment is stopped, and imports needed to complete the stunted industrialization, such as spare parts, can no longer be financed, this approach to industrialization in fact results in the opposite of what the credit was supposed to do, namely, in deindustrialization. It is scarcely possible to show more clearly or more dramatically how the growth model of Pax Americana leads to a dead end. The industrialization that was expected to come from external savings proved to be a bitter illusion. Industrial catch-up, at acceptable costs, is not possible in the framework of the hegemonic system built up after World War II. The debt crisis therefore demonstrates that the Fordist model is limited in both depth and, as shown earlier, width.

As long as there is no fundamental change in the situation that existed at the beginning of the 1980s, real interest rates will not fall to a level appropriate for the given phase of the economic cycle. This has negative effects on the industrialized countries as well, because the comparison of real productive investment and financial holdings will favor the latter, given that the pure profit—profit less real interest rates—is further reduced by high real interest rates.[23]

Problem," *Economic Journal*, 39:72 ff (1929); Gottfried Haberler, *Der internationale Handel* (Berlin: Springer, 1933).

22. Compare the analysis of Pierre Salama, "Endividamento e penuria urbana?" *Ensaios FEE*, 5(2):3-14 (1984).

23. See the OECD figures: *OECD Economic Outlook*, no. 33, p. 57 (July 1983).

CONCLUSION

Responsible for the long duration of the current phase of crisis and stagnation is the combination of structural factors leading to the decline of the profit rate, the unlinking of the monetary sphere from the trends in the accumulation of real wealth, and the erosion of the hegemonic power that used to regulate the capitalist world system. The contradiction between monetary and real growth can be eased either by reducing the monetary demands of the creditors or by increasing the ability of the debtors to generate real growth. Both the International Monetary Fund's programs for countries in debt crises and the agreements reached between the private banks and their borrowers are currently aiming at the latter. However, it is clear that social developments in the debtor countries and structural developments in world markets set limits on debt servicing. One must therefore consider the prospect of reducing the monetary demands. Some banks have already partly accepted this in that they have, in recent years, built up larger reserves in order to cope with cancelations of debt. All the same, the actual writing off of losses appears to hover, like the sword of Damocles, and could, with one blow, destroy the complex network of monetary links.[24]

This danger could be contained if the hegemonic power still had the institutional and instrumental capability of preserving—reproducing—the capitalist world system. Today this would above all mean gaining a consensus in favor of a scheme for sharing the losses rather than leaving to the market forces how monetary demands are brought back in

line with the real economy. In effect, this would only induce national governments to come to the rescue of their national capital. It would tend to divide the world system into a number of protectionist zones. If this were to happen, the international credit system certainly could not survive and would collapse for two reasons. Many debtors, such as Third World countries, transnational corporations, and maybe even the United States, would have to reduce or stop their debt service payments. In addition, however, the collapse would mean that the dollar would cease to be a world currency.

This points to the current danger of the capitalist world economy, which has an immediate impact on employment in the individual countries. The system is sustained by three different markets, those of finance, goods, and labor. While the labor markets are essentially national, goods and financial markets have, after decades of evolution, become international. Assuming, as one must, that labor markets are above all dependent on goods and financial markets—the hierarchy of markets—it is obvious that national employment is influenced by international markets and that the maneuvering space of national employment policies is limited. This dependence varies from country to country, but nowhere is it so small that it can be neglected.

The crisis can be overcome only when a way can be found to match monetary demands and real performance. This requires some form of consensus on the allocation of losses resulting from writing off some debt. What would then follow? The crisis has shown that the current form of economic reproduction in—and the political organization of—the world system prevents all those seeking employment in the industrialized countries from

24. See *OECD Economic Outlook,* no. 37, p. 55 (June 1985).

finding jobs in formal or typical sectors of the economy. It has also shown that it has been made impossible for the not yet industrialized countries to catch up with the specific Fordist form of industrialization of the existing industrialized countries. For these reasons one must therefore conclude that in the future the global society can only develop when it leaves the growth model of the past decades behind it.

ANNALS, *AAPSS*, **492**, July 1987

The Neglect of Employment in
the International Economic Order

By KURT W. ROTHSCHILD

ABSTRACT: The post-World War II international economic order obliged the nation-states to conduct their foreign economic policies according to binding rules. As employment continued to be a purely national responsibility of the individual countries, international obligations turned into serious constraints on the pursuit of national employment policies. International agreement should provide the possibility that countries disengage themselves from the restrictive influence of foreign obligations. In addition, international employment policies would be desirable. They should focus on a common commitment to the goal of full employment rather than on concrete policy measures. But broad international strategies, such as the assumption of locomotive functions by strong economies or massive financial support for Third World development, can—depending on various conditions—also be positive.

Kurt W. Rothschild studied law and economics at the University of Vienna (J.D., 1938). He studied economics and political philosophy at the University of Glasgow (M.A., 1940). From 1940 to 1947 he worked as assistant lecturer and then as lecturer in economics at the University of Glasgow. In 1947 he joined the Austrian Institute for Economic Research as a senior research worker. In 1966 he became professor of economics at the University of Linz, Austria, where he retired in 1985. He has been visiting professor in universities in Austria, Germany, Switzerland, Great Britain, Italy, the United States, and Australia.

WHEN it came to the question of economic reconstruction after the end of World War II, the developed capitalist industrialized countries of Western Europe and North America were overwhelmingly influenced by the traumatic experience of the 1930s' depression. The two phenomena from these earlier times that appeared particularly threatening were mass unemployment and the restriction and departmentalization of international trade through a network of protectionist and currency controls. The question of how a new world economic order might prevent a return to these conditions was therefore already at the center of public interest and official thinking in the democratic countries, above all Britain and the United States, long before the end of World War II. Sir William Beveridge's book *Full Employment in a Free Society*, published in Britain in 1944, found more of an echo in public opinion than almost any economics book that preceded it. Writers of the time, such as Clarence Streit and others, who emphasized not only the political but also the economic significance of the fact that we all have to learn to live in one crowded world, also found a similar interest.

These sentiments soon found their way into official texts, statements, and actions, partly out of a genuine desire for reform and partly for fear of pressure for revolutionary change. It was in this fashion that employment objectives became almost obligatory in the government statements and legislation in Britain and America, which then acted as examples for other countries. International conferences led to the establishment of the International Monetary Fund (IMF), the World Bank, and ultimately, after the failure of the Havana Charter, the first effort to establish a comprehensive regime for foreign trade, the General Agreement on Tariffs and Trade (GATT). Thus an institutional framework was created that was to prevent a relapse into the double catastrophe of the 1930s, mass unemployment and the progressive strangulation of international trade. It was also seen as a basis from which to make further progress.

From the very beginning, however, there was a significant difference between the way the two problems were addressed, a difference that could be only partly attributed to the different nature of the problems of unemployment and trade. The employment problem has from the start been seen as essentially a national problem to be resolved by national effort. Apart from relatively inconsequential summit and other declarations, there have been no significant international agreements on—or commitments to—employment objectives. In total contrast, there is an expansive network of—admittedly, not always effective—consultations, coordination, and regulations aimed at preventing the slide into protectionism, currency controls, and export subsidization. Included in this network are, among others, the IMF, the Organization for Economic Cooperation and Development, the GATT, and the European Economic Community.

As already mentioned, this difference is partly due to the nature of the problems and would exist whatever national policies were pursued or whatever international agreements were reached. Foreign economic policy inevitably involves numerous players and is therefore amenable to mutual agreement and quid pro quo agreements. In contrast, employment policies always appear to be seen as a domestic concern.

Things are obviously not always quite so simple. One could, after all, always adopt a totally unilateral standpoint in foreign economic policy. One could, for example, argue—as I do not—that, according to the widely represented free-trade equilibrium model, every move toward free trade improves productivity and resource allocation even when it is not reciprocated. Above all, however, although it seems hardly credible that employment is an isolated problem that can be resolved by national means alone, it is largely treated as such in the discussion and practice of economic policy. This phenomenon requires more detailed analysis.

From a theoretical point of view there is little call to distinguish, in principle, between employment and international economic policy problems. Both could be seen to have national and international components. The well-developed macroeconomic models and theories of the global economy do indeed suggest that there is a high degree of interdependence between all parts of the economy and that there is a circular chain of causal links between them. The degree and form of interdependence vary according to circumstances and theoretical approach and thus provide scope for differences of opinion and debate. But no model denies the existence of a direct and indirect—that is, inter- and intrasectoral—interdependence between changes in domestic and foreign employment and trade and capital flows. This is true whether or not there is labor mobility.

There are therefore no theoretical grounds for drawing a dividing line between domestic employment policies and the presumably necessarily global foreign economic policy. Employment policy measures of an expansionary or deflationary nature affect trade flows and therefore affect trade and employment in other countries. Equally, foreign economic policy measures also influence both international trade as well as employment in a number of countries, regardless of whether they are national/unilateral measures or global/multilateral measures. The subsequent knock-on effects can then have further—multiplier—repercussions in all countries and sectors. Therefore, the difference between macroeconomic models does not concern so much the question of whether domestic or internationally agreed-upon policies are appropriate for individual sectors. It refers far more to the possibilities in principle of an active employment policy, be it a national or an international one. We need not concern ourselves further here with this conflict, which runs under the slogan of "monetarism or rational expectations versus Keynesianism," because we shall work under the premise that an employment policy is possible and makes sense.

THE NATIONAL-INTERNATIONAL DICHOTOMY

How can one then explain why, despite the ease with which both theoretical and commonsense views of the world point to interdependence, such a widespread dichotomy exists between national employment policies and international foreign economic policy? There are a number of explanations that, as will be shown, all have serious consequences. The fact that theoretical and policy discussions prematurely and almost totally accept the existence of such a dichotomy is largely due to the origins of the modern theory of employment policy. These were decisively influenced by Keynes's famous book *The General Theory of Employment, Interest and Money*, which was published in 1936. Keynes wrote the book during the depression, when world trade was already shattered, and concentrated on the possibilities of expanding employment in what was a relatively large country under relatively strong controls on the balance of payments. While he did not neglect foreign questions, his approach was largely geared to a relatively closed economy that therefore had to pursue its own employment objectives. This approach meant a national employment policy and thus influenced the discussion for a long time.

Ten years later, during preparations for the establishment of the IMF, Keynes saw the coming open world economy and was thoroughly aware of the links between domestic and international employment and economic policies. He had ideas on how to address the question of such links, which can be found in the so-called Keynes Plan and which were presented to the IMF but got nowhere due to American opposition. In both theory and practice, therefore, employment policies remained constrained to the national model. External factors—in particular, the importance of exports for employment—were recognized but usually only as exogenous factors beyond national control that could either increase or decrease employment. In addition, politicians, bending to the forces of political expediency, tended to ascribe good results on the employment front to domestic policies and negative results to uncontrolled external influences. Little attention was paid to the common ups and downs in employment and to the mechanisms of transmission from one country to another, which might make common policy

approaches advisable.[1]

Things are very different when one turns to what was happening on the foreign economic policy front. Although there is a good deal of scope for unilateral actions in foreign economic policy, such as in the form of open or disguised protectionism or exchange rate policies, the philosophy of mutual and binding agreements is still seen as normal. This philosophy is supported above all by the trauma of the 1930s, when every country tried to improve its own economic and employment position at the expense of others by adopting protectionist measures in the pursuit of competitive beggar-thy-neighbor policies. The result was that world trade declined or stagnated while unemployment persisted. A repeat of such a self-destructive process was to be prevented by mutual commitments to open trade.

A second factor promoting bi- or multilateral approaches is the idea that unilateral action should be avoided. The trade and currency policy instruments that can discriminate against other countries are retained as bargaining chips, even when their unilateral removal is possible or even preferable for purely economic reasons, and are only negotiated away in return for reciprocal concessions. In principle, such an approach is also conceivable for employment policies. As every country is interested in higher employment, and demand, in other countries, a country could use its own employment measures as a bargaining chip in order to get other countries to introduce similar measures in international agreements. Of course,

1. On the question of the transfer mechanism, see Gerhard Graf, "Hypothesen zur internationalen Konjunkturtransmission,"*Weltwirtschaftliches Archiv*, 111(3):529-63 (1975).

the analogy does not hold in practice because employment is much too explosive an issue politically for such a policy to be practicable. The use of increased tariffs in retaliation against foreign protectionism and as a means of bringing pressure to bear on another country is not unknown, even when these initially damage the domestic economy. But it is unheard of to use the threat of increased domestic unemployment in an effort to bring about a change in another country's restrictive economic policies.

Whatever the causes of this nationalization of employment policy and globalization of foreign economic policy might have been, we are faced with the reality that the discrepancy between them remains and has become more entrenched. That this should have happened at all is significant and must be discussed, at least briefly, before the question of a global employment policy is addressed.

There appear to be two important issues. The first concerns the interests involved. It is in the interests of the ever more important and powerful multinational companies that countries should enter into internationally binding agreements requiring relatively free trade and capital flows that are not qualified by any international or national requirements concerning socioeconomic objectives such as employment, living standards, and the like. In contrast to the earlier pressure for protective tariffs from the ruling national monopolies and oligopolies, the multinationals seek a freedom to reallocate resources through their global transactions that is secure from sociopolitical interference. This is a political-economic fact of life that helps explain why the institutional hierarchy favoring economic or trade policies over employment policies has been

so stable despite significant changes in the economic climate.

The implications of this hierarchy bring us to the second reason why employment objectives have remained nationalized while foreign economic policy objectives are global. As already emphasized, it is not possible to compartmentalize employment and foreign policy. The objectives of foreign economic and employment policy are interdependent and cannot be carried out in isolation from each other. Therefore, when the foreign economic components of a policy are subject to international commitments without there being similar commitments to employment, there is clearly a hierarchy of policy objectives and thus of what can be achieved in pursuit of these objectives for every single country. A clear asymmetry prevails. Commitments in the field of foreign economic policy—free trade, free flows of capital, and so forth—impose constraints on national employment policies, while the globally conceived rules for foreign economic policy—as in the GATT, IMF, OECD, the European Economic Community, and others—are scarcely constrained by specific commitments on employment.

In other words, while there is an internationally sanctioned effort to prevent efficiency losses due to the uneconomic allocation of resources resulting from protectionist measures, there is no equivalent provision for losses due to underemployment and insufficient capacity utilization. Nothing illustrates the harsh reality of this hierarchy better than the way the IMF uses its internationally agreed-upon rules to prescribe national policies for indebted countries in order to get the current debt crisis under control. Monetary, credit, and trade criteria take precedence, with catastrophic consequences for employment, living standards, and social cohesion in the countries concerned. In the end, this has implications for the balance of the international economy.

This all suggests that, given the continued high levels of unemployment in many parts of the world, more attention should be given to the question of global employment strategies. In what follows, a modest attempt is made to describe what these might look like.

GLOBAL EMPLOYMENT STRATEGIES

First of all, one should consider the consequences for national employment policies if, as is quite likely, a move toward global employment policy measures is politically infeasible and the expectations of various countries with regard to employment policy become strongly divergent. In such a situation a country wishing to improve prospects can face a real conflict between respecting international treaties and the need to expand its domestic economy. A degree of disengagement from restrictive foreign influences must then be within the scope of internationally agreed-upon possibilities; otherwise countries may simply take unilateral actions to disengage.

A central problem is that, failing equivalent expansionist measures in other countries, an expansionist policy will result in balance-of-payments difficulties that can cut short any expansionist policy. The hope that the introduction of flexible exchange rates would contain this stop-go problem and create more scope for unilateral employment policies has only been fulfilled to a very limited extent. As things are, expansion creates increased demand for imports and results in devaluation, which can fuel inflation via the price-wage mecha-nism and thus cause serious problems—in addition to that of domestic inflation. Given the existence of free capital and currency markets, there are also likely to be strong speculative shifts in the value of the currency destabilizing both trade and economic policies. This then leads to dirty floating, or the reintroduction of fixed exchange rates, with which the balance-of-payments problem would again become acute.

It would therefore be desirable to provide for countries wishing to reflate in isolation the opportunities to take appropriate measures with regard to trade and capital flows without being too constrained by balance-of-payments and inflation considerations. This does not mean import controls but only the opportunity of preventing too big a gap from emerging between the expanding import growth and the stagnating export growth. In other words, the increase in imports resulting from increased economic activity should be acknowledged as an alternative to an increase in imports due to reductions in trade barriers. More consideration of such alternatives in international agreements could represent the first step toward a reduction in the asymmetry between the scope for employment and foreign economic policies mentioned earlier.

What possibilities are there if the transition toward more global concepts of employment policy should be seriously considered? First of all, it is important to take note of a fundamental difference between general policy goals and specific policy instruments and programs. To some extent, it is not possible to consider the latter without agreement on the importance of the employment objective. It is, however, possible to agree on a common goal of high employment without agreeing on the details of common and coordinated policy instruments.

One can argue that, given the current state of the world economy and economic theory, a diffuse agreement on policy objective does not only make sense but should indeed be given a high priority for economic reasons. First of all, history teaches us that such an approach promises not only the possibility of success, but success itself. There has never really been anything such as an internationally agreed-upon employment policy, apart from rhetorical fireworks. During the 1950s and 1960s, however, most developed industrialized countries gave employment objectives such a high priority that there was, in practice, an agreed-upon de facto policy objective for these countries. Every country could rely on the fact that others would strive for high levels of employment and demand, so that, in the medium term, domestic employment policies could be conducted in relative freedom and without fear of general disruption from foreign economic factors. The existence of common objectives therefore confirmed and endorsed national employment policy measures.

As is well known, the period after 1970 was characterized by a massive shift away from employment objectives as the top priority in economic policies moved toward the control of inflation, privatization, and the restoration of private capital. This meant the end of de facto global agreement on employment policy objectives. When devising employment policies, countries wishing to expand had to take account now of the lack of parallel action by other countries, the ensuing dissipation of demand into deflating countries, and the resulting balance-of-payments problems. This change in policy objectives was not solely or even predominantly responsible for the change from the full employment of the 1960s to the long-term unemployment of later years. There were numerous other, largely real economic, reasons for this change. There is, however, a case to be made that the existence of full-employment objectives on a global scale did help and that their absence has made things worse.[2]

This historical point should illustrate the importance of global agreement on policy objectives even when these are not accompanied by agreement on specific methods and timing. There are a number of reasons why a broad agreement on the objective of employment has advantages over a detailed global employment policy, whatever form this takes. The first, obvious reason can be found in the continued heterogeneous nature of national employment policies. Differences between national policies are so great, especially between developing and industrialized countries, that a common policy is not feasible. Even among the advanced industrialized countries the differences are such that the creation of common methods and rules for policy instruments would reduce their efficacy. Distinct differences between countries—such as the scope for public sector involvement, income poli-

2. In this context it is interesting to note the review of Sir William Beveridge's book *Full Employment in a Free Society* written by the English economist Austin Robinson in 1945. After discussing Beveridge's various proposals on employment policy, Robinson wrote, "They [the proposals] are not so very different from, nor so very much greater than those with which we failed to defeat unemployment in the 'thirties that one can feel absolutely confident of success. But what, more than anything else was lacking in the 'thirties was an overwhelming national determination to defeat unemployment." *Economic Journal*, 55:76 (Apr. 1945).

cies, the timing of political cycles, the structure of corporate organization, and the like—suggest that different instruments need to be used depending on the particular national characteristics.

Independent of such differences there are also other reasons why different methods should be used. A single, global employment policy would have to be based on existing national thinking on—and knowledge of—employment policies. Given new developments in both economics and technology, as well as the inevitable clash of interests over policy objectives, there exists no broad consensus on what such national policies should be. There are a range of strategies, some more controversial than others, but all of which are subject to a constant process of testing and evaluation. There is indeed scope for gaining new experience from the experimentation with different approaches. In this way a global approach that allows for variations is better than one that does not, and all countries can benefit from the lessons learned by others. Furthermore, variation in approaches ensures that the errors that will inevitably be made do not have a cumulative effect and provides for a certain degree of inbuilt correction of such errors.

One can make similar arguments with regard to the timing of employment policy measures. Given the difficulties in producing exact diagnoses and projections and the unavoidable lags with which decisions are taken and policies become effective, it would not necessarily make sense for all countries to act at the same time. Asynchronous action also means that the inevitable fluctuations in employment due to cyclical effects and structural change will be unevenly spread. This means that the weakening of an economy in one country could be more rapidly eased by increased exports to countries undergoing expansion than would be the case if cyclical movements in the respective economies ran parallel. Analyses of the developments in the 1960s suggest that asynchronous economic cycles in the different countries significantly shortened the downward movements.

There are thus a number of grounds for arguing that the agreement on a global employment policy should be limited to a general agreement on the overall objective. The details of how this objective is to be attained should be left to national policies. This, however, leaves one major problem unanswered. How does one ensure that each country actually pursues and sticks to the agreed-upon objective? It is well known how easily the rhetoric of full employment slips from the tongues of politicians for whom the use of such rhetoric will always pay. It will take more than noncommittal declarations of intention to make a genuine global dedication to the goal of full employment.

One possibility would be to make the policy objectives credible by actually acting on them. This was in fact what happened during the 1950s and 1960s. The basis for a genuine global policy would be established without prescribing specific measures or results if governments were seen to be acting clearly and quickly to deal with employment problems and if they were to give employment problems an important place in all economic policy decisions.

Where the basis of mutual trust is not—or no longer—sufficient, more concrete indicators will be needed. The most obvious way to create these is to lay down specific targets. Just as specific targets are set for inflation, there could be concrete targets set for employment.

If these targets were not met, there would then have to be an obligation to take additional employment policy measures. Such an approach was, for example, incorporated in the employment programs for Asia worked out by the International Labor Organization (ILO), which called for "comprehensive employment programmes, indicating specific targets to be progressively achieved" for the Asian region.[3]

There are significant difficulties caused by such commitments to targets in market-oriented countries due to the dynamism of market-oriented economies, their susceptibility to disturbances, and the limited effectiveness of economic policy instruments. Realistic objectives are difficult to set and are not independent of time. If they are set too low, so that they are easily achieved, they lose their effectiveness in tackling unemployment. If they are set too high, they will frequently not be reached, with the result that the approach would lose its credibility and effectiveness. But even realistic, flexible objectives will not be easy to achieve. What sanctions, for example, can one employ when a participating country does not hold to its commitments? As mentioned earlier, it is simply infeasible to take direct retaliatory action as one can in trade policy with retaliatory tariff increases. It is possible to devise other forms of penalty, but these are politically infeasible.

It is partly, but not exclusively, because of these difficulties in devising an operational set of policy objectives that concrete global measures and projects assume a complementary importance of their own, especially during times of persistent mass unemployment. There are three types of strategy deserving further consideration in this still underdeveloped but important area of policy.

One strategy would be to build on the very modest foundations of the existing multilateral instruments of employment policy. Its impact would be relatively limited because of the limited scope offered by these instruments. But as they already exist it would be relatively easy to pursue such an approach. In the first instance, one thinks here of the ILO, whose founding statute of 1919 included the objective of full employment. Although this objective has been regularly endorsed in ILO resolutions and programs ever since, it has not been backed by sufficient resources or political support from national governments to enable the ILO to do very much.[4] In addition to the ILO, and in conjunction with it, the employment policy elements in other international organizations must be strengthened. Here one is concerned with all the U.N. organizations involved in work with the developing countries, the World Bank, and, on a limited regional level, the European Social Fund and the European Regional Development Fund, which deal with the employment agenda in the European Community.[5]

All these existing approaches only play a minor role because their scale is limited and because there is often no

3. International Labor Organization, *Proposals for the Formulations and Implementation of an Asian Manpower Plan*, Report 4 (Geneva: International Labor Organization, 1968).

4. See International Labor Organization, *The World Employment Programme* (Geneva: International Labor Organization, 1969); idem, *Employment, Growth and Basic Needs: A One-World Problem* (Geneva: International Labor Organization, 1977).

5. See François Vandamme, "The Revised European Social Fund and Action to Combat Unemployment in the European Community," *International Labour Review*, 123(2):167-81 (Mar.-Apr. 1984).

additionality—that is, resources are used to finance existing national schemes. But they could become more important if they were expanded significantly. One should not, however, exaggerate the potential for expanding such instruments. The instruments themselves and the programs associated with them are devised to assist in the implementation of national programs and to improve the functioning of employment markets. The emphasis is therefore on research, the exchange of information, and the provision of finance for retraining and actions in special problem areas such as underdeveloped regions or youth unemployment. As important as these are, and as desirable as the easing of such special problems as youth and regional unemployment are, such action can at best be no more than a complement to a more substantial national or international effort. They are not a genuine alternative.

THE LOCOMOTIVE THEORY

To have the necessary impact on demand or cyclically induced mass unemployment, one must look to other strategies. In this context there are two possible approaches: the so-called locomotive theory and, in Bruno Kreisky's words, a "Marshall Plan for the Third World" or the Brandt Plan. The basic concept of the locomotive theory, which was ventilated in the middle of the 1970s mainly in the OECD setting, is very simple and, with the exception of the name, not new. The concept was inherent in the saying "when America sneezes Europe catches a cold," which was well known at the time of the 1930s' depression. It is based on the simple observation that, given differences in the size of economies, the same relative effort to

expand economic activity in countries has very different absolute effects on other countries' trade flows. Economic weight is not the only factor, and trade dependence and the multiplier effects of various measures also play a role. But by and large it remains true that actions taken by large countries have a greater impact on others than those of small countries.[6]

The basic idea behind the locomotive theory is therefore that common and strong expansionary action by, in particular, the large economies can increase employment at a time of global recession. This would then provide a positive impulse in other countries the cumulative effect of which would be to add more steam to the locomotive and thus to the world economy. A stimulus cannot be created by small individual countries. Expansion by such countries is too small in relation to the world economy to have any significant effect, and all that would result would be balance-of-payments problems for the countries concerned because of increased imports with more or less static exports. The only real alternative to the locomotive approach would be a coordinated expansion by all or most of the countries affected by high unemployment, whether large or small. But this would clearly present much greater organizational and political problems than would the locomotive approach.

6. The best example is the United States, which, because of its import propensity and size, has a profound impact on the activity of other countries. The theoretical discussion of the relationship between size, savings, and import propensity can be found in Martin Bronfenbrenner, "On the Locomotive Theory in International Macroeconomics," *Weltwirtschaftliches Archiv*, 115(1):38-50 (1979).

There is one important problem with the locomotive strategy. Even when the expansionary policy is successful, it can still cause a number of problems for the locomotive country or countries. These mainly take the form of budget deficits, the danger of inflation, and problems with distribution. Countries benefiting from a successful locomotive action experience only the expansion effect and avoid the problems, at least partially, or can more easily deal with them in the already expanding economy. With their export-led growth, these countries then become free riders of the expansionary policies, the costs of which are unevenly spread.

Such imbalances in the risks and benefits of locomotive policies can significantly reduce the necessary incentive for large economies to pursue them. In order to compensate for this it would be necessary to complement the global strategy based on a locomotive approach with commitments from the potential beneficiaries to contribute to global demand by taking respective national measures and thus taking some of the burden from the locomotive countries. The initial step cannot be taken by the smaller countries, because the tail cannot wag the dog. But these countries can play an active role once the process of growth has been started.

There is one further point to be made. The locomotive strategy is endangered if the locomotive countries seek to promote expansion mainly by means of export promotion, which is not an unusual occurrence. This is more likely to result in a relocation of employment or in the export of unemployment than in a general improvement in the global level of employment. This would in fact represent nothing more and nothing less

than the misery of a 1930s type of beggar-thy-neighbor policy.[7]

The locomotive strategy is best suited to a global economic climate, like that of the mid-1970s or any recessionary phase of an international economic cycle, when there is persistent unemployment affecting most of the major trading countries. The locomotive countries should get the others moving again or moving faster, and the whole process should then be mothballed until it is needed again.

This contrasts with the permanent programs first developed for the developing countries and then elaborated to meet employment policy objectives as called for in the so-called Brandt Plan[8] but also repeatedly by Bruno Kreisky and others. If properly executed, a global plan, involving the cooperation of the developed industrialized countries and the international organizations, including especially the IMF, the World Bank, and the United Nations, could provide the financial basis for permanent and significant transfers to developing countries that would provide the impulse for flows of supply and demand benefiting both sides.

It is not possible here to go into all the problems involved in the implementation of such a program, such as the technical difficulties, the danger of inflation, the selection of suitable projects, or

7. There is a similar problem today with the competition between countries in the provision of large subsidies and tax concessions to attract multinational companies. This results in the multinationals' making big profits, in fiscal problems for the countries involved, and in a shifting of employment from one country to another. It is doubtful that the net effect for the international economy is positive.

8. *North-South: A Programme for Survival* (London: Independent Commission on International Development Issues, 1980); see esp. chap. 3.

the political resistance. These problems are by no means insignificant, but they are of the same order of magnitude as those already faced by the national and international economic systems. Nor can the development policy questions relating to such a program, which are indeed important, be covered. Only the differences between such a program and the locomotive strategy, which are in their essence twofold, can be discussed here.

First, as already pointed out, such a program would be permanent. It would not compensate for cyclical events but would compensate for permanent trends in international purchasing power and demand weaknesses and thus in effect act as a floor for foreign trade and employment. On this base there would then be scope for other national or international employment measures whether expansionary or deflationary. The second important point is that, if the projects and structural policy measures are chosen in a more or less sensible manner, such a strategy could have an immediate impact on the extremely serious employment position in the developing countries. This would then help the developed countries cope with the difficult process of adjusting their employment markets to changes in trading patterns—the New International Economic Order—by facilitating a progressive change with a minimum of frictional losses.

Finally, it is important to stress that this article only meant to shed some light on the major aspects of the various employment strategies. No claim is made for comprehensiveness. It should be pointed out, in particular, that the various national and international approaches are not necessarily incompatible with each other and can be complementary. This is especially true when one distinguishes between employment policies and labor market policies more narrowly defined. There is certainly a need to look more fully at these problems. If any of these proposals are to be realized today, however, it will require a political change in the emphasis of economic policy as well as more knowledge about the mechanics of the strategies.

ANNALS, *AAPSS*, **492**, July 1987

The Neomercantilist Constraint

By WOLFGANG HAGER

ABSTRACT: Concern about competitiveness in high technology has induced the European countries to pursue a policy of accelerated modernization. Raising the level of investment has become first priority, which implies reduced individual and social consumption and a distributive bias in favor of capital at the expense of wages, government revenues, and externalities, or environment. In addition, labor-saving innovations in process technology are speeded up without demand for final products being allowed to rise proportionally. The policy model is therefore bound to tolerate mass unemployment. Worldwide, the neomercantilist strategy creates large-scale overcapacity and leads to a race of competitive downward adjustments vis-à-vis increasing low-cost competition. The preferable alternative for Europe is a combination of Continent-wide free trade and controlled external trade in order to achieve both industrial modernization and economic growth.

Wolfgang Hager holds degrees from the Universities of Göteborg and Pennsylvania and a Ph. D. from Bonn. Since 1970 he had been writing on international economic affairs as fellow of public affairs institutes in Brussels, Paris, and the European University in Florence and, as a visiting professor, at Georgetown. He is presently a partner in European Research Associates, a Brussels consultancy.

NOTE: A slightly modified German version of this article was published in *Der Kampf um den Wohlstand von Morgen*, ed. A. Pfaller (1986).

THE currently dominant paradigm for economic policy is expressed with particular clarity in the European Commission's Fifth Medium Term Economic Policy Programme, of 1981. Professing to be ideologically neutral with regard to demand versus supply-side policies, the former are de facto excluded by reference to present circumstances: (1) inflation is too high—economic agents would expect any stimulus to be quickly followed by contraction; (2) rigidities in the economy would lead to price rather than quantity responses to any monetary or fiscal stimulus; and (3) public deficits are unacceptably high.

The immediate—that is, medium-term—task is thus to get the supply side right, which above all means promoting investment, deregulation, and more flexible labor markets. While the latter term includes employment-promoting measures like training, mobility aids, and pay differentials in tune with market demands, there is an overall bias in favor of lower real wages—or of wages rising more slowly than productivity—and of accepting the unemployment-creating consequences of productivity-enhancing investment in the context of low growth.

This article argues that the motives behind this policy stance are not only to be found in the macroeconomic orthodoxy of the day, but in the pursuit of a new and quasi-existential goal, technological excellence, with competitiveness acting as both a means and an ultimate goal.

CONVENTIONAL RESPONSES TO
GROWTH AND INTERDEPENDENCE

Many of the intellectual foundations of the present orthodoxy, including the classical proposition that capital-labor substitution can only be arrested by lowering the price of labor, are often discussed by macroeconomists, using essentially static, slightly modified closed economy models. The foreign sector appears merely as the external constraint, notably in the form of import elasticities of domestic demand above unity, and export elasticities of world demand below.

The supply-side response to the external constraint lies in increasing the flexibility of the domestic economy overall and in changing the structure of production toward goods with high individual elasticities in relation to global demand. The fact that such cycle-sensitive goods, which allow growth opportunities to be seized, exhibit a symmetrical down-side risk in weak growth episodes tends to be neglected.

The demand-side approach to the external constraint lies in internationally concerted reflation. The question of how and who has found different answers in the seventies usually involves the Organization for Economic Cooperation and Development, with the locomotive—countries with good inflation and balance-of-payments records taking the lead—and the convoy—everyone speeding up in tandem—as alternatives. The recent past shows an odd mixture—without an international common strategy—of an extreme version of the locomotive approach in the Atlantic context and a convoylike joint deflation in the European context, echoed by debt-imposed austerity policies in the Third World.

As the accidental locomotive is running out of steam, the European convoy has to rethink its speed. The European Commission, long a champion of concerted austerity policies, suggests now a modern and cautious locomotive approach for the European Community. Countries that had brought their deficits soundly under control should pause in their fiscal consolidation and introduce some supply-side tax cuts. This would bring perhaps an extra 0.5 percent in growth.

The modern part of the prescription consists of making the fiscal stimulus conditional on simultaneous supply-side measures: a reform of payroll taxes, a reduction of employment security, more competition, deregulation in service industries, and so forth. These are thought to bring another 0.5 percent in growth. A total growth of 3.5 percent would begin to match productivity increase and hence stabilize unemployment at present levels. Thus the prospect of steadily worsening unemployment—and the risk of downright recession—have led the European Commission to modify slightly its deflationary stance of the last four years, while leaving its main thrust intact.

MACRO AND MICRO POLICIES UNDER NEOMERCANTILISM

To understand this persistence it is not enough to refer to the intellectual dominance of supply-side economics and to the death of Keynesianism, which, with a lag and with a vengeance has hit the European side of the Atlantic. There is a peculiar European motivation behind these policies, and their political salience is so great that even the politically weighty problem of unemployment takes second place. The term "neomercantilism" imperfectly captures an essential element in the new economic goal structure: the importance of the external environment in structural rather than aggregate terms.

The old mercantilism was designed to enhance the power of the state and to unify it, laying the basis for strengthened military power. A radical transformation of society to allow industrialization was part of that strategy. Some of these elements are still present today, as we will see, but to a much larger extent not only the means but also the ends of neomercantilism are economic. Yet, although trade competition plays a crucial part, it is not the kind that is carried out by the competitive devaluations, export subsidies, or protectionism, but by the competitive modernization of the economy.

What lies behind this concern? We can distinguish three related lines of argument. The first, vague but politically powerful, is a reaction to—or expression of—Europessimism: Europe is finished, the Pacific, including California, is the future. The main indicators of this—rediscovered—decadence are lags in the development of leading-edge technology in some areas of informatics and biotechnology and/or in their commercial application. The favorite stylized explanation is Eurosclerosis, stemming from rigidities above all in the labor market, but also in the regulatory environment, as well as in banking and management styles. The fact that this ossified Europe has had a better growth and employment performance than the United States until 1980 is conveniently forgotten.

The second strand relates to the unique opportunities that must be seized during the early stages of the third industrial revolution. A number of new base technologies, mostly related to the chip and the gene, are transforming the way we produce and what we produce. Bioprocesses are said to enter into 40 percent of material output. Informatics is blurring the line between goods and services, making knowledge, embodied or otherwise, the primary source of value added.

One of the most important tasks of economic policy, in this context, is to raise the level of investment: to incorporate technical progress into the capital stock and to offset the creative destruction of the existing stock. In the process, human capital is equally—creatively?—destroyed. Some reinvestment—training—is possible but scrapping seems increasingly to be the efficient option.

TRADE EQUALS HIGH-TECH TRADE

The implementation of the third industrial revolution is seen as a race between advanced nations, with the laggards and losers permanently locked in a vicious spiral of decline. History provides illustrations for this—Britain since the 1880s, for example—but more recently, catching up has more often than not provided a low-cost road to prosperity, as in postwar Europe and Japan.

The third related strand of thinking sees the world economy as composed of a large number of slowly growing or declining sectors and a few high-growth performers. Total economic growth can be assured by those nations that manage to capture large world—domestic and export—market shares in growth sectors. Since the total market for these fast-growing goods and services remains a small percentage of total world consumption—at most 10 percent—the competition for capturing these growth poles is fierce and, in the short run, zero sum. The acceleration of technical progress engendered by that competition may, however, in time trickle down to all participants.

If the mercantilist race were limited to high-technology products, its damage to the world economy and to the societies composing it would be limited. There would be excess capacity in, say, microchips or telecommunications equipment—more expensive perhaps than similar phenomena in steel or shipbuilding, but equally amenable to solutions combining protectionism and subsidies. This sort of generalized protectionism is familiar from developing countries, as well as procurement-related high tech in advanced countries. The nuclear power industry furnishes perhaps the best example.

In fact, the third industrial revolution extends the race to all tradable products, while creating new tradables in services. The reason is that it is, above all, a revolution in process technology. High tech becomes relevant to the most banal and traditional of products. Laser-guided automatic cutting of fabric for clothes furnishes a graphic example. Such advances are welcomed by national planners not only because they help the balance of payments and insulate a given activity from international wage competition, but also because this sort of investment creates a market for high-tech industries. Scale and learning effects resulting from rapid domestic introduction of new process technologies lay the basis for successful capital goods exports, reinforcing the scale and learning effects.

COMPETITIVE DEFLATION AND UNEMPLOYMENT

What are the consequences for employment policy? One immediate consequence is a neglect of the unemployment-generating consequences of the changes in process technology. The old word "rationalization" captures these consequences, but not the new motivation: saving labor by deepening capital is a half-welcome, half-unwelcome by-product of the real purpose, which is to stay in the top league of technological excellence. Since national power and the future welfare of society are thought to be linked to success, formerly dominant political goals like full employment become secondary.

The more subtle consequences for employment come from the macroeconomic stance associated with modernization-oriented neomercantilism. As pointed out earlier, investment is the crucial variable. In the present dominant pre-Keynesian perspective, investment is a function of expected profits. Profits are a function of costs—since prices are given by the world market, and demand is, in the first instance, neglected.

Costs are ultimately to be lowered by a technological progress function in the medium run, that is, via investment itself. The task of public policy is to reduce costs by acting in four areas: (1) deregulation, which may either involve a wholesome review of accumulated bureaucratic obstacles or a calling into question of nonmaterial aspects of the social welfare function; (2) corporate taxes, including social security contributions, which must be lowered or shifted to the consumer; (3) the share of wages in gross national product, which share must be further lowered by letting real wages rise more slowly than productivity; and (4) government spending, which must be curtailed to avoid crowding out, that is, to free savings from deficit financing to allow productive investment.

How about demand in this model, which is the familiar austerity model applied in virtually all Western European countries today? There are two answers. One is to expect investment to rise in proportion to the fall in final demand engendered by reduced government spending and in proportion to the squeeze on consumption caused by increased private taxes and lower wages. Such a closing of the model is indeed theoretically feasible, if we had a once-and-for-all shift in the relative shares of consumption and investment in gross national product, with both terms of the equation growing at a higher and equal rate after that. The problem with present policies is that they are medium term in concept, implying a slow and steady squeeze on demand. Moreover, as I will argue, they have long-term deflationary consequences in the present context of the world economy.

The second answer to the demand problem is exports: the increased investment will increase competitiveness. This will allow growth at least as strong as the world average (import and export elasticities = 1), or better (export elasticities ≥ 1). In many respects this is the familiar export-led growth model as described by Balogh in the early seventies: incomes in the exporting country rise more slowly than productivity and/or world income. Exports give an investable surplus to firms. This increases productivity, allowing a permanently lagged rise in worker incomes. This provides an additional and stable domestic element of growth.

What are the differences between the present strategy and the familiar export-led growth model? First, the lag between domestic productivity increases and income rises is stretched to the point where the essential domestic demand component of growth fails to materialize in time to vindicate the initial investment surge. That surge might therefore not take place at all. Second, a parallel strategy by all Western European countries, which carry out two-thirds of their trade with each other, leaves a small residual, in terms of gross national product of exports—± 10 percent—to the rest of the world. This becomes infinitesimal when reduced to net exports, that is, minus imports. If we moreover consider that many of Western Europe's third export markets are strictly dependent, as regards their ability to import, on Europe's conjuncture—for example, Eastern Europe, the Mediterranean rim, raw-material less developed countries—the proposition becomes even more doubtful. The poor growth and employment performance by one of the most successful practitioners of this strategy, Germany, which is once again piling up huge export surpluses, rather proves the point.

In fact, Western Europe as a whole has just lived through an episode that half vindicates the export-led growth strategy, increasing exports to the United States by 45 percent, as against Japan's 47 percent. A slowdown of U.S. growth or a fall of the dollar or increased protectionism in the United States—and potentially all three—will throw Europe back on its own resources for demand creation with a vengeance. At that point, the normal pattern of interaction between the world economy and neomercantilist Europe will become apparent.

Modernization, we recall, is to be achieved via investment. This is to be stimulated by higher profits on the supply side and exports on the demand side. The model seems to assume no capital mobility; otherwise, the equation of higher profits with higher investment would have to be complemented by the condition "provided returns on invest-

ment in domestic manufacturing are higher than alternative investments." In this context the flow of capital into foreign investment, direct or portfolio, is particularly relevant. Such investment will occur—under conditions of free trade—if the costs of manufacturing abroad are even lower than in a supply-side reformed Europe. For a very large range of products this seems to be the case. Leaving aside some high-tech areas where production in the United States enjoys an absolute advantage, in the standard products, including labor-intensive parts of high-tech production, the cost picture may look as follows.

Instead of lower taxes, as in Europe, there may be none at all for an initial 10-year period, which is longer than the lifetime of manufacturing plants these days. As regards labor, wages will be a fraction of European levels; however, moderate future pay claims and flexibility of labor use will remain much higher. Capital costs will be subsidized twice: by the home government and by the export credits from Western suppliers. The result is a no-growth rentier economy in Europe, which not only means a shift of income from workers to capital without the lagged income growth under the export-led growth model, but also higher unemployment and above all—from the standpoint of neomercantilism—a failure of the investment-led modernization strategy itself.

This picture seems to be in partial contradiction to what was said earlier on the properties of the third industrial revolution. New production technologies reestablish comparative—better: competitive—advantage to the rich countries. Labor costs become less relevant, but they do not become wholly irrelevant, except for wholly automated production, as in fibers. At that stage the employment problem is replaced by a pure distributional issue. In practice, manual labor remains important even in rapidly automating industries like automobiles. And even if wage costs ceased to matter, the European worker would retain a nuisance value that can be avoided by relocating to a trade-union-free environment; compare a similar north-south movement within the United States.

On a world level, the constellation outlined is severely deflationary in aggregate terms and prone to disequilibrium in structural terms. The structural effect derives from the global trend to subsidize industrial capital, leading to (1) overcapacity, that is, waste on a large scale; and (2) unemployment, since the artificially stimulated investment increases productivity without an offsetting growth in total output, or demand—pace Say's Law.

The aggregate effect results from a universal attempt to keep production costs—wages, taxes—low, destroying final demand. We argued earlier that already implied in the design of present policies is a long lag between the profit-induced investment rise and the eventual, productivity-derived rise in final domestic consumption, such as wages and government expenditure. In theory at least, that lag may have to wait until such distant times as productivity wages are equalized worldwide and full employment reached. The integration of world goods and capital markets implies the integration of world labor markets. Given the global labor surplus, the shadow price of labor is close to subsistence. Myriad market imperfections prevent, in reality, factor price equalization for labor. But the pressure operates clearly, at the margin, in that direction, although quantity responses—unemploy-

ment—are being preferred to price responses—lower wages—at least in Europe.

The renewed stress on industrial modernization has other, more subtle effects as regards public policy. In Europe, a comparatively large part of total investment has traditionally gone to long-term infrastructure: public and private building, roads, schools, and parks. In a mercantilist context, these investments are seen as frivolous unless they serve to lower industrial costs; investments in transport, telecommunications, some forms of education, and so forth would be reviewed as frivolous. In general, however, there is a shift in national resources toward the material end of the needs spectrum, and toward tradables in particular. Deregulation, as already mentioned, is in part a rollback of a century-old attempt to cope with negative externalities of industrialization. While initially this may remove a lot of deadwood, the need for international competitiveness in the end implies *harmonisation vers le bas*.

ARE THERE ALTERNATIVES?

The first alternative to competitive deflation is competitive devaluation. This can be a strategy for one country, but not for Western Europe as a whole, except vis-à-vis the United States and Japan. Devaluation is fairer than wage reduction as a means for reestablishing competitiveness, as the sheltered sector—dentists, bureaucrats—share the income loss. Those losses are, however, larger than necessary to the extent that non-price-sensitive exports and imports are involved, causing an excessive loss in terms of trade. Moreover, the resistance to such a general income loss has proved inflationary, unless accompanied by deflation.

Devaluation also fails to address the structural mercantilist objective, which, to repeat, is not competitiveness in the short term, but competitiveness gained by a shift of production toward the high-tech, high-value-added range of the spectrum. Making traditional industries competitive through devaluation can thus not be part of the strategy.

A second alternative is protectionism. This would raise profits for domestic industry, plus expectations of future profits that could translate into investment. The capital goods manufacturers would lose export markets, due to quantity effects and retaliation, but gain a more profitable and growing domestic market. Full-employment policies and growth would become feasible and imports would actually increase. The rapid and high-tech modernization of the textile industries of the countries of the Organization for Economic Cooperation and Development illustrates the structural case if not the aggregate one.

In addition to the familiar objections to this strategy, mercantilism adds a new one: world-class technological excellence cannot be reached unless firms are forced to compete in world markets. This proposition belongs not in the realm of classical economics, but in the realm of empirically testable industrial economics. We know that competition as a spur toward efficiency and the adoption of best practice has an upper and a lower bound. The upper bound is represented by an equalization of profit rates that inhibits innovative investment, as has been described by Schumpeter. The lower bound is monopoly, although American studies of monopolies such as the Bell system have shown an above-average introduction of new technology. Japan's protectionism can be maintained until a product reaches supercompetitiveness, while in the domestic market competition is modulated pragmatically over the life cycle of a sector; Japan's protectionism also inhibits blanket assertions.

For Western Europe, continentwide free trade and a mixture of Japanese-style internal competition and external protectionism would seem to provide an answer, however unpleasant, to the twin dangers of deflation and loss of socio-economic autonomy posed by the present mercantilist constellation of the world economy. This would not involve anything remotely like autarky: with the extension and tightening of the Multifibre Arrangement in the seventies, Europe's imports and exports in textiles have grown substantially relative to the sixties. Rather, it would provide that margin for macroeconomic policy and profitable investment without which neither the unemployment nor the industrial modernization problem can be tackled.

ANNALS, *AAPSS*, **492**, July 1987

Population, Labor Supply, and Employment in Developing Countries

By HILDE WANDER

ABSTRACT: Over the past thirty years, almost all developing countries have been suffering from severe underutilization of their rapidly growing work force, manifest in the first place in various forms of underemployment rather than in open unemployment. Prospective trends in the working-age population suggest an even steeper increase in labor supply and respectively rising employment problems for some time ahead. Policies promoting economic growth have proved insufficient to solve the problems. New strategies are called for, aimed explicitly at mobilizing the ill-used labor potentials for developmental purposes. This article consists of three parts. The first one gives a general outline of the relationships between population, labor supply, and employment, while the second one deals with empirical trends and structural changes in labor supply in the second half of this century. Both analyses bring forth the arguments for comprehensive approaches to the employment problem, which are presented in part three.

Hilde Wander is a former staff member of the research department of the Kiel Institute of World Economics and is particularly concerned with population, labor force, and migration issues. She has also worked for the United Nations in several developing countries. Since her retirement, in 1980, she holds lectures in population economics at the University of Kiel.

A MONG the many problems confronting the developing world, the persistent shortage of productive employment deserves particular attention. For demographic and socioeconomic reasons, large numbers of juveniles and formerly inactive women have been swelling the work force for many years and are expected to do so for some time to come. For most of the new entries, employment is not only a means of earning a living but also of acquiring useful skills. Moreover, steady improvement of skills is an important component of overall economic and social development.

The experience of the last three decades has shown that even with high rates of economic performance, large segments of the work force in most developing countries have remained without the chance to gain a decent living. Obviously, the prospects for economic growth to meet the quantitative and the qualitative needs for employment are gloomy under conditions of accelerating labor force growth. This task involves two conflicting objectives that do not spontaneously balance in a socially desirable way. Indeed, the recent pattern of capital formation and technological advancement has often resulted in extensive labor surplus along with shortage of skills. New approaches to the employment problem are needed that take account of population trends and of the welfare of the so far disadvantaged groups as part and parcel of general economic development.

This article will first deal with the relationships between population, labor supply, and employment as arising in the course of demographic and economic development. In this context, "demographic development" denotes the historical decline in birth and death

rates—called demographic transition— and the resulting change in growth and structure of the population, while "economic development"—in contrast to economic growth—stands for successive structural change toward an integrated modern economy, dependent on intensive use of human and physical capital and serving all population groups.

LINKAGES BETWEEN POPULATION, LABOR FORCE, AND EMPLOYMENT PATTERN

Nobody doubts that population and labor force are closely connected.[1] Concerning employment, however, the links with population and labor supply seem less clear. To many experts employment is mainly governed by economic potentials and only indirectly affected by population and labor force trends. While this assertion holds true for the highly industrialized countries, it is not generally applicable to the developing world.

Population growth and employment in the traditional economy

In all developing countries a major part of the work force is engaged in the traditional, or informal, sector of the economy comprising subsistence agriculture, traditional trades and crafts, and many sorts of personal services. Labor demand of this sector is often governed by social considerations rather than by strict cost-effectiveness calculations.[2]

1. The labor force includes all persons who—in a given period—are employed or looking for a job. The terms "labor supply," "labor potential," and "work force" are used interchangeably.
2. Hilde Wander, "Die Beziehungen zwischen Bevölkerungs- und Wirtschaftsentwicklung, dargestellt am Beispiel Indonesiens," Kieler Studien, Forschungsberichte des Instituts für Weltwirtschaft

Many of these branches have proved most elastic in absorbing rising numbers of job seekers through a mechanism constantly fed by rapid growth of population and labor supply. Increasing pressure on the land has not only led to widespread underemployment[3] and poverty in the countryside, but also to intensive rural-urban migration. Many migrants to the big cities enter the informal sector for employment. Supported by the simple demand for goods and services of an increasing number of poor people and by the growing supply of workers in need of any kind of job, this sector has expanded largely by its own dynamics. Although many firms are working quite effectively, this self-feeding, demographically induced process has tended to depress productivity and to raise underemployment in even the most active urban places. This fact does not rule out the possibility for many individual migrants to enjoy better working and living conditions than previously in their home villages.

Conditions in the informal sector have not left employment in the modern part of the economy unaffected. Branches such as textile, leather, construction, and commerce often make use of the cheap and flexible supply of informal labor by direct hiring on a casual basis or by subcontracting production or marketing to small employers.[4] This sort of cooperation, although profitable to modern firms, contributes to keeping regular employment low in the modern sector and to perpetuating poor working and income standards in the informal sector, thus hampering the most needed functional integration of the economy.

The various links between population, labor supply, and employment work both ways. The shortage of remunerative income opportunities and the lack of prospects to advance, which many informal workers experience, are among the factors that support high fertility and rapid population growth. In this way, population growth and underemployment tend to strengthen each other through a kind of vicious circle that is difficult to break.

Demographic transition and employment prospects

The linkages between population, labor supply, and employment tend to change with demographic and economic development. The individual developing countries have reached different stages in the process of birth and death decline; their economies are therefore differently affected by population trends.

It is not accidental that countries with still-high levels of births and deaths generally suffer from economic backwardness. High birth rates imply an age structure with relatively many children to be supported by a respectively small work force potential. High mortality, on the other hand, means that many children die before becoming economically productive. Consequently, large parts of the resources spent on raising the young generation are lost and not paying dividends. Both conditions, high child burden and wasteful investment in human capital, tend to hamper economic prog-

---

an der Universität Kiel, ed. Prof. Dr. Drs. h.c. Erich Schneider, no. 70 (Tübingen: J.C.B. Mohr [Paul Siebeck], 1965), pp. 72-73, 144 ff.

3. "Underemployment," in contrast to open unemployment, means that persons—although employed—are confined to short-term, unstable, unproductive, or other unremunerative work.

4. Alejandro Portes and Lauren Benton, "Industrial Development and Labor Absorption: A Reinterpretation," *Population and Development Review*, 10:589-611 (Dec. 1984).

ress by impeding improvements in skills and in labor productivity.

Arguments maintaining that it is cheap in poor societies to raise children rest on false judgment. It can be shown that, relative to available resources, a child in a poor country consumes as much as a child in a rich country, on the average.[5] To put children to work at an early age, which is still common in many developing countries, may help the individual family to make an excessive dependency burden bearable, but it cannot eliminate the fatal consequences on the formation of skills.

In order to reduce the waste of human investment, mortality must fall. Favorable effects can then accrue from the better chances to raise the physical and mental ability of the young generation and to accumulate more experience during a longer working life. True, these advantages are mainly latent and depend on sufficient employment to have an effect. However, where there is high mortality, even these latent forces are missing. In fact, almost all developing countries with low mortality are also economically more advanced than those with high mortality. Yet, this advantage has not prevented severe underutilization of labor, unless fertility has also effectively decreased.

A fall in mortality does not alter the age composition and the dependency burden to any marked extent. If fertility stays high, the potential advantages of low mortality in terms of smaller losses of human investment are largely compensated for by the larger number of children to be educated. Moreover,

5. Hilde Wander, "What Does It Cost to Support the Young and the Old Generation?" in *Economic Consequences of Population Change in Industrialized Countries*, ed. Gunter Steinmann (Berlin: Springer Verlag, 1984), pp. 238-57.

young people entering the labor force face greater difficulties in finding adequate employment, since fewer workers die during their working life than under conditions of high mortality. Hence, at high fertility, declining mortality implies greater unbalance between entries to and departures from the labor force. Fewer vacancies for a rising number of young people also means a waste of human investment, only at a later stage of life than occurs under conditions of high mortality.

Such chronic unbalance between entries and departures is hard to defeat with economic measures alone. The amount of capital needed to create enough productive jobs for a rapidly growing number of beginners is bound to compete with the task of improving educational standards. Ever more resources must be spent per child if the quality of the young generation and, in turn, the work force is to be raised. Needless to say, this task is easier to manage with low birth rates and smaller cohorts requiring education and employment.

Shifts in underemployment in the course of development

Underutilization of labor, which plagues all developing countries with high fertility, tends to assume different forms at different stages of development. Countries or areas at the beginning of development typically suffer from underemployment in agriculture in the form of low productivity and seasonal shortages of work. With an ongoing mortality decline and rising pressure on the land, underemployment tends to spread to urban places and to take such forms as short-term work, job instability, makeshift production, and subnormal incomes. Finally, at low mortality and more advanced economic performance, open unemployment tends to gain importance along with all sorts of visible and disguised underemployment, especially in the swelling metropolitan areas. Mismatch of supply and demand of skills, in consequence of inappropriate educational systems and the lack of chances to acquire useful skills, is a prominent feature at this stage of demographic transition and economic advancement.

The tendency for underutilization of labor to alter its form rather than to slow down as long as fertility stays high explains how difficult it is to speed up economic development against the forces of an excessive dependency burden. None of the apparently more advanced countries with high birth and low death rates was able to master their employment problems. Real improvements have only been achieved in countries with an effective birth decline and reductions in the relative burden of young dependents.

*Demographic numbers alone
cannot explain the
links with employment*

Clearly, a downturn in births and deaths is not enough to improve employment, but it leads to demographic conditions that give appropriate policies a better chance to succeed. Taiwan is a good example of how demographic and economic development can be brought into harmony through well-designed socioeconomic strategies aimed at improving productivity and employment in all sectors of the economy.[6] Where

such farsighted policies are lacking, even favorable demographic conditions can do little to support economic development. The countries of temperate South America are typical examples. It goes without saying that it is easier with abundant than with short capital to absorb a growing population at rising living standards. But even so, without effective fertility decline and concomitant change in social outlook, it is problematic to introduce modern lines of production and employment into a society favoring traditional ways of life. The oil-rich countries in the Middle East, especially Iran, are cases in point.

The linkages between population, labor force, and employment in developing countries are therefore not explained just by numerical issues. Age structures, level of skill, as well as prevailing attitudes and aspirations of the population come into play. The several causal factors must be taken into account when evaluating empirical trends in population and labor supply, the more so as the conventional definitions and concepts that underlie the respective statistics are not well suited to the employment conditions in developing countries.

TRENDS IN POPULATION AND LABOR
SUPPLY, 1950-2000

The following analysis is based on estimates and projections by the International Labor Office.[7] The estimates for 1950-70 are derived from census returns and surveys; the data for 1980-2000 rely on population projections assessed in 1973 by the United Nations.[8] Since then the United Nations data have been re-

6. Paul K.C. Liu, "Toward a Closer Integration of Population in Development Policies in Taiwan," *Industry in Free China.* 56(2):9-28 (Aug. 1981).

7. International Labor Office, *Labour Force Estimates and Projections, 1950-2000* (Geneva: International Labor Office, 1977), vols. 1-6.
8. For techniques, see ibid., vol. 6.

peatedly revised by taking into account more recent knowledge on birth and death trends. Nevertheless, use of the earlier assessment has not invalidated the labor force projections to any major extent. Recent declines in birth rates will not much affect the work force during this century. Moreover, overestimates of births were often compensated for by underestimates of deaths, thus leaving total population largely unaffected by the revisions.

In this article, developing countries[9] have been subdivided into three main groups in order to allow for some obvious differences in economic attainment and natural resources. The first group covers all countries that, in 1980, had a per capita income below $500. This group includes China and India, which are shown separately in Tables 1 and 2. The second group covers all other developing countries, except for the most important oil exporters, which form group three.

Major employment problems
are still to come

Table 1 shows that population and labor force have expanded rapidly since 1950 and will continue the upward trend for the rest of the century. Between 1980 and 2000, 653 million persons are projected to add to the work force; this sum is 119 million more than over the preceding thirty years. As explained before, labor supply will likely grow most in the low-mortality countries, which are predominantly to be found in the two better-off groups. In these groups a 70

9. Developing countries include Asia south of the USSR, except Japan and Israel; Africa except South Africa; Latin America except Argentina, Chile, and Uruguay. Polynesia and Micronesia are disregarded because of small size.

percent increase is foreseen between 1980 and 2000, as against 30 percent in China, 55 percent in India, and 63 percent in the other poor countries, on the average. This suggests that even in the richer countries the major employment problems may still lie ahead, in spite of a recent fertility decline in several of them.

In 1980, almost 60 percent of the Third World's work force was still engaged in agriculture, but there were, of course, marked regional differences, ranging from over 70 percent in the group of low-income countries, excluding China and India, to somewhat above 40 percent in the other two groups. Although this share has much declined since 1950, the volume of agricultural workers has continued to grow. For example, in the poor countries other than China, agriculture still had to accommodate, in the years 1970-80, half of the group's total work force gains, and that in spite of heavy out-migration.

It is difficult to foresee how the even greater increase in labor supply to be expected for the rest of the century will distribute between agriculture and nonagriculture. Following recent experience, it is likely that in the poorer countries, except China, agriculture will continue to absorb major proportions of total labor force gains, while in China and in the other two country groups the agricultural work force will probably shrink, with the effect that all new workers plus those leaving agriculture will look for nonagricultural employment.

The projections in Table 2 show net additions to the work force. They do not allow for already existing underemployment and therefore fail to denote the real number of jobs needed to cut down underutilization of human resources effectively. The volume of underemploy-

TABLE 1
POPULATION AND LABOR FORCE IN DEVELOPING COUNTRIES,
1950-2000(In millions)

Country Group	Estimate		Projection	
	1950	1970	1980	2000
Population (total)	1,630	2,498	3,156	4,832
Labor force (total)	696	1,010	1,230	1,883
Low-income countries*	555	798	955	1,398
China	242	365	422	550
India	160	218	266	411
All others	152	216	267	436
Medium-income countries[†]	105	158	206	358
Main oil exporters	36	54	70	128

SOURCE: ILO, *Labour Force Estimates and Projections, 1950-2000* (Geneva: International Labour Organisation, 1977), vols 1-3, passim. Copyright 1977, International Labour Organisation, Geneva.

NOTE: The countries included are: Asia south of the USSR, except Japan and Israel; Africa except South Africa; Latin America except Argentina, Chile, and Uruguay. Polynesia and Micronesia are disregarded because of small size.

*Countries with per capita income below $500 in 1980.

[†]Countries with per capita income of $500 or more in 1980, except for the rich oil countries.

TABLE 2
AGRICULTURAL AND NONAGRICULTURAL WORK FORCE IN THE THIRD WORLD,
1980 COMPARED WITH 1950 AND 2000 (In millions)

Country Group	Agriculture			Nonagriculture		
		Change between 1980 and			Change between 1980 and	
	1980*	1950	2000[†]	1980*	1950	2000[†]
Low-income countries	613	155	57	342	245	386
China	251	45	−44	171	135	172
India	173	47	37	93	58	108
All others	189	63	64	78	52	106
Medium-income countries	90	18	−15	116	83	167
Main oil exporters	30	5	−4	40	29	62
Total	733	179	37	498	357	615

*Estimates are based on ILO, *Labour Force Estimates and Projections, 1950-2000*, vols. 1-3 (Copyright 1977, International Labour Organisation, Geneva); World Bank, *World Development Report 1984* (New York: Oxford University Press, 1984), tab. 21; International Labor Office, *Year Book of Labour Statistics* (Geneva: International Labor Office, 1983), pp. 38 ff.

[†]Projections are based on the assumption that the share of agriculture in the total labor force will in each country continue to decline along a curve following the actual downtrend between 1950 and 1980.

ment is hard to measure, but there is general agreement that it includes several hundred million workers, equal to about one-fourth to two-fifths of the total work force in the Third World.[10] All this suggests that the progressive

10. M.J.D. Hopkins, "A Global Forecast of Absolute Poverty and Employment," *Interna-*

shift of workers from agricultural to nonagricultural activities, which is usually taken as a sign of favorable economic change, may just indicate, under conditions of excessive labor force growth, a redistribution rather than an alleviation of existing employment problems.

Rising unbalance between labor force entries and departures

To provide the young generation with adequate jobs is a major task in all developing countries. As mentioned before, with declining mortality and persistently high fertility, the discrepancy between new entries to and departures from the work force is due to rise. Calculations carried out by the International Labor Office in 1974 give some idea of the size of this unbalance. Part A of Table 3 shows that the ratio of new entries to departures by death, which was about 3.4:1 in 1970 in the developing countries, on the average, may go up to 5.5:1 in the year 2000. True, these estimates, which rely on some obsolete population projections, may not be fully in line with actual and prospective trends, but the general impact of falling mortality and retarded birth decline becomes nevertheless clear. East Asia, which experienced a similar downtrend in deaths to that of Latin America, but an earlier fall in births, shows typically smaller discrepancies between entries and departures by death. According to part B of the table, this advantage even persists when all departures from the labor force are taken into account. With ongoing economic and social development, voluntary retirements tend to compensate increasingly for fewer departures by death, but demographic trends still remain basic for the level of entry-departure unbalance as well as for respective historical and regional differences.

Moreover, the jobs left by the retiring workers are not always open to the new entries. Many of the older workers who were self-employed or unpaid family workers may withdraw from the labor force because their activities are no longer demanded; others may give up jobs for which young beginners are not yet qualified. Young workers need, in particular, employment as wage and salary earners in enterprises where they can acquire useful skills. This fact implies a further squeeze in job opportunities for the young generation and stresses the need for effective change in employment structure by status.

Such change depends on comprehensive economic development, in the course of which the share of self-employed persons tends to decline in favor of rising proportions of wage and salary earners with constant increases in competence and labor productivity. The skills required in a structurally changing economy are no longer limited to special crafts, but include much broader qualities. Apart from appropriate working behavior and sufficient understanding of modern working conditions, adequate technical, managerial, and organizational proficiency is needed for all medium and higher grades of the occupational pyramid. Due to rising pressure for income opportunities, such productive change in status and proficiency is still missing in even the more advanced Latin American countries.[11] The persistently high percentage of self-employed

11. Portes and Benton, "Industrial Development and Labor Absorption," p. 103.

TABLE 3
ENTRY-DEPARTURE RATIOS FOR MALE LABOR FORCE
IN DEVELOPING COUNTRIES, 1970-2000

Region	1970	1980	1990	2000
A. Entries per 100 departures due to death				
East Asia except Japan	326	369	398	435
South Asia	351	452	523	592
Africa	336	368	438	516
Latin America* and Oceania[†]	464	560	670	783
Total	343	420	483	550
B. Entries per 100 departures for any reason				
East Asia except Japan	214	213	191	178
South Asia	260	304	302	310
Africa	242	279	299	323
Latin America* and Oceania[†]	306	330	329	359
Total	241	268	267	273

SOURCE: "Labour Force and World Population Growth," *Bulletin of Labour Statistics,* special ed. (1974), pp. 75 ff. Copyright 1974, International Labour Organisation, Geneva.
*Except Argentina, Chile, and Uruguay.
†Polynesia, Micronesia, and Melanesia are included. Excluded are Australia and New Zealand, which are developed countries.

persons indicates clearly that many of them are workers on their own account in the informal sector.

ARGUMENTS FOR A COMPREHENSIVE APPROACH TO THE EMPLOYMENT PROBLEM

The previous discussion has shown that the links between population, labor supply, and employment work through all facets of socioeconomic development as well as through individual behavior. A proper approach to the employment problem should, therefore, take into account the needs of society as well as of the people, which are often conflicting. Economic development and expansion of productive employment on the macro level of society depend very much on responsible cooperation by the population with respect to consumption, savings, working habits, and acquisition of skills. Behavior, however, is largely subject to values, norms, and physical conditions that govern individual life. Consequently, desirable change in behavior presupposes that individual and social interests be brought into harmony; that opportunities opened by economic development reach the people in their immediate sphere of life and offer them realistic chances for personal advancement. Generative behavior is motivated by the same set of values, attitudes, and aspirations that guide social and economic actions of the individual and are, therefore, likely to respond favorably to improvements in personal welfare.

Upgrading of the informal sector

These interdependencies between individual well-being and overall development provide a strong argument for giving more attention to the informal sector, the more so as the modern sectors in the developing countries are still too small to offer sufficient employment and training to the young generation. In spite of low productivity, the informal economy in the urban and rural areas holds a great deal of potential, such as initiative, enterprising spirit, and various skills that can be mobilized for development purposes. Apart from measures alleviating access to capital, raw material, and markets, special advice is needed for more efficient use of capital and labor, for raising production and marketing standards, and for improving managerial skills.

As mentioned in another context, the informal sector largely meets the consumption needs of the population. Upgrading this sector depends, therefore, very much on rising purchasing power among these particular strata. Of course, more purchasing power requires more stable employment, but the connection works both ways. Higher consumption does not necessarily retard capital formation and economic advancement, as assumed in neoclassical theory. On the contrary, in many poor countries, improvement in health through better food and housing is basic for raising labor productivity. Moreover, the chance to buy more than mere necessities and acquire such goods and services that give pleasure and status may provide a strong incentive to the individual to save and to spend on education and training. Such behavior tends to support economic development along with personal advancement.

Not the struggle for mere survival, but realistic prospects for a better life are apt to release productive impulses. Higher consumption standards imply wider markets, more skill-intensive production, and more remunerative employment and—what is equally important—

provide an inducement to limit births. Without effective birth decline, especially among the poor majority, there will be no real solution to the employment problem. Examples for such a comprehensive approach to economic development utilizing the potentials of all population groups are to be found in East Asia.[12]

Upgrading of the traditional sector means a direct attack on underemployment, mobilization of unused resources, and promotion of economic integration. It has the advantage of immediately reaching large groups of so far underprivileged people in their capacity as workers and consumers, and it implies the chance of developing useful skills and working habits, of directing small savings into productive channels, and of stimulating enterprising spirits.

Although the need for employment and training may be most pressing in the big cities, the fact that urban and rural problems are closely related calls for simultaneous improvements in all areas. In fact, rising productivity in traditional agriculture and more remunerative nonagricultural jobs in the countryside are basic to solving urban employment problems. They can assist to check city-ward migration and to unburden urban labor markets. Rising demand for industrial products in consequence of higher income in agriculture is a prerequisite for more intensive exchange of goods, raw material, and capital between rural and urban areas and thus a necessity for economic integration.

12. Deborah S. Freedman, "Consumption Aspiration as Economic Incentives in a Developing Country: Taiwan," in *Human Behaviour in Economic Affairs*, ed. Burkhard Strumpel, James N. Morgan, and Ernest Zahn (Amsterdam, New York: Elsevier, 1972), pp. 229-60.

Need for communal development

There remains the question of how these far-reaching aspects can be observed in practical policy, in view of the large and growing labor supply. There is, of course, no general answer, since national conditions and potentials play a decisive role. The manifold direct and indirect links between population, labor force, and employment nevertheless make one point clear: the problems of underemployment in the developing world cannot be managed by way of conventional central planning alone. The interrelationships between the macro and micro levels of society call for delegation of part of the planning activities, down to the lowest administrative strata, that is, to villages, small towns, and appropriate subsections of larger urban communities.

Experience shows that it is often more promising to let people define their own problems and look for adequate solutions than to employ centrally organized measures that are not directly geared to their specific need. Disregarding the difficulties in promoting communal activities, the following viewpoints underline the general importance of decentralized development efforts.

1. It is the local rather than the national level where individual and social interests are immediately confronted and can best be reconciled. It is on this level that social pressure arises and can assist to release and strengthen cooperative and progress-minded attitudes.

2. On a communal basis, local initiative, skills, and savings can be used for productive purposes that meet the needs of the people. Such activities are also best suited to make the population understand existing possibilities for social and economic improvements and to keep aspirations within realistic limits.

3. It is within individual communities that the potential advantages of fewer children first have an effect. Small increases in purchasing power and rises in consumption accruing from lower dependency burden will especially benefit local craftsmen and traders.

4. Local self-help activities can be employed particularly to improve social and economic infrastructure in the communities. Those activities are generally labor intensive and therefore suitable to reduce underemployment. Carried out with local resources, they can help to save national funds for projects dependent on higher inputs of capital and qualified labor. Moreover, such costly projects promise greater success when they are placed in communities actively striving for higher welfare.

5. Communal activities have the tendency to spread if they are well planned and kept in line with overall social and economic goals. They are, therefore, no alternative to national policies, but a necessary part of comprehensive efforts to make better use of available labor resources and to promote social and economic progress.

ANNALS, *AAPSS*, **492**, July 1987

Unemployment and the Recomposition of Labor Reserves

By GUY STANDING

ABSTRACT: To understand unemployment in less developed countries, five forms of labor reserves should be distinguished: latent—not job-seeking but potentially available for the work force; stagnant—social dropouts; floating—moving in and out of the work force; active—job seekers; and employed—stop-gap reserves of enterprises. In the course of economic evolution people shift from one category to others. This continuous recomposition is heavily influenced by the economic strategies pursued. Entrenched landlordism and agro-export production end up bringing about an unintended increase in the active and stagnant labor reserve, which destabilizes the political order. Neopopulist autonomy slows down the recomposition process without stopping it. Import-substituting industrialization accelerates the formation of an active reserve without prospects of absorbing it. Export-led industrialization could provide such prospects but is feasible only for a few countries. While future perspectives for employment in less developed countries thus appear very bleak, the World Bank implies that most observed unemployment is voluntary. The underlying assumptions of this view are highly questionable because they neglect the social anatomy of the labor reserve and rely instead on abstract economic concepts.

Guy Standing is coordinator of labor market research in the International Labor Office's Employment and Development Department, Geneva. He has a Ph.D. in economics from the University of Cambridge, and among his publications are Labour Force Participation and Development; Labour Circulation and the Labour Process; *and* Unemployment and Labour Market Flexibility: The United Kingdom.

IN sheer numbers there are more people unemployed in the mid-1980s than at any other time in human history. But according to what could be called the World Bank view, expressed in various publications by the World Bank's staff members and associates, labor markets in low-income countries are operating "efficiently," while unemployment is "not a major problem" there.[1] It is also claimed that unemployment does not represent a serious welfare problem, that involuntary unemployment is unlikely because of "informal" labor markets and flexible working practices,[2] and that open unemployment is predominantly voluntary. This article explores the logic of this view after first presenting an alternative analytical perspective that focuses on actual social relations of production, which the conventional labor market view so conspicuously ignores. A basic difficulty with the World Bank view is the essentially dualistic labor market model that is used to reach conclusions—along with a somewhat selective use of data—which misrepresents the nature of the labor process in the development context.

OF LABOR RESERVES

There are various ways of conceptualizing surplus labor. The focus on unemployment has been criticized for being inappropriate, particularly but not only for low-income countries, or only partially relevant, and much effort has been devoted to visible and invisible underemployment or wider measures of labor underutilization. In considering unemployment per se, behavioral distinctions have been made between involuntary and voluntary unemployment, causal distinctions have been made between Keynesian and classical or between frictional, demand-deficient, structural, and technological unemployment, and functional distinctions have been made between natural and other unemployment. In industrialized, wage-based economies such classifications have their value, but they are less appropriate for economies undergoing transition between forms of production, where social relations of production change so dramatically. To give an example, one would scarcely expect to find much unemployment in a slave-based economy, whereas one would expect a great deal in one where casual wage labor was the main form of employment. It would not make a lot of sense to say the labor market of the former was relatively efficient because unemployment was lower.

An alternative perspective is to consider surplus labor in terms of five forms of labor reserve.[3] To do so should help to show why one expects unemployment to have been growing in many parts of the world. The first form is the one that is predominant in primitive-communal and quasi-feudal, agrarian-based societies. This can be be described as the latent reserve, which itself consists of three parts, all of which would provide labor if opportunities and needs emerged. There are those largely outside the labor force as conventionally defined, such as

1. See, for example, Lyn Squire, *Employment Policy in Developing Countries: A Survey of Issues and Evidence* (Washington, DC: Oxford University Press for the World Bank, 1981), p. 67.

2. Alan T. Udall and Stuart Sinclair, "The 'Luxury Unemployment' Hypothesis: A Review of Recent Evidence," *World Development*, 10:1 (Jan. 1982).

3. Marx outlined a threefold classification of the surplus population—floating, latent, and stagnant—plus "paupers." Karl Marx, *Capital* (New York: International Publishers, 1967), 1: 640-45.

those children and youths who are neither regularly in school nor in work, plus housewives and prematurely inactive older workers relying on transfers from relatives or others in the community. And there are the predominantly rural underemployed, ready to migrate to centers of industrial growth. This second group encompasses many who are visibly underemployed, who belong to kin-centered productive units, in which work, risk, and income are shared. In peasant-communal societies the latent labor reserve is preserved by social leveling mechanisms that inhibit individual aggrandizement. These mechanisms include structured reciprocities, rituals, and forms of communal redistribution, all of which restrict overall labor supply.[4] Finally, the latent reserve also includes those belonging to residual modes of production—tribal cultivators, nomads, and shifting cultivators, who typically survive through short working days, weeks, or years or who concentrate productive activities in seasonal bursts of work.

If the latent reserve is not "efficiently" employed in any meaningful sense of the word, that is even more so with the second form of surplus population, the stagnant labor reserve. This consists of social victims only marginally in the labor force, in reality if not statistically. Included are those who have been so long out of work that their productive capacities have been dissipated, so that they become almost unemployable in a short-term sense. Included as well are those who have drifted out of unemployment into crime, social illnesses or disabilities, prostitution, or other so-called

4. Manning Nash, *Primitive and Peasant Economic Systems* (San Francisco: Chandler, 1966), p. 35. They also inhibit technical advance and class differentiation.

illegitimate survival activities. The stagnant surplus population is essentially a lumpen proletariat, which imposes a drag on the realization of surplus because of the need for substantial transfers—indirectly from all forms of income—to ensure their survival and quiescence. In some contexts much of what is euphemistically called the informal sector consists of a stagnant surplus population. But while it is not part of the readily available labor supply—and is thereby excluded from some definitions of unemployment—its existence may increase some forms of labor supply, notably from others fearful of joining its ranks.

So the latent and stagnant surplus populations imply that the immediately available—or short-term—labor supply is less than the realistic potential—long-run—labor supply that could be mobilized for alternative development strategies, one group being partly outside the labor force, the other being part of the surplus population but not likely to supply labor effectively, at least not in the short run.

The third component is the floating labor reserve. This consists of those who move in and out of the labor force depending on specific work opportunities as well as the seasonally employed who face considerable unemployment and work only a small number of days a year. This form of surplus labor is critical for some forms of estate agriculture that rely on migrant laborers and for newly industrializing areas. In sum, the floating reserve consists of those intermittently in the labor market when and as needed—migratory laborers, labor circulants, those who do harvest work but who do non-labor-force work at other times of the year, and so on.

In many countries in the colonial era, state policies created labor reserve areas, allowing settler enterprises to draw on a floating reserve, thereby securing workers at less than the cost of reproducing labor power because wages were subsidized by domestic activities in the reserves. This practice has continued where estate or plantation agriculture has been extensive, and in the early phases of capitalist industrialization a floating reserve was vital, mobilizing labor power directly and acting as a disciplinary threat to workers in jobs. But for industrial capital such a labor force has drawbacks. It is essentially an unpredictable labor supply, requiring costly—surplus-reducing—labor controls or the loss of direct control through the need to resort to intermediaries; as a result, productivity is usually low and its growth restricted, with labor turnover and absenteeism reducing efficiency.

The fourth component is the active labor reserve, which is the part identified by conventional unemployment data. It comprises the job-seeking unemployed, though by no means all of those are covered by official statistics. The openly unemployed consist mainly of youths seeking entry into the employed labor force, as well as rural-urban migrants or those they displace, disadvantaged groups such as ethnic minorities, and the educated unemployed whose pre-labor-market schooling has left them ill-equipped for whatever jobs are available. Both the active and floating components are likely to be underestimated in censuses and surveys, particularly when short reference periods such as "the past week" are used to define active job seeking or when unemployment is narrowly defined both as being without any work and as being registered at an employment exchange. Similarly, both the floating and active labor reserves are functional in the process of proletari-

anization, that is, in the stage of development in which a disciplined, surplus-generating wage labor force is being created and molded.

Also functional in that context is the fifth component, the employed labor reserve, those with attachment to a job but with rarely much work or income. It includes bonded and some attached laborers, whose freedom to sell their labor power is heavily restricted even when not working. In general, an employed labor reserve complements the use of a floating reserve. Thus in many industrializing economies an employed reserve is used to compensate for the semiproletarianized or erratic character of wage labor supply, which is due to sickness, onerous or unfamiliar working conditions, low—efficiency—wages, conflicting claims on work time, or the lack of labor commitment, all of which are associated with high absenteeism and labor turnover. In such circumstances, employers commonly retain a pool of surplus workers, paid only for work they are occasionally required to do as stop-gap labor. An example is the use of *badli* labor in the Bombay textile industry, which one study estimated as comprising 20 percent of the work force. In general, this fifth component of the labor reserve has received little attention in the development literature, but it deserves to be taken into account for its welfare implications and for its role in increasing overall labor supply, directly in mobilizing extra labor power and indirectly through inducing greater labor supply from more regular workers threatened by possible displacement.

All five components of the labor reserve exist in all productive systems, but their relative extent as well as the absolute size of the total depend on the type of productive structure, the prevailing social relations of production, the development strategy being pursued, and the state policies accompanying it. As suggested in the next section, there are reasons to suppose that the tendencies in both the national and international economies are increasing the relative weight of the active part, thereby increasing the size of the stagnant surplus population as well.

DEVELOPMENT STRATEGIES AND THE COMPOSITION OF THE LABOR FORCE

Whether one accepts some variant of dependency theory or some perception of the old colonial international division of labor, one cannot hope to understand the dynamics of the labor process unless one starts from a consideration of the underlying social relations of production. In recent years the international division of labor has been changing in ways that have undermined precapitalist productive relations in many parts of the world and have resulted in widespread but not universal proletarianization. This has increased the likelihood of enlarged active labor reserves.

Linked to the changing technology and international redivision of labor, more flexible labor systems have emerged in both industrializing and industrialized economies, the latter often responding to pressures emanating from the former. This flexibility—for example, use of casual labor, indirect labor, and subcontracting—has limited actual and necessary proletarianization in industrializing economies. And it has contributed to deproletarianization in industrialized economies, in many of which there have been growing active and stagnant surplus populations—represented in part by high total unemployment and an unprecedented growth of long-term unem-

ployment—along with a shift toward casual labor, part-time working, labor subcontracting, and related forms of self-employment.

The following only presents a skeleton of a framework for understanding the dynamics of the labor reserve in low-income and industrializing societies. But even so, it is hoped that implicitly it will indicate the shortcomings of any simple labor market analysis.

In the colonial era, the international division of labor meant that except for urban enclaves the current low-income economies were kept as mainly agrarian. The predominant relations of production were either quasi-feudal or primitive-communal, the labor reserve in both cases being essentially latent, with some floating elements where plantations, estates, or mines needed a seasonal or fluctuating labor supply. Later, population growth, land consolidation, the closing of land frontiers, stress migration, and other developments generated active and stagnant surplus populations mainly around urban areas, but until fairly recently that was a fringe phenomenon.

However, in the postcolonial era one can distinguish five main development strategies that have been followed. They are, of course, ideal types, but they capture the broad tendencies. All but the first represent attempts to alter the international division of labor and have involved transformations of the social relations of production. As such, they each have distinctive implications for the level and composition of the labor reserve.

The first is what can be called entrenched landlordism. This occurs in mainly rural societies where governments attempt to preserve a quasi-feudal structure, consisting of landlords and estates controlling most of the land and other means of production, forcing the peasantry to combine small-scale subsistence production with labor for the estates. This setup—characteristic of much of Central America, for instance—implies chronic underemployment, the preservation of a rural latent reserve, and checks on population mobility. Landlords and their representatives have restricted urban industrial growth, but with land consolidation and population growth, a rural floating labor reserve has emerged; and as that has not been absorbed in industrial expansion, active and stagnant labor reserves have tended to follow. As that has contributed to mass revolt and in turn to more severe authoritarian policies, landlordism scarcely represents a viable development option for very long.

The second strategy is agro-export production, often stemming from landlordism, a shift to agro-exports reflecting the limited scope for industrialization. But whereas landlordism has tried to preserve an impoverished peasantry, this involves a move to wage-based labor, whether the shift to agro-exports occurs in peasant-communal or in landlord-dominated economies. In the latter case, peasants have been squeezed off the land, often being turned into a landless or near-landless floating reserve, sometimes located in urban areas, as with the *boias-frias* in Brazil. In peasant-communal economies, a shift from food crops to export crops has been associated with smallholder differentiation, with poor peasants being turned into wage laborers and thus converted from latent into floating and active reserves. In both cases there is usually considerable stress migration that augments an active urban labor reserve and undermines nonwage relations of production, because of the availability of low-cost wage labor. The agro-export strategy implies a disintegration of peasant productive units, and the village communities on which they are based, which in turn enlarges and reconstructs the surplus population. Members of rural families—notably children, the elderly, and many women—are pushed into the latent reserve, while youths migrate to join the urban unemployed or take jobs in place of urban youths. To the extent that industrial growth is checked by the landlord-dominated government, a stagnant surplus population grows with many eking out survival in the nebulous informal sector.

Whereas entrenched landlordism relies primarily on the peasants' dependent insecurity to generate and control labor supply, agro-export production relies more on the lack of access to means of production. Agro-export production depends on active and floating labor reserves, whereas landlordism depends more on preserving a latent reserve. But both tend to generate growing active and stagnant surplus populations, scarcely placated by government policies in the absence of a flourishing industrial sector.

The third development strategy, also rural oriented, ostensibly dispenses with such motivational factors as insecurity and the denial of means of production. It is best described as neopopulist autonomy, being an attempt to break from the international division of labor and secure accumulation through communal production and distribution. Examples of this strategy, to some extent at least, can be found in Tanzania, Guyana, and Cuba. A feature is a bureaucratization of production, with state-organized redistribution of surplus limiting income and class differentiation. Such systems have run into a motivational crisis, a limited labor supply leading to limited accumulation, and the growth of a large latent reserve mainly in rural underemployment, as well as a growing active reserve as people flock to urban areas, partly due to the absence of consumer goods in rural communities. So some of the symptoms of a surplus population in other agrarian structures emerge, even though populist anti-urban bias slows the growth of an active labor reserve.

The fourth strategy is import-substitution industrialization, of which there are several variants. It relies on the mobilization of an industrial labor supply through the growth of urban active and floating labor reserves. The strategy has inherent limitations. Here is not the place for an extended discussion, but we can say that they have fueled the growth of unemployment. One failing has been the low purchasing power of the emerging working class, since wages have been held down, both as a condition for attracting multinational capital and as a reflection of the growing active and floating labor reserves. Another has been labor market segmentation, with foreign firms attracting the relatively educated and technically qualified, thereby limiting accumulation and incomes outside the modern import-substituting sector. At the same time, the vertically integrated nature of multinational enterprises and the lack of an indigenous capital goods industry have limited the emergence of a male-dominated labor aristocracy of skilled crafts workers. The jobs that accompany this form of industrialization have been mostly process labor requiring little training and much discipline, given the work's intensity and monotony. Such jobs have been geared to women, who are habituated to relative docility by generations of oppression. The result is that a large part of the latent reserve is converted into active

and employed labor reserves, while many men join the active component without access to industrial jobs.

A criticism of the import-substitution strategy is that it is rarely based on the country's comparative advantages, involving an adoption of inappropriate factor proportions that contributes to unemployment as well as a shift of surplus workers into the ubiquitous informal sector.

The fifth development strategy, lauded as overcoming the shortcomings of import substitution, is export-led industrialization. This has sometimes been based on a phase of accumulation through import substitution, as exemplified by South Korea. In altering the international division of labor it has relied on low labor costs. To ensure a low-cost efficient labor supply, not only have wages been held down, but measures, often coercive, have been used to limit the freedoms of workers and their bargaining power over working conditions. To be successful, one condition has been the initial creation of a large labor surplus, and in particular active and floating reserves to provide a flexible labor supply and to act as a disciplinary force. Subsequently, there has been less need for an active reserve because the state performs the regulatory function directly.

To the extent that export-led industrialization leads to labor absorption, the operation of an efficient labor market could be expected to drive wages up, which would slow the growth of exports and help less developed industrializing economies acquire a share of the international market for such goods. However, where export-led industrialization has really flourished, the labor market has been heavily circumvented by the state's checking the incipient growth of labor's bargaining power. Means of restraint include suppressing trade unions, banning strikes, raising work intensity—through permitting long workweeks, for example—bypassing health and safety regulations, not providing unemployment benefits or pension schemes, and so on. Many workers have been overemployed, being forced to work 50 or 60 hours a week as a condition of employment.[5]

Even more than with import substitution, export-led industrialization has been geared to the absorption of female labor. Typically, hundreds of thousands of teenaged women have been brought into the urban-industrial labor market—often as little more than bonded labor—to assemble imported components or to work on semiautomated production lines. In industrial export zones women typically account for three-quarters of all employment. In the absence of a system of craftsmanship, no male labor aristocracy of the proletariat has developed, with the type of income and status associated with wives and children being outside the labor force. Indeed, the nature of the industrialization has meant a vast mobilization of labor supply, from women and children as well as men.

In sum, where the strategy has had some success, employment expansion has drawn from active and floating labor reserves, mainly rural-urban migrants, a majority of whom have been women and from a latent reserve consisting largely of women who would

5. For example, in South Korea the average workweek in manufacturing in 1982 was 55.4 hours for men and 56.3 for women, having actually increased over the previous decade. International Labour Office, *Year Book of Labour Statistics* (Geneva: International Labour Office, various editions).

otherwise have remained outside the wage labor force. As capital accumulation has progressed, open unemployment has fallen, female labor force participation rates have risen, and in several countries a perceived labor shortage has arisen.

Thus, of the five development strategies, export-led industrialization offers the best prospect for sustained labor absorption. But it is doubtful whether more than a few countries could successfully industrialize on that basis, if only because their share of world manufactured goods would have to rise so enormously that the industrialized countries would experience so much unemployment that they would limit imports by protective responses. Yet without export-led industrialization the projected scenario for the growth of unemployment in low-income countries must surely be pessimistic.

THE WORLD BANK VIEW OF UNEMPLOYMENT

Now let us turn to another perspective altogether. It may seem strange to associate a particular view of the labor market with an institution, but it is justified by the rigor devoted to this topic by economists in the World Bank and by those associated with it. In essence, the elements are that in most developing countries the labor market operates efficiently, that open unemployment is not high or worsening, that the welfare and resource costs are less than is implied by the unemployment that does exist, and that the unemployment is predominantly voluntary.

This view was presented in detail in a 1984 article that stated, "There is no evidence of a general deterioration of labor market conditions as judged by open unemployment."[6] The authors based that evaluation on a 1980 paper that claimed, on the basis of partial data from a selective group of 14 countries, that the figures were "suggestive" of improvement.[7]

The evidence on unemployment is examined elsewhere and is rather considerable.[8] The remainder of this article concentrates on the logic and assumptions underlying the view that because unemployment in developing countries is mainly voluntary, it is not serious.

Berry and Sabot dismissed "demand deficiency" as "the key to urban surplus labor in LDCs [less developed countries]" and asserted that "unemployment is a symptom of labour misallocation caused by the decisions of workers to forgo available low-income employment opportunities and queue for the limited higher-income positions available in a segmented labour market."[9] This dualistic model was then used to deduce that the resource costs were less than where demand deficiency prevailed, because such costs should be measured by "the marginal product of labour in the sectors where the unemployed would work in the absence of segmentation."[10] That last claim is moot, but the real difficulty is that the dualism and segmented labor supply are presumed, not demonstrated.

It seems merely mean to point out that if segmentation is prevalent, one should scarcely refer to the labor market as efficient. In any case, Berry and Sabot concluded, "Where unemployment is due to segmentation, the unemployed worker is less a victim of circumstances than he is when unemployment is due to an aggregate imbalance between labour supply and demand."[11]

Another widely read World Bank review argued that labor markets in developing countries operate "reasonably effectively" in that they respond to "forces of supply and demand," so that "attention should be directed to the factors determining labour demand and supply, rather than to the operation of the labor market itself."[12]

In these and related articles a common theme has been that the unemployment is voluntary. Because that assertion attributes responsibility for the unemployment to the unemployed themselves it deserves careful scrutiny, for if it were the case the state could legitimately downgrade policies to stimulate aggregate demand and work opportunities. Seven elements have been identified as indicative of voluntary unemployment, though many of those asserting that such unemployment is extensive mention few or none of them. Six are behavioral characteristics attributed to groups of workers; the other involves mechanisms by which voluntary unemployment is supposedly encouraged. Given the potential implications of this perspective, it is appropriate to examine the reasoning in each case, the assumptions involved, and by implication the type of data required to identify the

6. Albert Berry and Richard H. Sabot, "Unemployment and Economic Development," *Economic Development and Cultural Change,* 33(1):109 (Oct. 1984).

7. Peter Gregory, "An Assessment of Changes in Employment Conditions in Less Developed Countries," *Economic Development and Cultural Change,* 22(4):697 (July 1980).

8. Guy Standing, *Unemployment, Underdevelopment and Labor Process* (Geneva: International Labour Office, forthcoming).

9. Berry and Sabot, "Unemployment and Economic Development," p. 110.

10. Ibid.

11. Ibid., p. 111.

12. Squire, *Employment Policy in Developing Countries,* pp. 96-97.

extent and incidence of so-called voluntary unemployment.

Unrealistic wage aspirations

Perhaps the main contention is that many workers are only willing to work for a wage or income above a level they could reasonably expect. This raises several conceptual ambiguities.

The main difficulty is that of determining the reasonableness of wage aspirations. Is a worker expected to take any job paying an average wage, even if his or her skill corresponds to that of workers whose average wages are above that level? Or is a worker expected to take any job yielding an income adequate to meet some subsistence standard of living? There is by no means a consensus of opinion.

A popular variant of the excessive-wage-aspirations thesis is one most often suggested by World Bank analysts. Widely applied in the context of urban labor markets in low-income countries, the argument goes somewhat as follows. A minority of the labor force works in what is variously termed the formal, protected, or primary sector, in which wages are institutionally, or socially, fixed above an overall equilibrium—or market-clearing—level. The majority are in the informal, unprotected, secondary, or free-entry sector, where incomes are much lower and where no barriers hinder entrants from doing the work available. Proponents of this view argue that those who do not enter the informal sector must be voluntarily unemployed. In this way they almost define away the unemployed by making any unemployment voluntary. As one World Bank report, based on an assumed dualism, baldly stated,

The existence of free entry labour markets implies that observed unemployment must be of a voluntary nature. The idea behind this is that a worker increases the probability of his obtaining a job in the protected sector by being unemployed and investing in search. Unemployment is part of a process of job search, where the costs are the present forgone earnings in the free entry sector and the benefits are the present value of a higher probability of finding a job in the protected sector.[13]

This argument is built on several dubious assumptions. The first is that there is a large free-entry sector in which the unemployed could earn a subsistence income. Yet at the margin many informal activities may yield an insignificant net income, barely compensating for the risk, uncertainty, and effort cost of participation in such activities. Moreover, many activities that promise a moderate income are highly stratified, with clear barriers to entry, and requiring skills, experience, and contacts that most of the unemployed could not be expected to possess. For instance, petty production or trading often has highly structured labor, input, and product markets, with considerable costs of entry and low entry-level incomes.

Another assumption is that those who remain unemployed must be voluntarily idle, investing in prolonged job search. A problem here is that it cannot be presumed that an unemployed's expected wage is a positive function of duration of unemployment. Prolonged unemployment induces demoralization, anomie, and a loss of energy, which in

13. Sebastian Piñera and Marcello Selowsky, *Unemployment, Labour Market Segmentation, the Opportunity Cost of Labour, and the Social Returns to Education,* World Bank Staff Working Paper no. 233 (Washington, DC: World Bank, 1976), p. 7.

turn make many unemployable for a wide range of jobs. One review of youth unemployment in Sri Lanka observed, "The period of waiting for employment among these youths ranged from one year to five years and over."[14] One wonders what they were doing for five years and what five years of waiting were doing to them.

A further difficulty is that remarkably few studies have tried to ascertain the unemployed's wage aspirations to determine whether they were excessive. Admittedly, the methodological difficulties are real. One method of assessing the unemployed's wage aspirations was tried in two small surveys conducted in Kingston, Jamaica.[15] In this method, the unemployed's aspirations were compared with wages paid in jobs similar to those they were seeking. The aspiration wage was calculated by asking the unemployed how many hours per week they were prepared to work and the income they would require for that number. A comparison was then made between the aspiration wage and the employed's wages. The result suggested that if any voluntary unemployment existed it was among those seeking unskilled jobs, not among those seeking clerical jobs. Even so, the mean aspiration wage of 56 Jamaican cents an hour was by no means high; in 1974, when the surveys were conducted, many women in unskilled jobs in larger firms in Kingston were receiving over twice that.[16]

14. S. Ranasinghe, "Unemployment and Job Expectations Among Our Youth (Sri Lanka)," *Manpower and Unemployment Research* (Montreal), p. 26 (Apr. 1978).

15. Guy Standing, *Unemployment and Female Labour: A Study of Labour Supply in Kingston, Jamaica* (London: Macmillan, 1981).

16. For further analysis of one of the surveys, see Guy Standing, "Aspiration Wages, Migration and Urban Unemployment," *Journal of Development Studies*, 14(2):232-48 (Jan. 1978).

Unrealistic job aspirations

A related characteristic supposed to indicate voluntary unemployment is that many job seekers are only looking for certain types of jobs. It is commonly argued that unemployment is voluntary if a job seeker is not looking for "suitable" work, by which is usually meant a job corresponding to his or her skill level. This is perhaps the key aspect of recent neoclassical analysis.[17] But the voluntariness of unemployment should be judged only on actual refusal to take other types of available jobs, or at least a stated unwillingness to do so. It would surely be unwarranted to classify as voluntarily unemployed an unskilled worker who expressed a preference for skilled work if he were also seeking unskilled work, especially if he had no opportunity to decline work for which he was trained or suited.

Empirically, it is hard to devise an appropriate method to test whether many of the unemployed have unrealistic job aspirations. One commonly used method is to contrast the unemployed's schooling with that of the employed. Thus one labor market review asserted,

Higher unemployment rates among educated than uneducated workers are found throughout the developing world. School-leavers are faced with the choice of "queuing" for a job in the preferred occupation or of accepting a less preferred (lower wage) job. For some workers expected income will be higher in unemployment than in relatively low wage employment.[18]

17. See, for example, Berry and Sabot, "Unemployment and Economic Development," pp. 110-11.

18. Albert Berry and Richard H. Sabot, "Labour Market Performance in Developing Countries: A Survey," *World Development*, n. 86 and p. 1219 (Nov.-Dec. 1978). See also Mark Blaug, Richard Layard, and S. Woodhall, *The

The assumption that school-leavers have such a choice implies that not only are there less preferred or lower-paying jobs available but that the more educated are able to displace the less educated. Whatever their schooling, youths are often not regarded as substitutes for older workers, many of whom have higher productivity by virtue of on-the-job experience and training. Furthermore, for such substitution to take place, labor turnover must be high; but evidence suggests that in low-income urban environments and everywhere in times of high unemployment, turnover among older workers is normally very low, except for jobs being lost altogether.[19] In addition, employers may be reluctant to hire relatively educated workers to do routine, narrow jobs, partly because they could be expected to suffer from status frustration and could be less easily directed and controlled. For such reasons, showing that unemployment for those seeking or working in clerical jobs was above the average rate for all workers scarcely constitutes grounds for claiming that much of the urban unemployment in Colombia is voluntary.[20] The educated's best chance of getting a job may well be in seeking clerical or other white-collar jobs, as their potential productivity in manual work may be low and their time in school may even have made them incapable of retaining a physically demanding job.

In sum, while some unemployment might reflect inappropriate expectations, its extent and incidence can scarcely be gauged from the type of data typically available. Any claim that such voluntary unemployment is widespread should be regarded as a revealing or questionable opinion, not an established fact.

Inactive unemployment

The most basic claim is that some of those counted as unemployed do not actively search for jobs. However, by itself the job-seeking criterion should not be used to identify voluntary unemployment; it is unreasonable to expect workers to expend time, energy, morale, and money in searching for jobs known to be unavailable.

Moreover, many of those without jobs will be discouraged workers of one sort or another, part of the latent reserve, having given up searching either because of repeated failure to find suitable work or because there was no formal mechanism for job seeking in the area. Labor statisticians have long wrestled with these issues and with the classification of discouraged workers.[21] *Inter alia,* the number of discouraged workers is determined by the unemployment level and by the reference period used. Many labor force surveys merely attempt to ascertain respondents' "main activity" in the "past week"; as a result, those who

---

Causes of Graduate Unemployment in India (London: Allen Lane, Penguin Press, 1969), pp. 75-90; David Turnham, *The Employment Problem in Less Developed Countries* (Paris: Organisation for Economic Co-operation and Development, 1971), pp. 50-53; and Peter Lloyd, *Slums of Hope? Shanty Towns of the Third World* (Harmondsworth: Penguin Books, 1979), p. 145.

19. See, for example, Shygam B.L. Nigam and Hans W. Singer, "Labour Turnover and Employment: Some Evidence from Kenya," *International Labour Review,* pp. 479-93 (Dec. 1974).

20. R. Albert Berry, "Open Unemployment as a Social Problem in Urban Colombia: Myth and Reality," *Economic Development and Cultural Change,* pp. 276-91 (Jan. 1975).

21. For an analysis of categories of such workers, see Guy Standing, *Labour Force Participation and Development,* 2d ed. (Geneva: International Labour Office, 1981), chap. 5.

last sought work eight or more days before are automatically excluded from the unemployment count.

Casual or short-time work preferences

A fourth characteristic supposed to distinguish the voluntarily unemployed is a preference for work of short duration.

The difficulties with the short-hours criterion are like those raised with respect to aspiration wages and job suitability. Would those seeking part-time work accept full-time work if it were offered, or if they had time to adjust other commitments? Should the aspiration workweek be compared with some overall average workweek, or with the average in a particular job or range of jobs for which the worker is qualified, or with the average worked by some demographic social group to which the worker is supposed to belong? Just posing such questions should make it clear that this criterion too can only be applied using somewhat arbitrary procedures. There is no reason to regard any particular work duration figure as acceptable or as validly defining voluntary unemployment.

These conceptual points do not mean that distinctions should not be drawn between those seeking full-time and those seeking part-time employment. What is objectionable is the blanket description of the latter as voluntarily unemployed. Rather than excluding them from recorded unemployment, their existence suggests a need to measure unemployment in terms of a rate of labor underutilization as well as in terms of numbers of workers.

Turnover-induced unemployment

A fifth characteristic concerns the means by which workers become unemployed. Some claim that if workers voluntarily quit jobs, the unemployment is in effect chosen and therefore voluntary. Thus one analyst of urban unemployment in Colombia asserted that the rise "was not primarily a reflection of increasing scarcity of jobs but rather of more exacting job demands by the searchers," supposedly because "most people who leave their jobs appear to do so by their own choice, rather than through the action of the employer."[22]

It has also been argued that high labor turnover indicates voluntary unemployment.[23] But labor turnover combines quits, dismissals, and job completions. Besides, the notion of voluntary quitting is ambiguous. A man may quit under extreme pressure, or he may be given the option of resigning rather than being sacked; it is also common for workers who anticipate being laid off to leave in search of a longer-term job. Similarly, suppose someone is put on extremely short-term work because of lack of business; if he then quits because the income is insignificant, it would be a misuse of language to describe his ac-

22. Albert Berry, "Constant Utilization of the Labour Force Despite Rising Open Unemployment in Colombia?" *Journal of Economic Studies* (Oxford), p. 120 (Nov. 1975), citing a local labor market study that found that about two-fifths of the unemployed men and one-tenth of the women lost their jobs "through action originating primarily on the side of the employer." This does not imply that three-fifths of the men lost their jobs through action originating primarily on their side. Who originates the action if a seasonal job is merely finished or if a firm or even industry collapses?

23. S. Buckley, "Recent Canadian Experience with Unemployment," *Canadian Statistical Review* (Ottawa), pp. 4-5, 114-17 (Feb. 1974).

tion as voluntarily choosing to become unemployed.

Another objection is that even if a worker voluntarily quits a job, that does not mean he or she is not subsequently involuntarily unemployed. Most damaging of all, any such distinction breaks down for the unemployed entering or reentering the labor force. In sum, claims that voluntary unemployment should be measured by the proportion of the unemployed who quit their previous jobs are unconvincing.

Marginal workers

Some observers have claimed that many of the unemployed—for example, married women, students, teenagers indulging in career experimentation, and the elderly—have only weak labor force attachment, being casual or secondary workers prone to drop out of economic activity and typically dependent on the income of primary labor force participants. It has been argued that much of their labor force participation is voluntary, that unemployment only influences the timing of their participation, that the unemployment rate overstates the reliable labor supply, and that where these groups' share of the labor force has risen the social cost of unemployment has fallen.

Two points should be kept in mind in discussing so-called marginal workers. First, a distinction should be made between the determinants of the overall rate of unemployment and the factors influencing the incidence of unemployment. Some groups have higher unemployment rates than others. But this does not necessarily mean that if there is an increasing proportion of workers from such groups, unemployment will rise. Second, some groups, defined by

personal characteristics such as age, sex, marital status, or race, who exhibit chronic employment instability may have specific behavioral traits, or their unemployment, job instability, and limited labor force commitment may be due to persistent discrimination against the group to which they belong.[24] They may be marginalized by being pushed into unstable secondary jobs with poor promotion prospects, low status and income, and poor working conditions, generally being last hired and first fired. Given these possibilities, it is hard to determine the role of personal factors. Indeed, it is hard to test this hypothesis with the data typically available, for in part job instability is due to so-called marginal workers being among the first to be laid off, even in relatively good jobs; so econometric tests may show that outflows from jobs are linked to personal characteristics, without that necessarily meaning that those workers are particularly prone to job instability—or to so-called voluntary unemployment.

Another argument, used with particular reference to unemployment in low-income countries, is that the situation is less serious because many of the unemployed are non-family-heads who can indulge in prolonged job waiting.[25] One

24. "Inferring present-day labour force attachment from group's previous record of employment smacks of 'blaming the victim'. What passes for today's limited commitment may be the result of yesterday's discrimination." Teresa A. Sullivan and Phillip M. Hauser, "The Labor Utilization Framework: Assumptions, Data and Policy Implications," in *Concepts and Data Needs: Counting the Labor Force: Appendix,* by National Commission on Employment and Unemployment Statistics (Washington, DC: Government Printing Office, 1980), 1:258.

25. Turnham, *Employment Problem in Less Developed Countries,* pp. 45-47. In Colombia the small proportion of first-time job seekers who

difficulty is that most workers become heads of families only when they have employment or income. Thus to some extent cause and effect are mixed.[26]

Unemployment benefit mechanisms

Probably the most contentious issue arising from the notion of voluntary unemployment is the impact of income transfers. In support of their claim that unemployment is voluntary, Berry and Sabot assert, "Deprivation is also less than it would be in industrialised countries in the absence of formal social security systems because subjective costs are distributed beyond the persons without jobs to those with jobs, by means of intrafamily transfers."[27]

Personal transfers make survival possible, but for the unemployed assistance has costs, including reciprocal obligations and the "disapprobation cost"—in Adam Smith's words—of having to accept charity and being seen as a failure in the labor market. For their part, those providing transfers have a financial interest in prodding the unemployed to find work. So, for reasons on the side of donors as well as the unemployed, it would be unreasonable to presume that recipients of transfers are voluntarily unemployed, unless the contrary were demonstrated.

A second form of transfer is poor-relief schemes. These have often involved onerous obligations, including means tests or unpaid labor, making participation a humiliating experience and thus unlikely to induce voluntary unemployment. A third form, of minor significance in low-income economies, is severance pay. This has an impact by making job search more feasible than in its absence, but it has less disincentive with respect to job seeking than other forms of transfer by virtue of the fact that whether a worker stays out of work for 2 or 36 weeks he or she receives the same lump sum. The fourth form of transfer, unemployment insurance, is the most important in industrialized countries but of only limited relevance in industrializing economies.

In general, whether transfers come from family, employers, or the state, their availability could be expected to raise the unemployed's reservation wage and, by encouraging more job search, could increase the expected duration of unemployment. They may also be expected to encourage a substitution of leisure for work and job seeking.[28] However, these effects can easily be exaggerated. First, leisure-work substitution has costs that discourage it. Second, while unemployment benefits and other transfer mechanisms exert some pressure on wage rates, they may have little long-term effect on the relative incomes of the employed and unemployed.[29] Moreover, they may improve the allocative efficiency of the labor market by facilitating more rational job search,

were family heads was cited as supporting evidence that rising unemployment reflected "more exacting job demands by the searchers." Berry, "Constant Utilization," p. 120.

26. This point is often overlooked. See, for instance, David E. Goodman and S. R. Oliveira, "Urban Unemployment in Brazil," *Brazilian Economic Studies* (Rio de Janeiro), no. 4, pp. 79-103 (1978).

27. Berry and Sabot, "Unemployment and Economic Development," p. 111.

28. For the impact of unemployment insurance, see, for example, Gary Chapin, "Unemployment Insurance, Job Search and the Demand for Leisure," *Western Economic Journal*, 9:102-7 (1971); Mark M. Hauser and Paul Burrows, *The Economics of Unemployment Insurance* (London: Allen & Unwin, 1969), pp. 96-110.

29. George David Norman Worswick, ed., *The Concept of Measurement of Involuntary Unemployment* (London: Allen & Unwin, 1976), p. 45.

thereby reducing turnover unemployment, since those receiving transfers will be less inclined to take inappropriate jobs. Third, unemployment insurance schemes generally have regulations restricting benefits to the involuntarily unemployed. Unemployment benefits and personal transfers ensure that part of the latent reserve is converted into, or kept as, part of the active reserve. One important form of this arises in urban areas of low-income countries where the availability of kinship or work-group transfers enables unemployed migrants to remain in the active urban labor surplus rather than migrate back to the countryside.

CONCLUDING POINTS

The perspective that depicts unemployment as the active part of the overall labor surplus, and as the part likely to grow relatively as social relations of production change and as alternative development strategies evolve, seems more fruitful than one that considers labor markets simply in terms of demand and supply and dualism. The World Bank view almost defines away the problem of unemployment by means of an assumed dualism that makes practically all unemployment partially or wholly voluntary. At the very least, it is regrettable to find that perspective regarded as "moderate" and a "sign of the coming to maturity of the research programme on labour markets in LDCs."[30] It is nothing of the sort.

30. Berry and Sabot, "Unemployment and Economic Development," p. 112.

The Internationalization
of Global Labor Markets

By H. PETER GRAY

ABSTRACT: The rapid industrialization of labor-surplus countries will present serious problems for the achievement of high levels of employment in the industrialized world. The employment consequences of a flood of imports from developing countries is jeopardizing the liberal international trading system that has contributed to the world's prosperity since World War II. The argument for free trade and a liberal system of world trade is based on a static analysis that does not countenance the rate of change imposed on the importing nation. Some intermediate stance that avoids the employment costs of unimpeded imports and the rigidities that permanent, die-hard protection will inflict on an industrialized economy may prove desirable as an aid to the process of economic adjustment.

H. Peter Gray was born in England and was educated at Cambridge University and at the University of California at Berkeley, where he received a Ph.D. in economics. He is professor of economics and finance at the School of Business at Rutgers University in New Brunswick, New Jersey. His main research interests are focused on the excessive simplification of much of international economic analysis and its implication for international economic policy.

WHEN the factor-proportions theory of international trade was accepted as the basic explanation of the existence of benefits from trade among nations, the internationalization of input markets through international trade flows was recognized. Gains from international trade were perceived to be achieved by means of the exchange of relatively plentiful inputs for relatively scarce or expensive inputs through the exchange of goods that embodied different mixes of inputs. Each nation imported goods that contained disproportionately large shares of inputs that were in short supply in its own economy. The seminal essay of this approach saw that international trade would have the effect of reducing the disparity in payments for different inputs in different nations relative to the disparity that would have existed in the absence of international trade.[1] This same body of theory is used to validate the main policy recommendation that has relevance to international trade: unrestricted trade among nations will generate the most efficient global allocation of resources and will increase world output.

The assumptions that underlie and constrain a body of economic analysis limit the relevance of its conclusions for policymaking. The free-trade argument is constrained by many analytic assumptions and some of these are crucial. The argument assumes full employment in all trading countries, so that the existence of surplus labor in Third World countries is not in conformity with the analysis; the theory also assumes that labor markets clear at better than subsistence income. The analysis is static and precludes concern with the rate of change of foreign supply capabilities. The problem of short-run dislocational costs is not confronted. There is assumed to be no movement of inputs internationally, so that the transfer of technology and financial capital to labor-surplus countries by multinational corporations is excluded from consideration. Finally, the abstract economic analysis avoids concern with the internal political dimensions of the problems of adjustment: the reallocation of resources from contracting importing industries to expanding export industries. The analysis is concerned with global gains from trade in a world in which policy decisions are made by national sentiments and political pressures. The lack of success of recent economic summits and the nonachievements of UNCTAD VI in Belgrade in the summer of 1983 indicate that industrial democracies can only cooperate internationally to the degree that their electorates have been convinced that cooperation is in the national interest and does not inflict heavy costs in the short run. The concept of global good is less heavily weighted.

The importance of the neglect of national political pressures lies in the possible existence of dynamic instability. If the social costs of adjustment to a new set of international conditions are positively related to the level of protectionist sentiment in a country and if suppression of adjustment makes future costs still greater, the system is dynamically unstable. Protectionism—suppression of adjustment—will feed upon itself.

Currently, the integration of the global economy is proceeding at a pace that shows every indication of exceeding the ability of many industrialized countries to adjust to the new conditions without serious dislocation in input markets. Policymakers have not been given the

1. Eli Heckscher, "The Effects of Foreign Trade on the Distribution of Income," *Ekonomisk Tidskrift*, 21:497-512 (Sept. 1919).

analytic tools that will enable them to assess the benefits and costs of passive acceptance of the dictates of the market system when a liberal system is preserved—the free-trade position—and of capitulating to domestic political pressures that will inevitably seek to suppress change. If these two policies both engender substantial costs, then exploration of possible middle-ground solutions is required.

THE MECHANICS OF ADJUSTMENT

The danger of an excessive rate of change being forced on the industrialized countries lies in the combination of labor surpluses in many countries and the ability of multinational corporations—and owners of technology generally—to transmit modern know-how internationally. The countries that host the multinationals and that generate the exports will increase their spending with the developed world. The developed economies produce more efficiently goods that require relatively large amounts of highly sophisticated machinery and highly skilled professional workers. The labor-surplus countries will be able to export goods that require large amounts of relatively unskilled labor because such labor can easily be trained for repetitive production-level jobs. Harnessing labor surpluses in developing economies will displace production in the industrialized nations in those industries that use production workers and low-skilled workers intensively. The problems emanating from the international sector will be reinforced within the industrialized economies by the new technological innovations that will exert their first labor-saving effects on low-skill tasks.

Traditional economic theory postulates that economies will adjust to the new set of trading conditions by having labor become cheaper in the industrialized economies and by having machinery and skilled workers—respectively, capital and human capital—relatively better paid. The changes in relative costs of inputs will lead corporations to substitute the now-cheaper low-skilled workers for the now-costlier machinery and high-skilled workers to the extent that full employment will be generated. The static nature of the theory glosses over the time dimension and the size of the change imposed. Industrialized economies do have some inherent ability to adjust as older workers retire and new workers are admitted to the labor force. This ability is limited.

The longer the pressure of available cheap, labor-intensive imports from developing nations lasts, the greater will be the adjustment strain imposed. The duration of the import pressure might, at first, be thought to have well-defined limits: that quantity of standardized goods that could be sold through retail outlets. Most consumer durables and other so-called experience goods require after-sales servicing and marketing networks to provide the necessary maintenance and warranty support. Given that servicing and marketing networks are the essence of sophisticated distribution techniques and are very culturally sensitive, exports of consumer durables by firms based in developing countries will encounter serious difficulties.[2]

The ability of multinational corporations to link production units in developing countries with marketing and distribution outlets in the industrialized world will overcome the obstacle to a

2. However, note the recent successes in Canada of the Korean automobile industry.

steady increase in the volume of exports of manufactures. There may be no effective limit to exports from developing countries short of something approaching full employment in the Third World. This limit may be exaggerated because not all cultures will permit the acquisition of skills and the adaptation to conditions in a modern, manufacturing society at a rate sufficient to cause displacement pressures in the industrialized world. But there are many would-be developing countries just waiting for the day when they can supply manufactured goods to North America and Europe. The adjustment strains in the industrialized world can be expected to be severe and long-lasting.

Microeconomic adjustment

Microeconomic adjustment involves the reallocation of labor—and other inputs—from declining to expanding industries. The essential problem in the labor market is the change in the mix of workers required by skill and by skill level. High-technology export industries require highly skilled workers, and society must develop a labor force that adapts to the new pattern of demand at the same time that labor is being displaced by labor-saving technology.

Unless the analyst is optimistic about the degree to which industry can substitute low-skilled labor for highly skilled labor in response to changes in wage rates and salaries, there will have to be a considerable upgrading of skills. But workers either may not be tempted to upgrade their skills or may not be capable of so doing.[3] If workers are to have

an adequate incentive to upgrade their skills, the reward must be sufficient to warrant incurring the costs. This requires that the wage rates paid to low-skilled workers decline so that displaced workers are not tempted to compete in a job or skill stratum with lower requirements in which they will be relatively well qualified. This downgrading of the skill level of employment will oust, or bump, another worker to a still lower level. If displaced workers are not attracted to higher grades of work by wage-rate differentials or are incapable of financing the necessary training, then the downgrading mechanism will ensure that any surplus labor will comprise low-skilled workers predominantly.[4] The likelihood that displaced workers will try to upgrade their skills will be determined, in part, by the availability of publicly financed facilities for retraining.

Some writers have suggested that there will be an erosion of the middle class, which is loosely defined as workers or families earning within 25 percent of the median income.[5] If a substantial number of displaced workers choose downgrading and bumping, the industrialized economies may be faced with a severe bimodal distribution of income and a lack of upward mobility except through intergenerational change. What such a prospect, particularly if coupled with significant unemployment of the very low skilled, portends for the sta-

---

3. In this context, it is useful to distinguish between retraining a worker to acquire new industry-specific skills at the same level of sophis-

tication and retraining to attain a new, higher level of skill. The second task is more formidable and may be impossible.

4. The idea of bumping is developed in E. Ray Canterbery, "A Vita Theory of Personal Income Distribution," *Southern Economic Journal*, 45:12-48 (July 1979).

5. Vitor F. Zonanna, "Population Puzzle," *Wall Street Journal*, 20 June 1984.

bility of the social system is neither known nor foreseeable.

The required change in skill characteristics of the work force can contribute to unemployment in two ways.

First, the labor market will be less efficient as workers procrastinate in the decision to seek upgrading or to bump. In this the role of information is important. Knowledge of opportunities available after upgrading and of upgrading facilities will directly affect the likelihood that upgrading will be sought and the speed of decision making increased.

Second, the perceived capacity of workers to upgrade themselves may not be adequate to accommodate the new pattern of demands when society's concept of subsistence income sets an absolute floor to wage rates for low-skilled labor. The capacity of the labor force to acquire new skill levels depends upon the absolute capacity of each worker relative to the skill level already attained. Retraining in different industry-specific skills at the same level presents no problems of capability, but a worker's ultimate capacity to acquire skills depends upon the individual's genetic inheritance, the mind-set produced by schooling and peer-group pressures during the formative years, the present age, and the level of both formal and general education achieved. At any time, the work force has both an actual and a maximum attainable mix of skill levels. As the actual approaches the maximum attainable—as more and more workers are at their individual maxima—the difficulties inherent in overall upgrading of skills are increased. Thus the capacity of the economy to adjust to new conditions depends upon the magnitude and the duration of the disturbance. The process is cumulative since the early strains will be easily absorbed by up-

grading workers with significant latent capacity. As the need for adjustment accumulates over time, workers with smaller margins of latent capacity will have to be upgraded at ever increasing costs. Further, if the shift required in skill levels is large, then a process of upward bumping may be required as workers are trained up by one level each, until the entire required upgrading has been accomplished. The dangers that such a complex link could be broken are great, and so complex a phenomenon may well only be accomplished successfully within individual organizations.

It is possible that a combination of widespread bumping and an inability of firms to utilize low-skilled workers—perhaps because of the minimum wage or subsistence barrier—could create permanent unemployment. In this context, "permanent" should not be interpreted literally but as implying a condition for which no end is in sight. Some people may be unemployed for a lifetime and adjustment may be made intergenerationally.[6] Long-term, or permanent, unemployment is the more likely the higher the level of subsistence income in the importing country. While subsistence income could have a purely physiological definition, it is more likely to be defined in terms of national cultural values and past standards. Cultural values should be taken as including the level of safety regulations in force. What matters in terms of potential job displacement in industrialized countries is differences in the money value of subsistence income in developing and industrialized countries. Staples that are locally produced in developing countries tend

6. Intergenerational change assumes improvement in the skills developed in the formative years as a result of better educational and home support.

to be cheaper than their counterpart products in industrialized countries, so that with real incomes equal, there will still be a wage-rate advantage accruing to workers in poor countries.[7]

Required speed of adjustment

The required speed of adjustment depends upon the rate of increase in the capacity of developing countries—including such semi-developed countries as Mediterranean and Eastern-bloc countries—to supply exports that compete with and substitute for domestic production in the industrialized countries. The faster the rate of increase in the availability of potential imports, the more likely is adjustment to lag behind, and the degree of dislocation will grow through time.

Every nation has some innate ability to adjust without significant social cost. This capacity increases with the rate of saving and the percentage of the work force that retires each year. If the required rate of adjustment exceeds this capability, then social costs are incurred—unemployment will exceed the target rate. Even under such conditions, traditionalists may find grounds for optimism if the change in conditions is a one-shot phenomenon, implying a maximum availability of imports from developing countries, since the economy will steadily adjust and social costs will ultimately disappear. Given the large number of developing nations that actively seek to develop export markets and the danger of violating the subsis-

tence-income constraint, any such optimism would seem to be misplaced.

The greater the degree of dislocation, the more likely is the adjustment process to become cumulative. If the system cannot keep pace, the amount of excess unemployment will increase steadily. At the same time, the efficiency of the market mechanism as a means of channeling workers to productive outlets is likely to decrease. The larger the number of displaced workers, the larger is the number of workers who will need to upgrade their skill levels and the larger the amount of upgrading needed per worker. Given some finite capacity of training facilities, a higher rate of displacement will lead to a larger proportion of workers becoming discouraged about the advantages of upgrading and who will choose to bump a less qualified person. This, in turn, will lead to a larger pool of workers with very few skills who may be thought of as being all but unemployable. Fast rates of dislocation will also lead to congestion in the labor market as workers displaced will have quite similar patterns and levels of skills and will be geographically concentrated at the same time that such job opportunities as exist will be more or less haphazardly distributed over space and will have higher skill requirements. A concentration of workers with the same skills lowers the likelihood of a good correspondence between the mix of skills demanded and those supplied.

Dynamic instability

Dynamic instability exists when protectionist forces postpone adjustment and gain strength in the process. Resistance to adjustment will be positively related to perceived costs. If the resistance suppresses the effects of the change

7. Wolfgang Hager, "North-South Trade and Socio-Economic Autonomy: A Peace Formula," *Trade and Development Unctad Review*, vol. 3 (Winter 1982); Dan Usher, "The Transportation Bias in Comparisons of National Income," *Economica*, 30:140-59 (1963).

in conditions in international markets, the distortion between actuality and the free-trade—or nonsuppressed—state will increase over time, as foreign export capacity increases. The perceived social costs of adjustment will, then, grow steadily and the likelihood of acceptance of adjustment will decrease.

Political pressures for protection—for suppressing change—will be exerted by groups in danger of suffering economic loss as a result of that change. The more broadly based and the more politically active these groups, the greater is the likelihood that suppressive measures will be legislated. The breadth of opposition to a free-trade or hands-off policy can be easily identified by the number of people who are or perceive themselves to be likely to be displaced. The degree of political activity will depend upon the perceived costs for displaced and threatened workers. Four factors contribute to the perceived loss of income.

First, the expected duration of unemployment and the gap between unemployment compensation and earnings are crucial. Thus the generosity of unemployment compensation will ease political activity, and the size of any existing pool of unemployed will intensify it.

Second, the rate of pay in the foreseen alternative employment will also affect the intensity of political activity. If the disparity between the worker's skills and the available job vacancies will cause a large decrease in remuneration, the intensity will increase. In the same vein, pessimism about the opportunities for upgrading will also lead to resistance to change.

Third, if a job that a displaced worker might reasonably expect to find has suffered a reduction in the wage rate because of earlier changes in relative wage rates for high- and low-skilled workers, resistance to change will be higher.

Finally, if the existing occupation carries with it a wage premium attributable to experience within the industry and the acquisition of industry-specific skills, resistance to change will be more intense.

The internationalization of labor markets carries with it profound implications of both a quantitative and a qualitative nature. The essence of the process lies in the degree to which industry is capable of adjusting its requirements to comparatively small changes in the relative costs of labor and machines and in the remuneration for workers of different skill levels. The second dimension of importance is the degree to which the subsistence-income constraint may become effective. The process has dynamic dimensions and is directly related to the increase in the foreign capacity to produce goods for consumption and use in the industrialized countries. The degree of adaptability of other members of the industrial bloc can also affect the size of impact placed on an individual country as goods excluded from protected markets seek an outlet in the remaining open markets. There exists the possibility of severe protracted unemployment and for strong political pressures for protection against imports. Any such pressures are likely to be reinforced by the effects of the introduction of labor-saving technology in domestic plants.

Industrialized countries have not had experience in dealing with surplus population within the last forty years. If unemployment becomes chronic and income distribution markedly bimodal, a large shift in economic philosophy may be required.

POSSIBLE RESPONSES

The somber picture drawn in the preceding pages is taken as relevant, and the rest of this article assesses the competing sets of policy options that are available to governments in the industrialized democracies. The problems faced by politicians will be severe because of the seemingly inevitable clash between short-run loss avoidance and long-run costs—from suppression—and short-run costs and longer-run benefits—from acceptance of change. Convincing voters of the wisdom of a prescribed policy package will be far more difficult than the still-difficult task of selecting and legislating a good and consistent set of policies. To the extent that any collection of policy measures requires international cooperation, the difficulties of convincing voters of the benefits of collective action may be even greater. Nonetheless, this challenge of adjustment to the new conditions in global labor markets is likely to be the most difficult peacetime economic problem faced by the industrialized world since the Great Depression. Good policy may require a substantial shift in the accepted views of what constitutes appropriate economic behavior and appropriate policy.

Three categories of policy exist: negative or change-resistant policies, which seek to suppress the natural working of the market system; neutral policies, which accept the natural working of market forces but intervene to diminish the social costs of adjustment imposed by the pace of market forces; and positive or change-accommodating measures, which attempt to increase the efficiency of the economy to adjust to new conditions in global labor markets. Each set of policies may be considered against the probable outcome of a hands-off, laissez-faire policy.

Negative policies seek to limit, in part or completely, the impact on the domestic economy of increases in the capabilities of foreign economies to supply large quantities of manufactured goods. It will be more difficult to suppress labor-saving innovations that have their origin in locally available technological innovations.

Negative policies are those that are most likely to appeal to the electorate in the short run. The costs will be long run and will probably not be borne by those who agitate for the institution of the negative policies. Negative policies reduce or eliminate short-run costs of adjustment and diminish any socially disruptive increase in income inequality within the industrialized nations.

The costs of negative policies could become substantial with time. Foremost among them would be the strains induced between the home country and the developing nations whose exports were being curtailed. This set of strains would probably escalate into a straightforward rift between the bloc of industrialized countries—the North—and the bloc of developing countries—the South. Northern industrialized countries have a very real interest in the continued development and prosperity of the South in addition to any moral concern with the diminution of poverty in those countries. The other major cost derives from the effects of any suppression on economic rigidification that may develop in the North in response to the sheltering of embattled sectors. Any unwillingness to adapt in the face of change may confirm a resistance to change that is already active or that is latent in the economy. The so-called economic sclerosis of the European nations has caused comment in recent years as workers and governments try to withstand the effects of changing conditions on the reallocation of resources among sectors.[8]

Negative policies are unacceptable. They tend to lock the economy into a pattern of production that is likely to become progressively less consonant with underlying global conditions to the detriment of the long-run viability of the economy.

Neutral policies rely on market forces to effect change as dictated by new underlying conditions in world markets and seek merely to temper any adverse side effects that might be induced by the speed of change imposed by a hands-off policy. The benefits of such policies are self-evident. They allow change to take place and in this way avoid any increase in North-South strains and minimize any tendency for Northern economies to rigidify.

The unimpeded operation of market forces will undoubtedly generate unemployment as declining sectors lay off workers more quickly than expanding sectors can hire them and as the total demand for labor diminishes before any substitution takes place. Unemployment will also be enhanced because of the changed pattern of demand by skill level. This unemployment will be greater the greater are the rate of growth of imports, the duration of substantial rates of growth of imports, and the greater the rigidity of wage rates in threatened industries. In principle, the economic harm done to the displaced workers can be mitigated by generous transfer payments in the form of unemployment

8. Wolfgang Michalski, "The Need for Positive Adjustment Policies in the 1980s," *Intereconomics*, 18:42-48 (Jan.-Feb. 1983), develops the concept of the need for resilience if mature economies are to perform well.

benefits, redundancy payments, and income supplements.

One way in which employment rates can be kept at a higher level is for the pace of change to be slowed by the institution of commercial policies. The essential idea of such a scheme is much easier to set down on paper than to institute. By reducing the rate of change imposed on the economy from external sources, policies will diminish the degree of congestion in labor markets and will allow the labor market to work more efficiently by reducing the number of workers and vacancies that need to be matched. The basic policy requirement is that the effect of the market mechanism be slowed but not stopped. Temporary protection against imports must include strictly enforced and carefully defined provisions for phasing out the protective measures lest the incentive to adjust be eliminated in the hope that the temporary measures can be made permanent.

A second feature of this kind of protection is the simultaneous introduction of conditions on the award of phase-out protection. The threatened industry would only receive protection in the form of limits on the rate of growth of imports if both its management and labor undertook to make sacrifices to improve the industry's own price competitiveness with foreign goods in the short run. These conditions would make investment and employment in the industry less attractive. The more demanding the conditions imposed, the more gradual the phase-out protection could be. Conditional protection should have strong and broadly based political appeal since it finds common ground between the needs of the threatened industry and the welfare of the rest of the electorate.

The most difficult problem to be faced is the possible existence of chronic unemployment. This eventuality may only be considered at all probable when the joint effects of North-South trade in manufactures and the new labor-saving technologies are seen as being mutually reinforcing. Long-lasting, excessive unemployment may require a change in the nation's social values so that unemployment is not necessarily regarded as an inferior status. The implicit renunciation of the work ethic may have profound implications for the social order and can be expected to arouse strong opposition from people who are unable to conceive of the enormity of the problems that confront the industrialized nations.

When the possibility of chronic unemployment exists, optimists will argue for the creation of larger and more efficient means of retraining workers and upgrading their skill levels. But such steps may not be enough. Workers have limits to the skills that they can acquire. If the demand for labor has requirements for skill levels that exceed the maximum attainable supply of skills, then long-run or chronic unemployment is inevitable. The only way in which governments might manage to reduce the level of unemployment without resorting to make-work programs reminiscent of the depression is to attempt to subsidize the employment of low-skilled workers in all industries. This subsidization could be achieved by changing the structure of payroll taxes for firms—making the taxes more progressive—as well as by paying an actual subsidy per worker earning less than some specified wage rate. There would seem to be no problem with the processes of effort maximization and cost minimization in such a policy: firms would still minimize their own costs and the subsidy element would merely reduce the net cost of low-skilled labor. Workers would continue to seek employment, provided that the wage earned, after taxes, exceeded the dole paid to the chronically unemployed. There might be some income level at which subsidy would be eliminated. This rate would exceed the level at which bumping might be expected to occur. It would be necessary to apply any measure designed to reduce the cost of unskilled labor to all industries in order to prevent such measures from constituting a nontariff barrier against trading partners.

Neutral policies constitute the workable compromise between the possibility of total suppression of the forces of change from the international sector with all of the long-run costs of such policies, and the difficulties in an industrialized democracy of instituting positive, or change-accommodating, policies. The attractiveness of neutral policies is that they have obvious benefits in that they slow the rate of change, they ensure that wage excesses are diminished, and they cushion society against the individual and social costs of the inevitable dislocation that accompany too-rapid change. These policies provide politicians with a middle-ground position from which, it is to be hoped, the furies of extremists on both sides can be directed at each other.

Positive policies deliberately seek to diminish capacity in industries that are not internationally competitive, and they otherwise try to foster progress toward the new equilibrium that is compatible with the new conditions. Such actions are necessarily interventionist in the sense that they seek to allow the economy to expedite change and seek to aid the market mechanism to conform to the new underlying conditions. Such policies may be expected to encounter fierce opposition from those segments of the population whose private interests are destined to be damaged.[9] The political task is much greater than for neutral policies, which allow impersonal market forces to effect change. A decision to invoke positive policies assumes that there is no possibility—or only a negligible possibility—of significant chronic unemployment; positive policies accelerate the movement toward some new equilibrium. Their adoption must, then, assume that the new equilibrium is politically and economically satisfactory. Such an assumption is built into the traditional analysis that espouses free trade.

There are clear difficulties in instituting positive policies because it requires that government identify those industries that must have their capacity reduced or eliminated and, still more difficult, those sectors and industries that are likely to expand. While the former problem may be relatively straightforward, the problem of picking winners is something in which governments have little skill.[10] Interventionist, or positive, policies are therefore likely to be limited to aiding the market in curtailing capacity in industries that have lost their international competitiveness.

Where such industries are privately owned, positive policies can be effected through incentives and disincentives: phase-out protection for senile industries can be tied to the closing of specific, very high cost plants. The release of any protectionist measures currently in force,

such as government preferences in purchasing and any tariffs or quotas that may have been instituted to allow the industry to reduce its costs, can be introduced at the same time that limitations on wage and salary increases in designated industries are legislated. When the industries are publicly owned, the process becomes more direct but not necessarily easier. Closing down high-cost plants, instituting wage and salary freezes, and reducing protection all lie within the purview of the authorities, but the resistance of employees may be even more vehement than in the private sector. In positive, as in neutral, policies, the question of the rate of change that is being inflicted on the economy is important. Opposition will be less when change is gradual, especially if displacement is accompanied by generous redundancy payments, if only because the task of an entrenched power group is to safeguard the welfare of its members and membership will decline quickly with golden handshakes and gradually with the passage of time.

A second dimension of positive policies is the degree to which the authorities facilitate relocation and retraining. If the market mechanism works imperfectly in transferring resources among industries, the causes may be an excessive rate of change, the failure of potentially expanding industries to institute expansion quickly enough, and constraints on the ability of displaced workers to acquire the skills that enable them to relocate in order to conform to the needs of the new industrial profile. Government has a responsibility to provide goods and services with a public-goods component. Retraining facilities, aid in relocation, and information on the existence of vacancies of various kinds in different regions are all activi-

9. The French experience in steel and the British experience in coal in the spring of 1984 are cases in point.

10. See C. L. Schultze, "Industrial Policy: A Solution in Search of a Problem," *California Management Review*, 25:5-15 (Summer 1983).

ties with a public-goods component. Positive policy can, then, involve creative measures that improve the ability of the economy to adjust to change. In such a schema, it is important that conditionality apply, just as in phase-out protection. Financial assistance must be closely tied to retraining commitments and relocation and must be independent of the source of dislocation. This conditionality is particularly relevant for workers who enjoyed wage premiums in their original employment. The existence of such generous wage rates will encourage workers to cling stubbornly to the idea of a resurgence of their own industry and to avoid a commitment to retraining and relocation.

CONCLUSION

Given the magnitude of the changes that actually or potentially will confront the economies of the industrialized nations over the next 15 years or so, it is important that policymakers be provided with analyses of the various options that they may legitimately consider and analyses of the costs and benefits of such options. The arguments presented in this article suggest that die-hard free-traders and obdurate protectionists do not provide policymakers with the tools of analysis needed for good decision making in a period of rapid change.

This article argues for allowing change to take place at a rate that is consistent with high levels of economic activity. Intervention, then, is to slow the rate of change, but the measures adopted must not abort the change. Such policies would lead to dynamic instability and fortify the popular resistance to adaptation, with all of the dangers of excessive economic rigidity in the industrialized countries.

The danger that haunts the analysis of the global internationalization of labor markets is the possibility that the integration of labor-surplus economies with those of the industrialized North will engender chronic unemployment in the North. This process will be reinforced by the effect of the new technologies that are already displacing workers, with a preponderant impact on production workers.

Chronic unemployment with the likelihood of mismatch between the pattern of skills demanded of the work force and those supplied by it will require intergenerational change. Some people will be destined to face a lifetime of unemployment. And successful intergenerational change will require a fundamental rethinking of educational systems, at a minimum. The economic hardships of protracted unemployment can be mitigated, but this process will require a fundamental change in established concepts and values with regard to the role of economic policy. More important and more difficult will be the concomitant reformulation of socioeconomic standards and values with respect to the status of unemployed workers by both the employed and the unemployed. If the system will not allow full employment at an income level deemed appropriate by national consensus, there should be no stigma attached to unemployment.

So profound a change in values as the effective renunciation of the positive social role of gainful employment will not be accomplished either quickly or easily. The change will take time, and, in the interim, it will be necessary to achieve some compromise position between the rigors of a simple hands-off policy and the short-run comforts of suppression. Such policies will need to be thought through long before the problem reaches its maximum severity. These policies will need to be tailored to fit national idiosyncrasies. Outright subsidization of low-skilled workers, directly or indirectly, will work only to the degree that industry can substitute among gradations of labor skills in response to changes in relative costs. Such policies may be valuable in the short run. Work sharing or a shorter workweek seems to have better long-run potential as a means for absorbing otherwise surplus workers but has two serious questions: how are workers to be remunerated for their enforced leisure and how can such workers be prevented from bumping other workers in the regular or in the underground economy?

When world labor markets are fully internationalized, the growth of the population in the developing world cannot be allowed to continue unhindered. The industrialized nations cannot serve as a sink for the productions of future unrestrained growth of Southern populations and it remains to be seen whether they can successfully adapt to the integration of the extant surplus labor into the world economy.

The final implication is normative. Those workers likely to be displaced by new technology and by exports of goods from labor-surplus nations are at the low end of the income scale. They are also the least likely to be able to take advantage of such opportunities for upgrading as exist. They deserve better than parsimonious treatment by governments elected by a majority of the more prosperous and more fortunate. While this argument has universal applicability, it is particularly relevant to countries in which the bottom end of the income scale is populated by ethnic minorities with past histories of discrimination.

ANNALS, *AAPSS*, **492**, July 1987

International Employment Competition

By ALFRED PFALLER

ABSTRACT: As countries assume more and more the character of regions within one integrated world economy, the conditions and the level of employment in the individual nation-state become increasingly dependent on the country's competitiveness. The wealth of nations becomes a matter of securing for the country—and the population that is confined to the national territory—a favorable position in a worldwide spatial hierarchy of market chances. Therefore the industrialized countries today face a double challenge. The industrialization of formerly backward, labor-abundant regions in the South threatens to displace high-wage Northern labor. This threat can perhaps be kept in check for the time being through an increasing destandardization of industrial production, which, in turn, gives rise to increasing intra-North competition. In this context, which in itself means more displacement and less job security, national employment goals are largely sacrificed to the priority goal of international competitiveness. National employment becomes the hostage of the country's success in the struggle for high-technology market shares.

Alfred Pfaller studied sociology and economics in Munich, Mannheim, and Pittsburgh, where he received a Ph.D. in 1973. He worked for five years as a research fellow of the West German Friedrich Ebert Foundation in Chile and Ecuador and is currently head of the foundation's Research Group on International Economics and Development Policies in Bonn. His scientific interest focuses on the relationship between international economic dynamics and national societies and on the politics of economic policymaking in the West and the South.

THIS article develops the following argument: the transnational integration of markets makes the conditions and level of employment in the individual nation-state increasingly dependent on the country's competitiveness. Moreover, as countries assume the character of regions within an integrated world economy, the expansion of economic activity and employment in one country can very well be at the expense of employment in other countries, without the equilibration of exports and imports tending to restore employment in the initial loser country.

Major displacements are likely to occur if technological breakthroughs make available new competitive production capacity elsewhere in a relatively short time. This can be the case when foreign competitors conquer a sectoral market due to freshly gained technological superiority, as Western manufacturers did vis-à-vis craft production in backward countries. It can also be the case when foreign countries with abundant labor supply gain access simultaneously to competitive technology and to established markets. Thus the industrialization of formerly backward and therefore low-wage regions in the so-called Third World has a displacing effect on high-wage labor—and immobile business—in the Northern Hemisphere. To maintain their income position, Northern producers would have to move into markets not yet threatened by low-cost Southern competition, or else they would have to try to stay in their current market by drastically adjusting their income expectations downward.

To succeed with the first alternative is a matter of entering and expanding in already contested markets or of developing so far uncontested market niches.

Quantitatively, the adjustment potential provided by this avenue is limited. Whether it will be sufficient for the North as a whole depends on the extent and the speed of industrial relocation to the world's low-wage regions.

There are good reasons to expect that this process of relocation will not gain momentum in the foreseeable future. But the destandardization of industrial production, which is most responsible for the reinforcement of Northern competitive advantages vis-à-vis the less developed South, also gives rise to increasing intra-North competition and decreasing continuity in the intra-North distribution of competitive advantages. As a consequence there is more displacement and job insecurity. In addition, competitiveness must become the top priority for each nation's economic policy, with the implication that macroeconomic demand maintenance is subordinated and largely sacrificed. National employment becomes the prize and the hostage of the country's success in the struggle for market shares.

Our "theory"—used in the unpretentious meaning of the word—should be seen as a proposal to give explicit recognition to the factor of internationalization when dealing with the present employment problems in the industrialized world. It tries to shed light on the ways this factor is related to other more commonly considered aspects of the employment issue, namely, aggregate demand, wages, productivity, and structural change. Internationalization denotes a new contextual dynamic that interferes with the macroeconomics of the classical open economy and that reshapes the dynamics of structural change.

The argument is developed mostly in a deductive fashion, starting from a basic consideration of the spatial distribution of economic growth. It offers a theoretical perspective that would in principle be applicable to a broad range of empirical realities. But it also claims particular empirical relevance for the post-1970 employment problems. It permits a coherent interpretation of the reduced effectiveness of old-fashioned macroeconomic demand management, of the difficulties that most countries of the Organization for Economic Cooperation and Development seem to have with the much-heralded structural adjustment, of the insufficiency of innovation in bringing about a new supply-side boom, and of the increasing importance of downward wage flexibility despite rising productivity.

THE SPATIAL DIMENSION OF ECONOMIC COMPETITION

Orthodox macroeconomic theory—Keynesian as well as neoclassical—treats national economies as systems in which all economic transactions together form a circular flow of production, income, and demand. The growth of such systems is basically considered as a process by which production is expanded so that more goods and services are made available to satisfy national demand. Economic exchanges with other economies, as they are dealt with in the theory of international trade, complicate the functioning of the system, but they do not alter its logic of circular flows. A great deal of attention has been devoted to the problem of how to secure the demand that would support satisfying levels and growth rates of production. The match between the structures of demand and supply is also perceived as a relevant aspect for the smoothness of the circular flows within the economic system. But it

remains always a fundamental idea that the market serves—or could serve if properly tuned—as a mechanism of coordination within the system, ensuring that the country's economic potential is most fully used in accordance with the preferences of the national population. Thus national full employment and high national growth rates appear dependent on the adequate coordination of the acts of supply and demand that make up the national economy. The country's endowment with physical and human resources appears as the only kind of external constraints.

I shall argue in the following that the system's perspective just outlined is inadequate for understanding the wealth of nations in today's international context and that it is the particularistic perspective of the market participant that has become increasingly relevant. First I shall elaborate somewhat this particularistic perspective, which can be seen most clearly when we take the position of an individual economic agent.[1] It is then the market itself that adopts the character of an external constraint, limiting the individual's income chances. The market attributes a scarcity value to the individual's resources—for example, his or her working ability—and decides at which condition the individual is admitted to the social process of production. For the individual, the market is in many respects a hierarchical structure of income-yielding positions. Access to them follows a selection process, which sets competing applicants against each other. By advancing into a relatively privileged posi-

1. See also Michael Dauderstädt and Alfred Pfaller, *The New Zero-Sum World: International Competition and Global Economic Growth*, Analysis and Information Series (Bonn: Friedrich-Ebert-Stiftung, 1985), pp. 9 ff.

tion, the individual excludes other applicants—maybe because what they offer is qualitatively inferior.

The competitive selection process is about distributing production assignments and hence income sources among the various applicants. A successful bid for a production assignment is the decisive step for a market participant to secure his or her income. For the economy—that is, the whole market-coordinated system—it is important that there are bids, but it is irrelevant who is successful and who is not. Collective prosperity depends on the adequate functioning of the circular flows of the market; individual prosperity depends on the advantageous placement within them. However, a distinction has to be made between those market participants who bid for production assignments within a given task structure and those who introduce new productive tasks, thus adding to the economy's wealth-creating apparatus. The first category is everywhere the large majority of the economically active population. It includes those who offer their factor services to enterprises and other entities of organized collective production, such as administration. It also includes most independent businesspeople who try to attract largely given and predefined demand to their offers. The second category comprises the true entrepreneurs of the Schumpeterian sort.[2] By bidding for a better place in the market structure they change and expand this structure. In a way they put themselves, at least temporarily, above the competition of assignment bidders.

2. On the fundamental scarcity of entrepreneurship in any society, see, for example, Harvey Leibenstein, "Entrepreneurship and Development," *American Economic Review*, vol. 64 (June 1968).

Our next analytic step is to relate the individual's perspective to a larger and internally differentiated group of people as a nation. For this purpose we have to introduce the concept of space. One can group the individual bidders for production assignments and the attached income chances within the overall market system according to their spatial affiliation. The spatial entities that we consider are smaller than the total space covered by the integrated network of market relations. That is to say, the circular flows that make up the economy typically cross the boundaries of spatial entities. In addition, we assume that the individuals of different spatial entities compete to a considerable degree for the same production assignments. I shall term such spatial entities, which from an economic point of view are arbitrarily delimited subunits, regions.[3] For the prosperity of a region—as I just specified it—basically the same perspective applies as for the individual market participant. Regional prosperity depends on how successfully the region's inhabitants bid for production assignments—whether they get highly remunerated jobs and whether they secure for themselves highly profitable business. In other words, for a region's prosperity, how the production assignments of the larger

3. To avoid misunderstandings, let me give an example: the New York metropolitan area would be such a region, the Pacific Basin would not. The definition of "region" for the purposes of this article is also distinct from Ohlin's concept of regions as economically homogeneous spaces. Bertil Ohlin, *Interregional and International Trade*, revised ed. (Cambridge, MA: Harvard University Press, 1967). Our integrated, supra-regional economic space, in turn, resembles in some respects a "region" as understood by Ohlin and by August Lösch, even though we shall later restrict their common condition of complete factor mobility.

market system are spatially distributed is important.

Considering the spatial distribution of production assignments, our attention is directed to the decisive process of the creation and destruction of productive capacity. That the market assigns production tasks to a spatial entity implies two things: (1) productive capacity is created in the region; and (2) the market underwrites this capacity by accepting its output. The first element can be the result of a successful bid—for instance, when supraregional business managers decide to build a new production plant in the region. It can also constitute part of the bidding act itself—for example, when local entrepreneurs start a business, hoping that they will be successful. In both cases something enters the picture that can be called the competitiveness of the region and that has to do with geographical characteristics—like closeness to important markets or endowment with natural resources—as well as with individual and social characteristics of the population and with previous investments in the region's productive potential, or infrastructure. If the set of preconditions called regional competitiveness does not favor such an undertaking, the risk of creating productive capacity is less likely to be taken—by local as well as by foreign entrepreneurs. If it is taken—that is, if failure is not being anticipated—the second criterion, acceptance of the output by the market, must still be met.

The market does not only assign production tasks associated with income chances; it also withdraws them. This is the case when new productive capacity elsewhere leads to superior offers. Physically, the old capacity continues to exist, but economically it becomes worthless.

Figuratively, it is being destroyed. The result is that the region has become poorer as a consequence of extraregional competition, while another region has added to its income-generating productive capacity. Especially vulnerable to such substitution cum invalidation of capacity are regions with a highly specialized productive structure, which face, in addition, the danger of shifts in demand to different categories of goods and services. If they do not adjust in time these regions can be left with a tremendously reduced productive capacity.[4]

The amount of market-proof productive capacity, embodied in locally owned and foreign-owned enterprises, constitutes the wealth of a spatial entity. And from a spatial point of view, the competition for production assignments is competition between spatial entities for the allocation of such market-proof productive capacity. Endowment with productive potential, which plays so crucial a role for neoclassical explanations of trade and the corresponding allocative prescriptions, must thus in an important aspect be seen as a result, and not as a determinant, of competitiveness. It is the prize for which spatial entities, implicitly or explicitly, compete.[5]

4. The impact of adverse market developments on a spatial entity is only in degree, not in principle, different from that on a firm. As Nelson and Winter say, "The 'gales of creative destruction' blow down the incomes not only of capitalists and managers but also of workers whose skills have become obsolete and of people who were unlucky enough to live in places where industry has become obsolete." Richard R. Nelson and Sydney E. Winter, *An Evolutionary Theory of Economic Change* (Cambridge, MA: Belknap Press, 1982), p. 369.

5. One could even say that from a policy perspective the nexus of endowment arising out of trade chances is more important than the classical and neoclassical nexus of trade chances being implied in endowment.

Now, it is well known that productive capacity tends to become unevenly distributed over space. Some locations are naturally more advantageous than others. But most important, the advantages of agglomeration reinforce spatial concentration once it has started. Thus economic growth gives rise to spatial structures of centers and peripheries; for our purpose we neglect here all the finer subdivisions and complications.[6] At a given point of time—with the exception of revolutionary changes, of which we shall speak later—most production assignments go to centrally located bidders rather than to peripheral ones. This applies also to the newly created assignments, so that production and income tend to grow more rapidly in the central spaces. But the increase in demand that derives from economic growth in the centers also benefits the periphery as the scarcity value of peripheral goods and services—for example, agricultural products, raw materials, tourism—increases and as central production extends into the periphery.[7]

However, the most decisive benefit of central growth for peripheral population has always been the chances it provides for emigrants. For the distribution of income chances among the economically active, the spatial dimension would become nearly irrelevant to the degree that migration became feasible

and financially and psychologically without cost. But suppose migration beyond certain distances is a rather difficult—in the extreme case, prohibited—option for most people. Then the spatial dimension of competition for production assignments is a very significant one. Spatial affiliation determines then the income chances of the non-entrepreneurs because it limits their access to productive capacity, on which in turn the value of their work depends. Moreover, a region's competitiveness, as specified previously, determines to a considerable degree the chances that local entrepreneurship can build up market-proof productive capacity, thus creating regional wealth as well as assuming the function of a growth engine for the whole supraregional economy.[8] To the degree that migration barriers are effective, the unequal spatial distribution of production implies privileged and underprivileged work force segments, the latter being confined to regional labor markets with relatively few highly productive jobs, a relatively low marginal productivity at full employment, and hence a relatively low average wage.

To recapitulate, a spatial hierarchy, which is so decisive for a region's and its inhabitants' prosperity, evolves on the basis of two preconditions: (1) an integrated supraregional market, which sets bidders for production assignments from various regions in competition with each other so that competitively disadvantaged regions get fewer and less privileged assignments; and (2) barriers to migration that prevent the population

6. One of the first to bring up this proposition was von Thünen in his *Der isolierte Staat in Beziehung auf Landwirtschaft und Nationalökonomie* (1842). Elaborated to a high degree of sophistication by August Lösch—see, for example, his *Economics of Location* (New Haven, CT: Yale University Press, 1954)—it served later as theoretical pillar for the dependencia approach to Third World underdevelopment.

7. On the other hand, demand that arises in the periphery tends to be absorbed to a much larger degree by centrally located producers.

8. However, this does not rule out the possibility that entrepreneurs in relatively poor peripheral regions do highly profitable business, especially if they control a significant part of the region's productive capacity.

of disadvantaged regions from competing in the labor markets of the advantaged regions for access to income-generating productive capacity.

But to what extent would regional income privileges emerge if these two conditions prevail? Competition is an equalizing mechanism, more or less forcing competitors to adjust to the quality and price standards set by others in their bid for production assignments. This individual adjustment tends to keep everybody in the market or to return those who have been pushed out. Spatially it means that the competitively weaker—because somehow disadvantaged—regions take over production assignments under less favorable conditions, as less skilled individuals do. If large-scale migration is ruled out, this downward adjustment goes on, in theory, until everywhere everybody—whose preference for idleness is low enough—is occupied. Production is spread over the space evenly in accordance with locational advantages and disadvantages, exhibiting a division of labor in line with the logic of comparative costs. Individual wages vary according to a center-periphery pattern, reflecting the true economies of agglomeration. Central growth dissipates to the periphery as soon as the cost of central labor surpasses the economic value of these economies of agglomeration.[9]

SHIFTING COMPETITIVE ADVANTAGES

Interregional equilibrium considerations lead, thus, to results that are not

9. On the other hand, if there is general unemployment—due to a malfunctioning of the overall system's circular-flow mechanism—it is rather likely that it becomes spatially concentrated in the periphery.

too different from the international division of labor as envisaged by the modern versions of classical trade theory. But major differences emerge when we consider changes in the spatial structure. If we look at classical economies with their own, basically independent, dynamic of accumulation, we will see changing comparative advantages and corresponding structural adjustments as relative factor endowments, including skills, change. On the other hand, if we look at the hierarchical spatial structure of one integrated supraregional economy, we will instead see improving and deteriorating market positions of spatially identifiable population segments, as competitive advantages shift from one region to another.

The immediate effect of a shift in competitive advantages from A to B is that B takes over production assignments from A and receives the corresponding income. Seen from a spatial perspective, population segment B, which lives in region B, takes over the jobs of population segment A, which lives in region A. The A people are being pushed out of the market. To get production assignments anew, they would have either to

—regain their old competitive advantage through improvements in the region's performance potential—more efficient local enterprises or increased attractiveness of the region to supraregional enterprises;
—compensate the loss of competitiveness by adjusting wage demands downward;
—compete successfully for newly—in the way of general growth—arising production assignments; or
—take over production assignments formerly held by others.

The last possibility would correspond to the shift in comparative advantages emphasized by classical trade theory. It presupposes that the B people, who take over the A people's production assignments, give up *uno ictu* some other production assignments since they cannot do everything at once, or in other words, as the economy works at the limits of its capacity. But often this is not the case. A competitive substitution of production typically proceeds by creating new capacity and simultaneously devaluating capacity elsewhere. It enables one segment of the work force to produce more while diminishing the productive potential of another segment. The A people can only hope that by adjusting their wage demands downward they will attract new investment in the next round of general growth or capacity renewal. But it is also possible that the initial loss of production and income may make region A less attractive in terms of agglomeration. The region then moves, so to speak, toward a peripheral position in the spatial structure and faces the necessity of even more pronounced downward adjustment.

Now consider the case of several regions that have been largely protected against substitutive external competition and that, therefore, have experienced their own autonomous accumulation processes. If these regions are exposed to each other's competition—because trade restrictions and geographic distances matter less—major dislocations are quite likely to occur. And it would be pure chance if in each region losses and gains of production assignments were balanced. Thus, on top of large-scale structural adjustment, one or some regions will have to cope—at least in the first round of spatial reshuffling—with a loss of production, employment, and income.

Two sorts of losers should be expected. First, relatively inefficient local production capacity tends to be invalidated by newly created superior capacity elsewhere. The region's per capita income shrinks or—in the context of general growth—experiences relative stagnation. Part of the population reduces its consumption. The other part buys and sells more outside of the region and less within the region—that is, it gets more integrated into the supraregional economy—while the region itself becomes economically disintegrated.

The other sort of losers are those who suddenly face the competition of almost equally efficient, but much cheaper, production elsewhere, as the new mobility of capital and technology erodes former efficiency advantages and the income privileges based on them. The region as a whole, if it cannot attract or create sufficient production assignments in other sectors, loses part of its inherited central position to a catching-up periphery. As in the previous case, the circular flows of economic exchanges are redirected across the regional borders, while part of the regional population is being excluded.

Having discussed so far *in abstracto* the implications of market integration for spatial subunits, I shall now apply the results of the analysis to the reality of today's international economy. It is the thesis of this article that the Western nation-states have been caught in a process of increasing exposure to external competition for many years and that the process is gaining momentum, so that their economies resemble less and less the integrated-circular-flow model of orthodox theory and more and more the regional model previously outlined. But while they become integrated into a supranational world economy their national boundaries continue to constitute effective barriers to labor migration. Contrary to the formation of integrated supranational market networks, nation-states continue to pursue in a sovereign way the collective national interest. They turn, economically speaking, more than ever into regions with their own political will. The wealth of nations becomes a matter of securing for a country a favorable position in the supranational spatial hierarchy. It is in the national economic interest to attract favorable production assignments to the national territory—and to the national population, which is confined to this territory—and to prevent the world market from withdrawing the assignments.[10] Therefore the highly industrialized countries face the challenge of increasing exposure on three fronts:

1. Countries with roughly equally efficient, albeit differently structured, industries invade more and more each other's traditional markets. This challenge is in principle being handled by increasing intra-industry specialization without excessive dislocations.

2. The bulk of industrialized countries face the competition of superior innovators in some other countries, most notably Japan.

3. They all have to cope with a loss of industrial production to new low-cost locations in the former periphery of the world economy.

The last challenge is potentially the most threatening one for the old industrial countries.

THE NEW LOW-WAGE COMPETITION

In those areas of the world where the stock of productive capital per inhabitant is very low—due in part to the late start of industrialization and in part to the very dynamics of center-periphery relations—and where, therefore, average labor productivity is very low, too, a large ill-paid or outrightly unemployed labor force has emerged that is kept by national boundaries from migrating to the world's high-wage areas.[11] In the course of the past decades this labor reserve has increasingly become available for industrial production as a substitute for high-wage labor in the regions of the world's industrial centers. The preconditions for this new availability are: decreasing costs of long-distance communication and transportation, improved physical infrastructure in the low-wage countries, improved education of the labor force, emergence of large-scale urban labor markets due to internal migration, guaranteed stability of the social relations of production, and accessibility of the important markets. To the degree that these conditions are fulfilled, the old disadvantages of industrial production in the periphery—espe-

10. In other words, the national economic interest calls, under the conditions of integrated supranational markets, for an essentially mercantilistic policy orientation. The argument, which guides policy practice all over the world but which is vehemently opposed by mainstream economic theory, is more fully developed in Alfred Pfaller, "Internationale Produktionsstruktur, nationaler Wohlstand und neo-merkantilistische Politik," in *Der Kampf um den Wohlstand von Morgen: Internationaler Strukturwandel und neuer Merkantilismus,* ed. A. Pfaller (Bonn: Neue Gesellschaft, 1986). See also Harry Shutt, *The Myth of Free Trade: Patterns of Protectionism since 1945* (Oxford: Basil Blackwell, 1985).

11. For the dynamics of unemployment in the less developed part of the world, see Hilde Wander, "Population, Labor Supply, and Employment in Developing Countries," this issue of *The Annals* of the American Academy of Political and Social Science; Guy Standing, "Unemployment and the Recomposition of Labor Reserves," ibid.

cially distance—disappear. The potential productivity of peripheral labor makes a big jump.

But the scarcity value of labor, as well as of land and environment, in the periphery stays much below that in the industrially central countries. Thus peripheral labor is more and more in a position to bid successfully for production assignments. The once rather closed labor market of the highly industrialized areas are being opened up to low-wage competition, in spite of the barriers to migration in the form of national frontiers. The tendency toward wage equalization, which corresponds to the decreasing productivity differentials of industrially employed labor, imposes itself through the mobility of technology, capital, and goods. For certain jobs high-wage bidders do not have a chance any longer. They have to adjust their demands to the low standards of the newcomers if they cannot secure other exclusive production assignments.[12]

But the relocation of industries from high-wage to low-wage regions does not in itself contribute to the likelihood of new high-wage jobs becoming available. The immediate effect is rather that certain population segments of the periphery become included in the circuit of economic exchanges while inhabitants of the central regions are left out. The low-wage bidders replace their competitors not only as sellers in the labor market but in part also as buyers in the goods markets. The other part of the contested chunk of income goes to the customers of the relocated industry who benefit from lower prices. National accounts will show more trade, as more

goods cross national frontiers, but the volume of goods produced and exchanged in the overall system does not increase.[13] In a static context, the low-wage countries experience a predatory growth at the expense of the high-wage countries. In the context of systemwide economic growth, one would have to register a dissipation of growth from the central countries to parts of the periphery.[14]

The empirical manifestation of this replacement process is being blurred, however, because at the same time there is another process occurring that corresponds to the orthodox notion of a rearrangement in the international division of labor in line with changing comparative advantages. Such rearrangements can be triggered by economic growth in the industrialized central countries that leads to capacity bottlenecks there and requires the mobilization of peripheral reserves. They can also be triggered by autonomous accumulation processes in Third World countries that increase there the demand for imports—as autarky is neither feasible nor desirable—and hence the necessity to increase production for exports.[15]

---

12. It should be noted that this result corresponds to the theorem of trade-generated factor price equalization, which is derived from the assumptions of neoclassical trade theory.

13. See Alfred Pfaller, "The New Protectionism and the Limits of Structural Adjustment," *Intereconomics*, 18:5 (1983), for further elaboration of this argument.

14. The notion of international crowding-out, as it has been developed by Michael Beenstock and Patrick Willcocks, reflects the predatory character of relocation-based growth of less developed countries even though these authors confine their notion to the manufacturing sector and assume that the deindustrialization of the North leads to the concomitant expansion of other activities there. See Beenstock and Willcocks, *The Cause of Slower Growth in the World Economy*, Economic Forecasting Unit Discussion Paper no. 76 (London: London Business School, 1980); Beenstock, *The World Economy in Transition* (London: Allen & Unwin, 1983).

15. For a more elaborate presentation of the overlapping process of growth-induced rearrange-

If these two autonomous sources of economic growth were powerful enough, industrial relocation would not constitute a threat for Western high-wage labor, except for the essentially temporary problems of structural adjustment.[16] Then indeed a new division of labor between old industrialized countries and newly industrializing countries would emerge, with the former specializing more in production at the high-technology end of the industrial spectrum and the latter dominating the technically mature production processes. The problem with this harmonious picture of the evolving North-South trade is that it is dependent on sufficient growth. The forces behind the wage-difference-induced relocation process do not become weaker when economic growth slows down. The replacement of Northern high-wage labor by Southern low-wage labor goes on even when the growth-dependent demand for high-tech goods and nontradables can no longer provide an adequate compensation for the displaced producers. As a consequence, part of the Northern work force is then eliminated from the high-wage job market. In an analogy to spatial considerations one could say that these job seekers move to the economic periphery, even though they live in highly industrialized countries. Like the academic who has to gain his income as night watchman, they will have to bid for low-wage jobs or stay unemployed.[17]

But there is a counterargument that carries some weight. It says that the low-wage advantage of the periphery matters much less than the idea of rapidly decreasing diseconomies of distance would suggest. Two lines of reasoning can lead to this conclusion. One emphasizes the decreasing importance of labor costs as many standardized production processes become more and more automatized. Other advantages and disadvantages associated with certain locations therefore have more weight. Higher requirements are to be met in terms of infrastructure, productivity, and reduced transport costs before a peripheral location can compete with the central ones.[18] The other line of reasoning maintains that many production processes become destandardized again as new quality and

ments in the international division of labor and wage-difference-induced relocation, see Alfred Pfaller, "The Changing North-South Division of Labor: Promises, Threats and EC Policy Options," *Kyklos*, 39:1 (1986). See also Gray's distinction between pull and push disturbance in Peter Gray, "Towards a Theory of Adjustment Policy," mimeographed (New Brunswick, NJ: Rutgers University, 1986).

16. As Gray shows, even these temporary adjustment problems can be rather intractable and can spell permanent unemployment for quite a number of workers. H. Peter Gray, "The Internationalization of Global Labor Markets," this issue of *The Annals* of the American Academy of Political and Social Science. Beenstock and Willcocks also attribute a large part of the present unemployment in industrialized countries to the short-term intractable adjustment problems caused by rapidly increasing competition from less developed countries. See Beenstock and Willcocks, *Causes of Slower Growth*.

17. For a similar assessment of what may be called the low-wage threat, see John M. Culbertson, *International Trade and the Future of the West* (Madison, WI: 21st Century Press, 1984).

18. Also, it is less easy for local enterprises of the peripheral countries to compensate for the advantage the large established firms have in terms of internalized—and thus not readily transferable—organizational expertise. See on this point, for example, Michael E. Porter, *Competitive Strategy: Techniques for Analyzing Industries and Competitors* (New York: Free Press, 1980); Boston Consulting Group, *Les mécanismes fondamentaux de la compétitivité* (Boulogne-Billancourt: Editions Hommes et Techniques, 1982); Nelson and Winter, *Evolutionary Theory of Economic Change,* chap. 5.

performance dimensions are added to mature goods. Thus competitiveness demands higher levels of technological and organizational sophistication than the notion of standardized production know-how implies. This is a matter of expert personnel, of a network of sophisticated auxiliary services and supplies, and often of closeness to the market, due to the required intensity of communication.[19]

Neither the decreasing importance of labor costs nor the new importance of sophistication and local agglomeration can immunize the old industrialized regions completely against the threat of low-wage competition.[20] But both certainly raise the threshold of preconditions that have to be fulfilled before industrial relocation to the periphery becomes advantageous. And for the time being they probably exclude many Third World countries from the circle of candidates for large-scale relocation. On the other side, the formula of low wages plus sophistication plus social stability should be considered a rather good recipe for competitiveness. Accordingly, the most developed among the newly industrialized countries are serious rivals to the old central countries when it comes to the future location of many industries.

HIGH-TECH COMPETITION AND THE REDUCED PRIORITY OF FULL EMPLOYMENT

If we want to speculate about the quantitative impact on Western employment of future low-wage competition, we must not only take into account the reinforcement of old central advantages but also the new trade restrictions that artificially increase the home advantage of national production and that evidently slow down the process of industrial relocation.[21] Under these circumstances, the danger of the replacement of high-wage jobs in the North by low-wage jobs in the South may appear as rather limited. Unfortunately, however, the transnational integration of markets has created a context that prevents national employment security in the North from being restored that way.

Trade barriers do not protect export markets. They do free the industrialized countries of the necessity of competing with foreign bidders for production

19. The automobile is an example of such destandardization. See, for example, David Friedman's critique of the production strategy of U.S. car-makers. Friedman, "Beyond the Age of Ford: The Strategic Basis of the Japanese Success in Automobiles," in *American Industry in International Competition: Government Policies and Corporate Strategies*, ed. John Zysman and Laura Tyson (Ithaca, NY: Cornell University Press, 1983). Also mentioned in this respect must be the notion of decreasing economies of scale in modern manufacturing and the increasing importance of flexibility, as it has been elaborated, for instance, in Michael J. Piore and Charles Sable, *The Second Industrial Divide: Possibilities for Prosperity* (New York: Basic Books, 1984). As Junne emphasizes, flexibility depends very much on the "economies of scope," that is, on a locally concentrated, diversified network of production, which makes all sorts of supplies readily available. Gerd Junne, "Reregionalisierung: Chancen regionaler Reintegration von Produktion und Konsum als Folge der Entwicklung neuer Technologien," in *Jahrbuch Arbeit und Technik in Nordrhein-Westfalen*, ed. W. Fricke et al. (Bonn: Neue Gesellschaft, 1985).

20. See Hartmut Elsenhans's argument on the limited effect of labor-saving technologies in undoing the competitive advantage of low-wage locations. Elsenhans, "Absorbing Global Surplus Labor," this issue of *The Annals* of the American Academy of Political and Social Science. See also Pfaller, "Changing North-South Division of Labor," pp. 95 ff.

21. The avoidance of trade barriers is, for instance, a major consideration guiding the investment policy of transnational corporations.

assignments in order to keep their work force employed at the high wages they are used to.[22] The promise of continuing competitiveness in a broad range of industries despite the periphery's low-wage advantage hinges on the condition that production becomes destandardized, that it moves ahead to ever new levels of quality and sophistication before standardization catches up. Not only must standardized products remain largely unacceptable to the market—otherwise high-wage employment has to retreat into niches—but the pace of national innovation also has to keep up with that of foreign competitors. The strategy that can protect against displacement from the low-wage side also makes a country vulnerable to displacement from the high-tech side. Competition is no longer an equalizing mechanism, which by and large forces every bidder to conform to the standards of the market, but a race. Being outbid is not just a signal for adjustment but

easily means elimination from the contest. There is no given comparative advantage that assures to, say, the Belgian or the British workers the competitive edge that is necessary to bid successfully for production assignments in the high-tech sector. The endowment of all industrialized countries with a relatively large amount of human capital—highly educated workers, many engineers, a highly developed research-and-development apparatus, and so forth—does not endow them automatically with market-proof high-tech productive capacity. It entitles them to participate in the contest but does not guarantee success.

And it is not surprising at all that innovative capacity is significantly higher in certain regions of the industrialized West—as well as the newly industrialized South—than in others and that the local preconditions for that new type of production are much better at certain places than elsewhere. It is not only the dynamics of agglomeration that matter here, but also the social, political, and cultural determinants of the way production is organized.[23] In those countries where enterprises are systematically slower in adjusting to continuous changes and/or that are less attractive to innovative enterprises, it will be increasingly difficult for the population to find jobs at all, let alone find jobs at the relatively high wages of the past. The countries that lag behind in the technological race become increasingly deindustrialized.

22. As far as the reservation of home markets for national suppliers is concerned, it might save jobs as it spreads the costs of low competitiveness over the whole national population. But collective impoverishment will not be avoided that way if the lame ducks cannot be pulled along by other, highly competitive national industries. See Dauderstädt and Pfaller, *New Zero-Sum World*, pp. 45 ff. Thus reducing foreign exposure for the sake of maintaining social stability at home—as it is proposed, for example, in Harry Shutt, *Myth of Free Trade*; Wolfgang Hager, "Free Trade Means Destabilization," *Intereconomics*, 19(1) (Jan.-Feb. 1984); David Gordon "Do We Need to Be No. 1?" *Atlantic Monthly*, (Apr. 1986)—can make sense as a way of dealing with an existing competitive situation or of improving the preconditions for future competitiveness. But as an alternative to competitiveness—as a recipe for escaping in the long run the dictate of international competitiveness—it is extremely risky because the comparison with the outside world will be increasingly disadvantageous for the particular nation and this will be less and less socially acceptable.

23. This proposition has been central to modern social science, the landmarks of the debate being associated with names like Adam Smith, Max Weber, Friedrich Hayek, and more recently Mancur Olson. For a very perceptive discussion, see Nelson and Winter, *Evolutionary Theory of Economic Change*, part 5. It is also central to the ongoing policy debate about the appropriate ways of promoting industrial competitiveness, organizing enterprises, and so forth.

As a whole they move toward the periphery of the transnational economy, with all the consequences of internal disintegration.[24] If nontradables absorb a relatively large part of rich countries' or regions' demand—a trend toward services!—a decline in manufacturing competitiveness may not appear that important at first. But since nontradables flourish there, where income is concentrated, they also reinforce the decline of a region and the rise of another one once the process has gained a certain momentum.

International competition for high-technology market shares is not a zero-sum game of the static sort, because the competitors also act as growth engines, continuously creating new production assignments. But in the context of worldwide labor abundance this competition is not a cooperative game either. It does know losers, and not to end up among them must have the highest priority for the economic polity of the high-wage countries, because national prosperity is at stake in the most fundamental way.[25]

This priority of competitiveness in the context of rapidly changing market conditions implies that less emphasis can be put on employment security and stable working conditions than it used to be up to the mid-seventies. Societies have to be prepared to accept large-scale displacement for the sake of rapid adjustment.[26] The priority of competitiveness also implies that the governments try to provide rather favorable conditions for innovativeness and flexibility in the adjustment of national enterprises as well as for inward investment by transnational enterprises. Measures to achieve these goals vary, but in general they have an austerity bias. Resources must be diverted from collective and individual consumption to investment. Profits must be boosted, wages and nonwage labor costs be kept rather tight. The tax load on enterprises should be lower rather than higher. There should not be too many restrictions on entrepreneurial freedom, neither from government nor from organized labor. The stimulation of demand has to step back wherever the corresponding measures, like fiscal expan-

24. What Nelson and Winter say about the evolution of firms is—by virtue of aggregation—equally valid for the spatial entities whose productive capacity is embodied in these firms: "Some firms track emerging technological opportunities with greater success than other firms; the former tend to prosper and grow, the latter to suffer losses and decline. Growth confers advantages that make further success more likely, while decline breeds technological obsolescence and further decline." Nelson and Winter, *Evolutionary Theory of Economic Change*, p. 325. For the anatomy of regional decline in the United States, see, for example, Barry Bluestone and Bennett Harrison, *The Deindustrialization of America: Plant Closings, Community Abandonment and the Dismantling of Basic Industry* (New York: Basic Books, 1982).

25. Although orthodox macroeconomics has relatively little to say about the competitiveness of a nation—and much more about the balance of foreign trade—the concern about it is very promi-

nent in the considerations that guide the actual economic policy of the Western nation-states. Some—such as Japan or France—proceed in an openly neomercantilistic fashion; others, like West Germany or Switzerland, are more subtle about it.

26. See in this respect Michael J. Piore, "Perspectives on Labor Market Flexibility," *Industrial Relations*, 25(2) (Spring 1986). The far-reaching consequences this may have for the Western welfare societies are provocatively laid out in John Goldthorpe, "The End of Convergence: Corporatist and Dualist Tendencies in Modern Western Societies," *New Approaches to Economic Life: Economic Restructuring, Unemployment and the Social Division of Labour*, ed. B. Roberts, R. Finnegan, and D. Gallie (Manchester: Manchester University Press, 1985). See also R. D. Norton, "Industrial Policy and American Renewal," *Journal of Economic Literature*, vol. 24 (Mar. 1986).

sion or disproportional wage increases, conflict with the instrumental requirements of the priority goal. Thus the goal of full employment must be largely neglected in practice. Moreover, full employment itself must be considered as ambivalent, because it increases the power of labor at the expense of profits and entrepreneurial freedom.[27]

The fact that the increasingly integrated transnational economy continues to be fragmented in sovereign nation-states does not only politicize the competition for privileged production assignments, it also reduces seriously the political capacity of macroeconomic management. Countries whose economic polity is oriented toward the priority of national competitiveness are induced to tolerate more economic slack at home than they would under different conditions. And they are not inclined at all to take over responsibility for the stimulation of economic activity on a worldwide scale, as it would correspond to the transnational nature of the relevant market circuits.[28] Thus the new kind of international competition brings about

unemployment not only for the losers but for all countries who struggle against being pushed to the losers' side. Here seems to be one fundamental cause of the end of stable full employment as the Western countries knew it before the 1970s. The circular-flow logic of accumulation must be politically neglected because the spatial hierarchy of market positions has been shaken up thoroughly and the particularistic competitor's logic has become salient.[29]

Circularity is also affected in the social organization of production. The end of stable full employment at rising real wages threatens the historical compromise between labor and capital, which was the social base of rapid accumulation after World War II.[30] The ensuing conflict, in turn, puts at stake not only further national accumulation but also national competitiveness. To organize a competitive economy would then require either a new kind of social discipline, independent of the former quid pro quo, or an uninterrupted superior competitiveness, which ensures continuing full employment at rising wages for the national segment of the global labor force.

27. See on the last point Michal Kalecki, "Political Aspects of Full Employment," *Political Quarterly* (1943). The austerity bias of competitiveness-centered—and thus mercantilistically inspired—policies is the central theme of Wolfgang Hager, "The Neomercantilist Constraint," this issue of *The Annals* of the American Academy of Political and Social Science. I have adopted Hager's argument and integrated it into my line of reasoning.

28. From this point of view it only follows that Japan and West Germany refuse to give in to U.S. demands that they should pursue a more reflationary economic policy. The transition from export-led growth to a growth regime that rests basically on internal demand is no longer the

crucial point. It is the new conflict in priorities between demand stimulation and competitiveness.

29. See Dauderstädt and Pfaller, *New Zero-Sum World*, pp. 9 ff.

30. This perspective is owed in large part to the pioneering work in David Gordon, Richard Edwards, and Michael Reich, *Segmented Work, Divided Workers: The Historical Transformation of Labour in the United States* (New York: Cambridge University Press, 1982); Thomas E. Weisskopf, Samuel Bowles, and David Gordon, *Hearts and Minds: A Social Model of US Productivity Growth* (Washington, DC: Brookings Institution, 1983).

ANNALS, *AAPSS*, **492,** July 1987

Absorbing Global Surplus Labor

By HARTMUT ELSENHANS

ABSTRACT: Capitalist economies need rising wages to keep up demand for increasing output. But the increasing availability of Third World surplus labor for world-market production threatens to uncouple wages from the development of productivity and to create, thus, a global deficit of demand that will profoundly disturb the growth mechanism of the capitalist world economy. None of the counterarguments that are brought up in the debate on the low-wage danger stands up to a closer examination. In order to check this danger, surplus labor in the Third World must be absorbed through inward-looking development. This requires that LDC demand structure be adjusted in a government-controlled way to the LDC supply potentials—relatively simple goods for mass consumption. The North should push such strategies in the South according to the leitmotiv "resources for reform—reforms against resources" thus strengthening reformist Southern elites.

Hartmut Elsenhans graduated from the Free University of Berlin. He has been teaching in Berlin, Frankfurt, Marburg, Montreal, Salzburg, and Dakar, and is professor of international relations at Constance University.

NOTE: A slightly modifed German version of this article was published in *Der Kampf um den Wohlstand von Morgen,* ed. Alfred Pfaller (1986).

N ORTH-South relations have been marked since the beginning of the 1970s by the rise in oil prices. The leverage obtained by Third World countries has been used to start a North-South dialogue, which up to now has not achieved concrete results. But the oil-price rise has been only the most visible stake in North-South relations. Less debated has been the very much more important change in international competitiveness of Third World labor-intensive industrial production. Effectively, there has been a real push of Third World low-cost industrial exports. It is not the subject of this article to criticize the geographical limitations of this push or the rather narrow range of products concerned, coupled with an even narrower range of products exported by each of the leading countries of export-led growth. My contention is that even if this export-led growth has been limited, it is sufficiently important to disturb the fundamental mechanisms of growth in the industrial countries and hence also in the Third World countries pursuing this strategy, because the push is insufficiently important to transform Third World labor markets. Export-led growth in Third World countries engenders and reinforces underconsumptionist tendencies in the international economy because it diminishes the bargaining power of the working class in the center without creating bargaining power of nascent working classes in the periphery. By the implied shift of bargaining power from labor to capital, capital's role of implementing cost-reducing strategies is insufficiently matched by a consumption-increasing labor strategy of sharing in increased output through rising real wages.

EXPORT-LED GROWTH LEADS TO A
CONTRACTION OF WORLD DEMAND

Basic to the argument is a Keynesian model of growth, the general implications and theoretical foundations of which are not to be discussed here. Profit depends on realized net investment, but the propensity to invest depends on the expectations about profits and markets. Capacity-increasing investment will not take place if consumption does not increase. Capital-deepening investment without capacity or without wage cost increases can only occur if total factor costs fall and hence if total factor income decreases. There is no such growth as proposed by Marx and Lenin, as well as by neoliberals, whose shared contention can be read as follows: if labor cost is sufficiently low and hence surplus value sufficiently high, capital-deepening investment may clear the labor market. Evidence supports my contention. Clearly, capital intensity of production as measured by capital goods in constant prices employed per worker has risen in Western industrial countries. But capital goods even at constant prices incorporate labor at secularly rising real wages. The contention that capital deepening or a rise of the organic composition of capital—the Marxian version of capital deepening—occurs has to be established by comparing direct labor and indirect labor units employed in production. The most convenient indicator is the capital-output ratio, which—at a constant share of labor in national income—follows the movement of the ratio of the cost of capital goods employed in production to the wages paid to workers and employees. The historical stability of the capital-output ratio in most industrial countries need not be further elaborated.

Contrary to planned economies of the East European type, capitalism cannot grow by capital deepening, because such growth would mean either that the rate of accumulation would constantly outstrip the rate of production growth or that production growth rates increase in a geometrical manner. If the rate of production growth is outstripped by the rate of accumulation, an abrupt fall of the rate of profit is necessary; if production growth follows the rate of accumulation, the increased surplus in case of stagnant real wages requires that in any period the rate of capital growth has to be higher than in the previous one, until the share of labor in national income becomes negligible.[1] Capitalist societies require rather stable capital-output ratios and hence rather stable capital-wage ratios, if we discard the idea that capitalists use increasing shares of profit for nonproductive luxury consumption. Capitalist societies have historically been dependent on markets for mass-consumption goods; their coming into being required a balance of power rather favorable to the lower classes.[2] Capitalist

1. The point is elaborated in Hartmut Elsenhans, "Der Mythos der Kapitalintensität und die notwendig falsche Technologiewahl der Entwicklungsländer," in *Technik und internationale Politik*, ed. Beate Kohler-Koch (Baden-Baden: Nomos, 1986), pp. 267-90, originally published in a more simplified version in Elsenhans, "Das Gesetz vom tendenziellen Fall der Profitrate," *Leviathan*, 7(4):584-97 (1979). Conclusions are similar to those achieved in Alain Lipietz, "Conflits de répartition et changements techniques dans la théorie marxiste," *Économie appliquée*, 33(2):511-39 (1980).

2. Cf. Hartmut Elsenhans, "Grundlagen der Entwicklung der kapitalistischen Weltwirtschaft," in *Kapitalistische Weltökonomie: Kontroversen über ihren Ursprung und ihre Entwicklungsdynamik*, ed. Dieter Senghaas (Frankfurt: Suhrkamp, 1979), pp. 103-50.

growth was tied to lower-class resistance in the form of wage bargaining and struggle for shorter work hours and improved labor conditions. Powerful labor organizations or other mechanisms that increased the negotiating strength of labor are constitutive elements of capitalist growth. If Rosa Luxemburg had admitted increasing real wages as a reality in capitalism—which she discarded in her model of the capitalist growth process—she could have resolved the realization problem she detected in Marx's reproduction schemes. The noncapitalist sector she required for maintaining growth is the working class of the industrialized countries—and not the periphery. Labor is sold and bought in a capitalist economy, but it is a very special commodity, the price of which does not depend on its cost of reproduction but on bargaining.

Until recently, industrial countries have all been characterized by the common feature of having different, but to some extent comparably powerful, working-class organizations. Productivity growth may have differed, but everywhere real wages tended to rise with productivity and until the 1929 crisis, even downswings led to rising real wages because prices fell more rapidly than nominal wages, due to workers' resistance.

If such types of societies coexist with societies in which wages do not increase, and if technology in the form of know-how or in the form of machinery is mobile, the societies with stagnant wages will acquire cost advantages in those branches where productivity is increasing less rapidly than the average: labor costs follow the average increase of productivity, hence unit costs rise in branches with low productivity growth. If this rise is sufficiently high, the low-wage economy will become competitive even if productivity per man-hour is lower than in the industrial countries. Historically, this has been the case first in raw-materials production, where the depletion of low-cost deposits in the industrial countries limited productivity growth by technical progress. Today, this is the case of a great variety of eventually labor-intensive, often assembly-line-type—and then relatively capital-intensive—production lines.

The industrial countries' working classes' advance in productivity compared to the Third World workers' productivity is lower than the respective advance in real wages. Technology transfer as well as labor-intensive processes of production allows high-productivity employment of Third World workers in industrial production. The wages of these workers rarely amount to more than feeble fractions of wages in industrial countries. This development is not entirely new. Textile production in India had grown already in the 1880s and efficiently undersold British textiles on East Asian markets. But this process was halted by the convulsions of the world economy during the world wars and the protectionist tide of the interwar period. This process of growing cost efficiency of Third World low-wage industries had inexorably to start in the relatively open post-World War II economy and has found its manifestation in the actual export push of the so-called newly industrializing countries, as well as of other low-wage countries that strive to obtain this status. The level of real wages arrived at in the industrial countries is, however, necessary to clear the market and to guarantee full employment.

The working classes of the industrial countries are caught in the following dilemma if the previously mentioned process gains momentum: if working-class organizations continue to raise wages—or to lower hours—the difference in unit costs in relation to Third World sites of production increases and becomes lethal for a further number of production lines still established in the West. New industries are running away. The export of jobs is accelerated. If working-class organizations follow the advice of conservative governments and employers' organizations, underconsumptionist tendencies will develop and will actually lead to economic crises.

The metropolitan working classes can no longer balance productive potential and consumption in the world economy. Are the working classes in the Third World in a position that makes them able to contribute to raise world consumption? Export-led growth has too little impact on Third World employment and cannot change the fundamental imbalances in the structures of Third World labor markets. The free export-processing zones employ some million mostly low-paid workers whose salaries, however, constitute already the bulk of the retained value. At least, in this sector, multiplier effects of creating induced employment are low. But the free export-processing zones are not the only sites that participate in export-led growth. On the basis of employment in Hong Kong textile manufacturing and the level of manufacturing exports of the Third World, the following estimate of employment is possible: in 1977 there were 234,000 jobs with $3 billion worth of exports. Disregarding price rises for export-led produced goods and disregarding also higher output-labor ratios in other countries—such as South Korea—and, in particular, in other branches, $112 billion of exports in manufactures from Third World countries may have led to a maximum of 9 million jobs. This number decreases to 6 million if the estimate is based on the South Korean output-labor ratio of 1977, and it decreases to 5 million if price rises of 5 percent are included. Indirect employment seems not to exceed direct employment. Empirical investigations on multiplier effects have shown rather low values, unless employment in the production of raw materials, previously exported without further transformation, is included. A most optimistic view may lead to 10 to 20 million jobs created by export-led growth directly or indirectly.

Even this probably exaggerated number is totally insufficient in relation to total unemployment in Third World countries, which will increase in the last two decades of the twentieth century from 350 million to at least 700 million.[3] Wage increases for workers in some plants in the Third World are matched by further relocation within the Third World. Increasing relocation of industry to Third World countries will create incentives to adapt technology to prevailing factor costs and remove the bottleneck of the lack of qualified workers. This will further diminish the bargaining power of workers in export-oriented plants, to the extent that such power exists. Unless the misery of the mass of the population, especially the rural population, is overcome, the unlimited supply of cheap unqualified labor is left unchecked. And to date, the process of relocation leads to the replacement of well-paid Western labor by low-paid Third World labor with the inevita-

3. Cf. William R. Cline, "Can the East Asian Model of Development Be Generalized?" *World Development*, 10(2):81-90 (Feb. 1982).

ble consequence of a contraction of total world consumption demand.

CONSIDERING SOME OPPOSING ARGUMENTS

Governments in Western countries adhere to the view that the danger of losing employment to Third World countries should be met by a change of industry mix in the industrial countries. Although it is not necessarily true that productivity in those branches is sufficiently higher in the industrialized countries than in Third World countries, a rise in productivity requires a rise in consumption. There may be doubts as to whether there is a sufficient number of industries in which the level of productivity allows the required wage rises and will lead to full employment.

It should be added that Western industrial countries are affected to different degrees by Third World competition. The less advanced countries and regions within countries in the West have historically specialized in the same labor-intensive products that the Third World can offer today at lower cost. They are caught between the anvil of Third World labor-intensive exports and the hammer of high-technology exports of the leading industrial countries. The ensuing decline of the absorptive capacity of their markets leads to fewer outlets for high-technology exports from leading industrial countries and diminishes the chances of structural change even there.

It is sometimes contended that the use of microelectronics will stop, slow down, or even reverse the relocation of production to the Third World. But microelectronics raises the productivity of labor. Either consumption is increased or hours of work are diminished.

Both measures counteract the hoped-for tendency toward falling unit costs and remove the expected increase in competitiveness. Microelectronics can be used also in Third World countries and will save relatively high-qualified labor there, so that the comparative advantage of Third World sites of production may even increase.

Obtaining fair labor standards in affiliates of transnational corporations (TNCs) located in Third World countries will have little impact. Export-led manufacturing is organized by TNCs to a very small degree.[4] TNC foreign direct investment is directed to areas where TNCs have an enterprise-specific comparative advantage in relation to other, national enterprises. The comparative advantage of a country due to its wage level is accessible also to national producers who are normally less vulnerable to critique for the exploitative character of the production concerned. Rising real wages in some TNC plants in Third World sites of production do not contradict the scenario sketched here because they are limited in extent and because they concern but a small fraction even of the industrial working class in the Third World—less than 10 percent of Third World manufacturing employment in the TNC affiliates—and an even smaller fraction of the potential work force.

The low volume of Third World manufactured exports compared to the consumption of manufactured goods in the Western industrialized countries is underlined by a number of authors. This share, however, rose rapidly until protectionist measures were enacted in the 1980s. But it is absurd to defend a model of world growth by asserting simultaneously that it will lead ultimately to overcoming underdevelopment in the Third World and that its impact is negligible.

The often voiced argument that more jobs have been lost in the West due to rationalization of production than due to Third World exports is irrelevant. In a closed economic system, rationalization-based losses of jobs can only occur if an insufficient expansion of real wages impedes capacity-increasing investment in the rationalized and other branches of production. Only then will the job-killing outrunning of productivity compared to production take place.

There has been the contention that increased Third World manufactured exports will not decrease total world consumption, as increased earnings of Third World countries would be used to offset imports of the same amount.[5] The argument would only be consistent if prices for goods, the production of which is relocated, remain stable. This is not a very realistic assumption, as relocation takes place in order to lower costs and hence prices, at least in competitive markets. If relocation lowers prices, the real wage increase in industrial countries would have to follow not only the increase in productivity but also the amelioration of the terms of trade between the remaining industrial branches and the relocated industry.

4. Cf. Angus Hone, "Multinational Corporations and Multinational Buying Groups: Their Impact on the Growth of Asia's Exports of Manufactures," *World Development*, 2(2):145-49 (Feb. 1974); Deepak Nayyar, "Transnational Corporations and Manufactured Exports from Poor Countries," *Economic Journal*, 88(2):59-84 (Mar. 1978).

5. P. de Grauwe et al.,"Trade Expansion with the Less Developed Countries and Employment," *WWA*, 115(1):98-113 (1979).

Some statisticians want us to believe that there is still a positive balance in favor of the industrial countries in the West-South trade in manufactures. As long as the Third World remains an exporter of raw materials—even of high-priced ones such as oil—this is inevitable. But the argument is vitiated in a more fundamental way: such statistics normally include very highly priced imports from the Organization of Petroleum Exporting Countries. I do not deny that higher raw-material prices could counteract the underconsumptionist threat of export-led industrialization by redistribution between the West and the South, although this type of redistribution would probably benefit upper- and eventually middle-income classes in the Third World. Such statistics include also the newly industrializing countries with high and increasing international indebtedness. Debt-financed balance-of-payments deficits of that category of underdeveloped countries have certainly reduced the slackening of capitalist growth in the industrial West during the greater part of the 1970s. But the end of this type of demand creation has been demonstrated. The balances of trade of the countries concerned are now characterized by high surpluses, even if the balances of payment are still in deficit because of the charges of debt servicing.

Neoliberals may argue that the new competitiveness of the Third World countries will not influence Western industrial employment because changes in rates of exchange will rebalance trade flows. But the push of Third World export-led industrialization was based on devaluation. Changes in rates of exchange will probably not be admitted because the slackening of the export demand will endanger the whole growth

model of this type of economy. It would further increase the competitiveness of products of the industrial West in Third World markets and change relative prices between Third World labor and Western products, thus creating a tendency toward higher real mass incomes in the South. This model hence implies that incomes in the Third World reflect productivity. But rises in income without bargaining power of mass organizations can theoretically be deduced only if a short supply of labor requires employers to raise the offered wage above the opportunity wage that a less productive plant can pay. The mechanism implies consequently a situation of nearly full employment, which quite obviously does not exist.

In a situation in which the price elasticity of the mix of products is low—a situation that Third World countries can offer—there is even a great incentive to subsidize exports in new product lines. This is the case if the opportunity cost of substituting essential imports by local production is high in relation to additional exports. State trading firms can tax some more conventional exports and allow the export of new goods by financing measures such as the training of workers and the creation of infrastructures. Singapore and Hong Kong, where there is state auctioning of export licenses,[6] are already engaging in such types of measures, which broaden the range of products offered at low cost on world markets.

The mollifying arguments about export-led growth do not contradict the described scenario. Export-led growth may help to trigger growth processes in

6. Morris E. Morkre, "Rent-Seeking and Hongkong's Textile Quota System," *Developing Economies*, 17(1):110-18 (Mar. 1979).

the Third World only to the degree that multiplier and linkage effects are high. This strategy can be complementary to efforts to overcome the unemployment problem by creating jobs in inward-looking strategies, but it cannot resolve the employment and poverty problem of Third World countries on its own. With the exception of Hong Kong and Singapore, success has been achieved by countries, like South Korea and Taiwan, that have had parallel strategies of implementing agrarian reform and raising rural incomes.

CONDITIONS FOR ABSORBING SURPLUS LABOR IN THE THIRD WORLD

The fundamental contradiction of Third World economies is the divergence between the structure of demand and the disposability of required factors of production. Overcoming underdevelopment cannot be achieved if changes in the structure of demand and changes in the availability of factors of production do not lead to a narrowing of the gap between the two elements of the problem. Development policy up to now has been mainly concerned with changes in the availability of factors of production. Training programs, technical assistance, and concessional as well as nonconcessional resource flows were considered as means to bring people into employment that was considered to be productive. Productive employment is employment in lines of production for which there is a solvent demand at the prevailing prices. The productiveness of employment changes if the system of relative prices and relative quantities of products in demand are changed by alterations of the demand structure.

The highly skewed income distribution in most of the Third World coun-

tries has led to a demand structure where modern, mostly capital-intensive goods predominate. The quantities produced of each item are low; production costs are often high. The local production of required investment goods is discouraged by the low quantities needed and the rather high degree of sophistication of the machinery employed in such lines.

On the contrary, the demand basket of low-income receivers predominantly contains food and simple industrial goods. Parts of these goods can be produced by local artisans of the so-called informal sector and small and medium-sized enterprises. The local content is high; imported technology, low; the capital-output ratio, rather low; and a high proportion of the work force consists of unskilled workers or workers who are trained in this very sector of production. But poor people also tend to consume modern industrial products. However, at a constant level of national income and an identical marginal propensity for people with high incomes and those with low incomes to consume products of a modern industrial sector, redistribution in favor of the poor creates a structure of demand where fewer articles are bought in larger quantities. Economies of scale can be used as well as full-capacity utilization for cost reduction and foreign exchange savings. A more homogeneous consumer demand leads to a production pattern in which fewer articles are produced in larger quantities. Fewer different technologies have to be learned in comparable time periods. Greater production runs in fewer lines render the demand for machinery more homogeneous: more identical machines are needed in greater numbers. A more homogeneous final demand for modern industrial products leads to a more homogeneous demand for investment goods and lower costs for local production of investment goods.

Moreover, demand from people with lower incomes for modern industrial products is less characterized by a desire for conspicuous consumption. A tape recorder or a transistor radio is valued less for the eventual capacity to impress friends and foes than for its original use, if bought by a rather poor person. Models can be democratized by removing gadgets. Production technology can be downgraded within the same product group—such as television sets—or within the same product family, as in the case of transport equipment, where a bicycle with a small engine might be produced instead of a sophisticated car.

Lower technology requirements because of lower quality requirements in the sector of modern industrial products or because of the production of industrial products by small-scale and medium-scale enterprises are an essential aid to promoting local machinery production of the necessarily low quality, which can be achieved initially by the local work force. The training obtained by such local machinery production is the basis for creating the capacity to assimilate more sophisticated machinery and hence to switch over from technology import as technology consumption to technology transfer as capacity to repair, to copy, and to adapt imported technology to local needs—and hence to comply to market forces.

A strategy of absorbing surplus labor by adapting demand to resources instead of adapting resources to demand has to be centered first on the rural sector. The mass of the low-income receivers are rural, and the mass of additional consumer incomes in case of redistribution will be spent on food. Agrarian reform is necessary so that proprietor-peasants use the available land more effectively. If grouped in loose cooperatives, they are capable of adopting yield-increasing innovation, but they will articulate a less diversified demand for new inputs and machinery than big landowners will and they will buy less new machinery and inputs for the same amount of agricultural production. This is so because they will never replace their own labor time, which in their calculation costs nothing, as long as they are poor and as long as there are no other opportunities for gainful work.

Certainly, land reform has to be rather radical. It should give access to rural production to the mass of the rural population even if marginal product decreases.[7] If peasants are to increase production by increasing work time, they have to be offered material incentives. The mostly corrupt state-owned trading organizations should be cut back, and free marketing of at least part of the production should be allowed in order to have the peasants produce a marketable surplus. Price efficiency does not necessarily mean that peasants will obtain the actual world market price, which may include a taxable rent, or that they will no longer have to buy the right to enter the market by delivering part of their harvest at reasonable prices to state trading organizations in order to contribute to basic needs satisfaction of the poorer segments of society.

If peasant initiative is to be mobilized, two axes for industrialization

7. N. Georgescu-Roegen, "Economic Theory and Agrarian Economics," *Oxford Economic Papers,* 12(2):1-40 (Feb. 1960); Ajit S. Bhalla, "On Nurkse's Concealed Saving Potential," *Indian Journal of Economics,* 40(159):305-10 (Apr. 1960).

become visible. First, local agricultural input and eventually transformation industry are necessary to complement additional rural work on scarce land with new inputs to increase yields more effectively and to utilize the possibilities of more efficient marketing. Second, production capacities for industrial consumer goods should become operative, because peasants will not increase their efforts if they receive only paper money and no goods.

In order to prepare redistribution of incomes, the possibilities of the informal and small and medium-sized industrial enterprises have to be evaluated in order to determine which type of locally produced machinery would allow an increase of production and which type of consumption goods in demand can only be produced in modern industrial plants. From these evaluations a profile of the modern sector can be drawn that includes its contribution to inputs and machinery in agriculture, to inputs and machinery for the expansion of the informal small and medium-sized industry, to the modern sector itself, and to the consumption by various classes of society as a function of the projected evolution of mass incomes.

What is needed is a restructuring of the productive apparatus from high-income to low-income demand. This restructuring cannot be obtained only by redistribution of income. Simple redistribution measures will lead, at least in part, to inflationary pressures and/or increased imports because the productive apparatus of underdeveloped countries does not—and, by definition of underdevelopment as disarticulation or structural heterogeneity or sectoral divergence of productivity,[8] cannot—

react flexibly to changing demand.

Planning is necessary, but implies dangers, which I have described extensively elsewhere,[9] in analyzing the contradictory orientations of the dominant state-classes in most of today's bureaucratic development societies in nearly all underdeveloped countries.

Such restructuring of the productive apparatus will allow the absorption of surplus labor by the following means:

1. The out-migration from the countryside will be slowed down because the rural-urban gap in conditions of living will be narrowed. It can be shown that in an agriculture with evenly distributed holdings, labor time—the marginal product of which is below-average subsistence earnings—will be mobilized because additional product will be above zero, although below marginal cost. Peasants see only the additional surplus of supplementary work, not its cost. In a cooperative of peasants, nobody knows who the marginal worker is. Capitalist big landowners maximize surplus or profit; peasants maximize production[10] by increasing time spent for work. The rational peasant is fairly well established by empirical research.

2. The increase of demand for industrial products from the agricultural population increases the outlet of the labor-

8. Hartmut Elsenhans, "Rising Mass Incomes as a Condition of Capitalist Growth: Implications for the World Economy," *International Organization,* 37(1):30 (Winter 1983).

9. Hartmut Elsenhans, *Abhängiger Kapitalismus oder bürokratische Entwicklungsgesellschaft: Ein Versuch über den Staat in der heutigen Dritten Welt* (Frankfurt: Campus, 1981), pp. 118-92; idem, "Capitalisme d'état ou société bureaucratique développement," *Études internationales,* 13(1):3-22 (Mar. 1982).

10. Hartmut Elsenhans, "Agraverfassung, Akkumulationsprozess und Demokratisierung," in *Agrarreform in der Dritten Welt,* ed. H. Elsenhans (New York: Campus, 1979), pp. 505-672.

intensive, informal, small and medium-sized industrial sectors, which train their own labor force. Increasing numbers of outlets lead to increasing employment at wage rates slightly higher than incomes in agricultural production. This growth enlarges the market constituted by mass incomes and leads to a demand for simple technology, on which the growth of local production of machinery can be based.

3. A more homogeneous final demand allows a more efficient use of capital in the modern sector, with higher local content—or more forward linkages. Scarce foreign exchange earnings can be used to create more jobs in the modern sector per unit of money spent.

4. The establishment of local production of machinery, even if initially of low quality, creates the basis for assimilating selectively realized technology imports and contributes to the further integration of the more modern with the more traditional economic sectors. Such a proposal does not imply that the South should imitate the West in consumption patterns and styles of life. It implies, however, that the elites in the South no longer hide their privileges behind the pretense of maintaining the cultural identity of their countries by defending their own privileges. Mass consumption can take various directions. National identity in the West continues to exist. Why should Indian consumers adopt Western habits of clothing and eating in order to produce locally the machinery for increasing their cloth and food production? And are there culturally meaningful differences in ways of tilling the soil or working metal pieces for mechanical purposes? Differences are due to technical development, and low-income classes of the population in the South are especially eager to adopt low-cost products and toil-diminishing instruments and machinery.

Would such restructuring lead at least temporarily to increasing competitiveness of Third World countries? Certainly to some extent, but as full employment can be achieved rapidly, the new Taiwans and South Koreas would experience rising wages because there would be no reserve army of unskilled labor.

THE CONTRIBUTION OF INDUSTRIALIZED COUNTRIES

Restructuring the productive apparatus of underdeveloped countries will require money. Such restructuring is also composed of the establishment of plants that can produce products for which demand would increase if incomes were redistributed. Such restructuring also requires planning and political commitment of those parts of state classes in Third World countries who take essential decisions on development policies. These three requirements determine the eventual contribution of Western industrial countries.

In everyday development policy, the projects that should be given priority are those that can be used also in case the focus of the development policy changes from elite to mass needs.

In the North-South dialogue, the Western industrialized countries should not simply oppose a refusal to the demand of the South for global negotiations but should consider their own definition of the global character of negotiations, which must include the necessary reforms in the economic and social structures of the South.

The leitmotiv would have to be "resources for reform—reforms against resources."

State classes in the Third World are

not only cynical. They are segmented. Some segments do realize that development requires redirection of the productive apparatus to mass needs. As segments of state classes will couple their own interests in more power, income, and prestige only with such strategies, if there seems to be a chance of realizing them, a firm commitment of Western industrialized countries today to give priority to reform directly or indirectly through appropriate project selection would therefore greatly influence the outcome of the rivalries between segments of state classes in favor of the reforms without interfering in an illicit way in the internal affairs of such countries. It should be noted that the lack of commitment of Western countries to reformist policies in the Third World has certainly discouraged such strategies and strengthened anti-reformist segments of state classes.

The probably time-consuming absorption of surplus labor in such a mass-consumption-based development strategy would remove the inexhaustible supply of low-skilled cheap labor. By creating productive employment with rising mass incomes, increases in exports through local or foreign enterprises will exert pressure on the labor market and bring labor markets to a form of functioning where increased demand for labor leads to increased wages and where working-class organizations do possess some leverage.

This outline of a new development strategy will not lead to a bureaucratic world economy. On the contrary, increased mass consumption will allow increasing reliance on market mechanisms after restructuring is achieved and will integrate the mass-consumption-based economies of the South into a liberal world economy, because full employment and rising mass incomes will create the objective conditions for mass incomes to follow productivity increases.

The mechanism of maintaining the conditions of existence of free-market economies—that is, that final consumption, especially mass consumption, is increased in order to create outlets for more efficient production—will then be extended also to the underdeveloped world. The South would become ready to be fully integrated into an open world economy where capital's and labor's power are balanced.

ANNALS, *AAPSS*, **492**, July 1987

Creating New Jobs in the Service Sector

By MANFRED WEGNER

ABSTRACT: The U.S. experience in the decade since 1973 shows that slow economic growth is compatible with the large-scale creation of new jobs. The contrast with Europe is accounted for by the service sector. In Germany, where overall economic growth was no slower than in the United States, the growth rate of service sector jobs was about one-quarter of that in the United States. The dramatic and continuous employment gains in the United States are often explained by the higher flexibility of its labor market, by higher labor mobility, and by fewer social regulations and protections than in Europe. There are many institutional and socioeconomic influences and demographic pressures that have pushed low-skilled labor, such as women and young people, into poorly paid service jobs. Most of the European countries, and especially Germany, have provided service outputs by less labor-intensive production processes promoted by the rapid growth of real wages and nonlabor costs in the 1970s. But there are many unsolved questions concerning the main underlying causes of the divergent employment patterns in the United States and Germany that justify a comprehensive research agenda.

Manfred Wegner graduated from the University of Heidelberg in 1954 and was engaged in economic research from 1954 to 1963 at the University of Heidelberg, Tübingen, and the Department of Applied Economics in Cambridge, England. He held several posts in the Commission of the European Communities in Brussels between 1964 and 1983, finally as deputy director-general for economic and financial affairs. In 1983 he joined the IFO Institute for Economic Research in Munich, where he is responsible for international and European research activities.

THERE is a danger that despite the improvement in the general economic climate there will be no fundamental improvement in the labor market in Europe. At the end of 1984 more than 11 percent of the total labor force was out of work, and the trend toward continued reductions in employment in agriculture and pronounced reductions in industry still prevails. Only in the service sector is there still a net increase in new jobs. The creation of a service-based economy is seen as one of the great hopes for solving the problem of unemployment in Europe.

Hopes of more jobs in the service sector were above all aroused by the employment miracle in the United States. This miracle began in the 1960s.[1] Although the United States has suffered two major economic shocks since 1973 and faced a long economic recession between 1980 and 1982, the trend in employment creation in the United States has still continued upward throughout the last ten years. Between 1973 and 1983 more than 15 million new jobs were created, almost exclusively in the service sector. The steep reduction in the number of employed people during the period of stagnation in 1982 has long been made good by the exceptionally strong upward swing in the economic cycle. From the depths of the recession in December 1982 until December 1984, a total of about 7.3 million jobs were added, of which 70 percent were in the service sector. The rate of unemployment, which was still 10.7 percent in December 1982, had fallen to 7.2 per-

1. Manfred Wegner, "The Employment Miracle in the US and Stagnation Employment in the EC," *Economic Papers,* no. 17 (July 1983); idem, "Growth and Job Creation in North America, Japan and Europe," *IFO Digest,* pp. 3-7 (Feb. 1984).

cent by the end of 1984.

The picture in most of the industrialized countries of Europe is totally different. The global picture of stagnation in total employment for Europe as a whole hides a significant reduction in employment in the United Kingdom and the Federal Republic of Germany. The number employed in the Federal Republic of Germany has fallen by 1.7 million over the last ten years and by 2.2 million in manufacturing industry alone. This compares with about 1.0 million new jobs created in the service sector over the same period. The rate of unemployment in Germany was about 4 percent following the first oil shock, but this grew to more than 8 percent, where it stayed for a long time, up to 1984. The position for employment only began to improve slightly in 1985, but one still cannot speak of an actual easing of the labor market.

How can this persistent divergence between developments in the U.S. and European labor markets be explained? Are there lessons to be learned for European employment policies from the American experience or is the U.S. employment market simply flooded with hamburger stands and security guards as some critics maintain?

The difficulties in analysis begin with the definition of what in fact the service sector consists of. There is no clear-cut answer to this question because of the existence of only inadequate data and the complex interdependence between industrial production and services. Services are characterized by their multiplicity of forms. Services can, for example, be contained in goods, such as films, books, or phonograph records. They can be complementary to goods, such as in transportation and distribution; can substitute for capital value, such as with leasing or repairs; or can have no direct relation to goods, such as with some areas of banking and insurance, consultancy, information services, and tourism.[2]

In what follows we shall use the classical institutional classification of the sectors of the economy for analytical and statistical purposes. In many ways this is a negative definition because it comprises branches of the economy in which no material goods are produced. Furthermore, the growing employment in the black or shadow economy, which has probably largely taken the form of service sector jobs, tends to be neglected. Employment in services, of course, includes more than just the jobs in the service sector. The statistical delineation of service activities varies significantly from economy to economy, with differences in coverage as well as in degree of specialization and expenditure.

In the following section, the " promise of the service society"[3] will be analyzed in order to clarify where and in which form the new service sector employees or professions have emerged. To help in this analysis a comparison of the very diverse examples of the United States and the Federal Republic of Germany is made. In what follows, therefore, an attempt is made to pinpoint some important causes and differences.

2. See, for example, Victor R. Fuchs, *The Service Economy* (New York: National Bureau of Economic Research, 1968); Thomas M. Stanback, Jr., *Understanding the Service Economy: Employment, Productivity, Location* (Baltimore, MD: Johns Hopkins University Press, 1979); Jonathan I. Gershuny and Ian D. Miles, *The New Service Economy: The Transformation of Employment in Industrial Societies* (London: Praeger, 1983).

3. Peter Gross, *Die Verheißungen der Dienstleistungsgesellschaft. Soziale Befreiung oder Sozialherrschaft* (Opladen:Westdeutscher Verlag, 1983).

DEVELOPMENTS IN THE UNITED STATES AND THE FEDERAL REPUBLIC OF GERMANY

During the 1960s the prophets of the postindustrial society fed the expectation that the share of the service sector in the economy would inevitably grow with increased prosperity. Both the French economist Fourastie and the American sociologist Bell developed theories for the service economy that pointed to fundamental changes in the future. Fourastie saw the service economy as "the great hope for the 20th Century." For him and others who have based their work on the three-sector model of the economy, developments were seen as following a typical development pattern. According to this model, employment was initially in the primary sector of agriculture and mining. With industrialization there was a growth in the secondary sector, which reached its peak in the middle of the twentieth century with a 40 to 45 percent share of total employment. Fourastie predicted that the tertiary sector's share of total employment would reach 80 percent by the end of the twentieth century. There can be no doubt that such a trend took hold in all the industrialized countries during the 1960s and has continued, or indeed accelerated in some cases, during the slower and changed economic growth conditions following 1973. (See Table 1.) The tertiary sector has consistently increased its share of total employment, and during the recent years of recession the service sector has been the only source of job creation.

These averages hide significantly divergent trends in the individual industrialized countries. The comparison of the United States with the Federal Republic of Germany itself points to irregularities

TABLE 1
EMPLOYMENT BY MAJOR ECONOMIC SECTOR
(Average annual rates of change, in percentages)

	United States	Japan	Federal Republic of Germany	Total OECD*
Agriculture				
1960-73	−3.4	−4.8	−4.8	−3.4
1973-83	−0.1	−2.8	−3.3	−1.7
Industry				
1960-73	1.5	3.4	0.2	1.3
1973-83	0.0	0.2	−1.9	−0.7
Services				
1960-73	2.9	2.7	1.3	2.3
1973-83	2.6	2.1	0.8	2.1
All sectors				
1960-73	2.0	1.3	0.2	1.1
1973-83	1.7	0.9	−0.7	0.7
1984	4.2	1.2	−0.3	1.5

SOURCES: *OECD Economic Outlook,* no. 36 (Dec. 1984); Organization for Economic Cooperation and Development (OECD); *Labour Force Statistics, 1962-1982* (Paris: OECD, 1984).
*OECD = Organization for Economic Cooperation and Development.

that cannot be explained by the three-sector model.

So far the United States has gone further down the road to the service society than all the other industrialized countries. In 1983 nearly 70 percent, or according to some definitions more than 70 percent, of total employment was working in the private and public service sectors, in which the growth in employment slowed only slightly after 1973. The share of employment in the service sector in the Federal Republic of Germany is about average compared to the shares in the other industrialized countries, with about 52 percent in 1983. In Germany, however, the number employed in the service sector has only grown half as fast since 1973 as it did before.

The United States

Which branches of the service sector in the United States have exhibited the most rapid growth since 1973? The public sector services, especially those outside the federal government, made a relatively modest contribution up to 1979. Since then, employment in this sector has more or less stagnated. Between 1973 and 1983 the number employed in the public service sector, including the resident armed forces, grew by roughly 2 million and thus contributed 13 percent of the growth in total service sector employment during the period.[4] There has been a strong growth in the number of self-employed in the various branches of the service sector: 1.7 million between 1973 and 1983, which is equivalent to 85 percent of the total growth in the number of self-employed.

In this analysis we shall consider only the figures for the employees in the

4. The increase amounted to 1.8 million calculated in terms of the equivalent of full-time employees—that is, an annual rate of 11.5 percent.

private service sector. Part-time employment will also be excluded because the U.S. data are based on full-time equivalence. The number of full-time employed increased by a good 10 million between 1973 and 1983, which is equivalent to an annual growth of 2.6 percent and thus only slightly slower than during the period 1960 to 1973 even though the rate of economic growth was only half as great after 1973 as during the 1960s. (See Table 2.)

A somewhat more detailed analysis enables one to make the following observations:

1. Distributive services—transport and communications, wholesale and retail trade, and catering[5]—grew in line with the average rate of growth of the economy and in 1983 accounted for 25 percent of the dependent—that is, non-self-employed—labor force.

2. The numbers employed in education and health and especially in the private health sector grew at an above-average annual rate of 4.4 percent and by about 2.3 million people between 1973 and 1983.

3. The greatest growth in employment was in producer services, such as those in which consultants, financial institutions, and insurance brokers, among others, are represented. Here the annual rate of growth after 1973 was nearly 4 percent, as high as it had been during the 1960s. In the last ten years the increase in the number of full-time employees in these branches was 3.8 million.

4. The real surprise is that employment in the consumer services, such as hotels, repairs, entertainment, and recre-ation, has grown relatively slowly—at an annual rate of 1.4 percent.

The Federal Republic of Germany

Employment has grown significantly more slowly in the Federal Republic of Germany than in the United States. This was particularly apparent during the period after 1973. The only exception is so-called other services, including real estate. As in the United States, most of the jobs created during the period 1973-83 were created in the production-oriented services and health services. Of particular importance have been service activities previously provided in-house that are now increasingly farmed out to outside contractors as well as new services such as software production and leasing. The importance of household-oriented services appears to have further decreased.[6] The number of people employed in wholesale and retail, transport, and communications has been declining since 1973, and the number of salaried employees in private services has only grown at an annual rate of 0.7 percent over the period 1973-83. That is only a quarter the pace in the United States and less than half the pace in Germany during the period 1960-73.

It is noticeable that the rate of growth in the public sector in Germany had been relatively strong, at an annual average rate of 1.8 percent, but this weakened after 1980. Nevertheless, between 1973 and 1983 the state contributed about 60 percent of all the service sector jobs created. The share of public sector employment, including military personnel, in total employment was 16

---

5. From 1973 to 1983, employment in eating and drinking places increased at about 5 percent per annum.

6. See Johannes Heinze, "Strukturwandel in der Bundesrepublik (Eine Auseinandersetzung mit der Drei-Sektoren-Hypothese)," *IFO Schnelldienst,* no. 33, pp. 17 (1979).

TABLE 2

SECTORAL EMPLOYMENT OF EMPLOYEES IN THE UNITED STATES
AND THE FEDERAL REPUBLIC OF GERMANY, 1960-83

(Average annual rates of change, in percentages)

	United States*		Federal Republic of Germany	
	1960-73	1973-83	1960-73	1973-83
Manufacturing industry	1.5	−0.9	0.4	−1.9
Total private services	2.8	2.6	1.5	0.7
Distribution	2.7	2.1	1.5	−0.4
Transport and communications	1.0	0.6	0.4	−0.4
Financial services and real estate	3.4	3.2	4.5	1.1
Other services	4.7	3.9	2.5	2.5
Private households	−3.7	−2.3	−0.7	2.0
Public sector	2.6	0.9	3.7	1.8
Total services	2.7	2.1	2.3	1.0
Total employees in all sectors	2.2	1.2	1.0	−0.4
Self-employed in services	−0.3[†]	3.3[†]	−1.2	−0.8
Self-employed in all other sectors	−2.0[†]	0.9[†]	−4.0	−3.2
Total employment	2.0	1.7	0.2	−0.7

SOURCES: U.S., Department of Commerce; Federal Republic of Germany, Federal Statistical Office.

*Converted into full-time-equivalent employees.

[†]Full-time and part-time employment.

percent in 1983 and had therefore tripled since 1960. At the same time the number of self-employed, including family workers, declined, albeit more slowly than during the earlier period, and stood at only 1.5 million compared to 1.9 million in 1960.

POSSIBLE EXPLANATIONS FOR THESE DIFFERENCES IN EMPLOYMENT

Most empirical research into employment in services is limited to presentations of factual differences or, at best, efforts to uncover only very general factors influencing employment. Efforts to explain the new service economy deal with either the European[7] or the American[8] examples.

7. See Gershuny and Miles, *New Service Economy.*

8. Thomas M. Stanback, Jr., et al., *Services: The New Economy* (Totowa, NJ: Allanheld, Osmun, 1981).

As far as we know there exists as yet no detailed comparative study of the American and European developments. The following remarks are therefore nothing more than an initial checklist for a larger research program.

Macro and sectoral demand factors

The dominant factors in the demand for employment are often taken to be the conditions for economic growth and global demand. But as a comparison between real growth in the United States and the Federal Republic of Germany during the period 1973-83 soon shows, these cannot explain the differences in the developments of the respective employment trends. The annual growth in real gross domestic product, about 2 percent, was almost identical for the two countries for the period 1973-81 and differed only very slightly for the period

1973-83. These rates of growth are about half what they were during the 1960s. However, the growth in service sector employment in the United States hardly changed at all while it was halved in Germany. (See Table 3.)

It is conceivable that a larger share of total demand was accounted for by services in the United States, whether in the form of final or intermediate demand, than in the Federal Republic of Germany. The share of private household expenditures for services has increased in both countries since 1973. The overproportionate increase in the growth of services corresponds to the three-sector model of the economy in which the income elasticity of services is higher than that of agricultural or industrial products. The growth and structure of private sector services depends on many factors. One factor is, for example, the size of households; small households tend to use more market-determined services. Another is the degree of urbanization; rural households are more self-sufficient. Another is the age structure of the population, as the demand for social services is greater with an older population. A fourth is the degree of female employment; the greater the degree, the more housework functions are brought in the form of services. (See Table 4.)

A global comparison of the expenditure on private services belies, however, the view that the private household's demand for services in the United States grew relatively faster than in the Federal Republic of Germany.

It is somewhat different when one considers the growth in demand for intermediate services. There are a number of reasons for believing that the division of labor between industrial enterprises and the tertiary sector is consid-

erably more advanced in the United States than it is in Europe and the Federal Republic. These include, for example, the rapid increase in employment in producer services, the spread of multinational enterprises on world markets, and the expansion of exports of service. From the input-output tables of the 1960s one can see that in the United States almost 40 percent of the output of the tertiary sector took the form of intermediate services compared to only 22 percent in the United Kingdom.[9] Stanback attributes a decisive role to the producer services in the spread of innovation and new technologies as well as the conquering of new markets. Is the lag in the development of services in the Federal Republic to be attributed to a lack of dynamism in private enterprise and unresolved structural problems, or is it an expression of the export dependence of the German economy, which is ultimately due to the continued undervaluation of the deutsche mark?

Labor productivity growth

In the 1960s there was a clear slowing in the growth of U.S. productivity as a whole, and at times it even came to a standstill. In Europe and above all in the Federal Republic of Germany the fall in the growth of labor productivity was less pronounced despite the fact that real growth was only about half that in the United States. This has stimulated a lively debate that has, however, not adequately explained or empirically demonstrated these differences.[10] In gen-

9. See Gershuny and Miles, *New Service Economy.*
10. Wegner, "Growth and Job Creation"; Douglas Todd, "Some Aspects of Industrial Performance in the European Community: An Appraisal," *European Economy,* no. 20 (1984);

TABLE 3
REAL GROWTH AND EMPLOYMENT IN SERVICES
(Average annual rates of changes, in percentages)

	United States		Federal Republic of Germany	
	1960-73	1973-83	1960-73	1973-83
Real gross domestic product				
All sectors	4.1	2.0	4.4	1.6
Services*	4.2	2.7	4.6	2.8
Total working population				
All sectors	1.9	1.8	0.2	−0.7
Services*	2.9	2.7	1.6	0.8

SOURCE: OECD, *Labour Force Statistics* (Paris: OECD, 1984).
*Private and public services, excluding real estate.

TABLE 4
EXPENDITURE FOR PRIVATE SERVICES IN CONSTANT PRICES
(Average annual rate of growth, in percentages)

	United States		Federal Republic of Germany	
	1960-73	1973-83	1960-73	1973-83
Services	4.5	3.4	3.5	2.8
Goods	3.9	2.2	5.2	1.5
Total expenditure*	4.2	2.8	4.6	1.9

SOURCES: U.S., Department of Commerce; Federal Republic of Germany, Federal Statistical Office.
*The weighted averages of the growth rates for services and goods.

eral, productivity growth in services has been slower than in manufacturing.[11] This is not true for all services, and certainly not true for capital-intensive service sectors such as transport and communications.[12] Nevertheless, the

trend in the United States during the 1973-83 period showed the expected underproportional increase in labor productivity, as well as a clear decline in dynamism compared to the 1960s, especially in retail and other private services. (See Table 5.)

The growth in labor productivity was comparatively rapid even though the growth in real value-added in private services between 1973 and 1983 was about the same in the Federal Republic as it was in the United States (see Table 2). The comparison shows up a double divergence: (1) a much higher rate of growth in the United States; and (2) a slower weakening during the period 1973-83 compared to the 1960s.

Assar Lindbeck, "The Recent Slowdown of Productivity Growth," *Economic Journal*, no. 369, pp. 13-34 (Mar. 1983).

11. The debate about differing measurement procedures of service output is left out of consideration here, although it could probably explain some of the differences appearing between industrial countries. See Gershuny and Miles, *New Service Economy*, p. 33; Fuchs, *Service Economy*.

12. Ronald E. Kutscher and Jerome A. Mark, "The Service-producing Sector: Some Common Perceptions Reviewed," *Monthly Labor Review*, pp. 21-24 (Apr. 1983).

TABLE 5
LABOR PRODUCTIVITY BY MAJOR DIVISIONS OF THE SERVICE SECTOR
(Average annual rate of growth, in percentages)

	United States		Federal Republic of Germany	
	1960-73	1973-83	1960-73	1973-83
Manufacturing industry	3.5	1.8	5.8	3.5
Total private sector services*	1.7	0.5	4.4	3.0
Distribution	1.9	0.3	4.5	2.2
Transport and communications	4.1	1.9	4.9	5.2
Financial services	0.9	0.4	5.1	3.6
Other private sector services	0.8	0.1	3.5	2.0
Public sector services	0.3	0.4	1.8	1.0
All services	1.4	0.6	3.6	2.4
Productivity of total economy	1.9	0.8	4.5	2.8

SOURCES: *Survey of Current Business* (1984); Federal Republic of Germany, Federal Statistical Office; Institut für Arbeitsmarkt- und Berufsforschung, Nuremberg, Federal Republic of Germany.
NOTE: Labor productivity measured in real gross domestic product in hours per employee.
*Exclusive of real estate.

In other words, the provision of services has remained more labor intensive in the United States than it has in the Federal Republic. There are few solid facts to explain this divergence, but the German experience is interesting for two reasons. First, it disproves the hypothesis that productivity growth is always slower in the tertiary sector than it is in industry. Second, it points to a growth pattern in the Federal Republic totally different from that in the United States and Japan. The experience of the Federal Republic may be an extreme case, but it can be found, to a lesser degree, mirrored in many other European countries.[13] The question of why Europe should have had such a different pattern of growth and whether it can be changed is of major relevance to theoreticians, historians, and empirical economists alike.

13. Centre d'études prospectives et d'informations internationales, *Économie mondiale 1980-1990: La fracture?* (Paris: Économica, 1984).

The most popular explanation for this relatively rapid growth in productivity is that, compared to goods, services are too expensive and that there is therefore a partial substitution of goods for services. Gershuny suggested that the three-sector model overlooks an important countertrend, which is that although services are income elastic, they are at the same time price elastic. The more expensive they are the less the relative demand for them. As labor productivity grows more slowly in most service sector activities than in industry, relative prices must increase for services, at least as long as wage rates are the same for both the service sector and industry. This results in a tendency for private households increasingly to cover part of their demand for certain service functions by purchasing relatively cheap goods. A washing machine replaced the washing maid, the television replaces the theater and cinema, and the purchase of a car covers transport needs. The service economy thus becomes a self-service economy in which there is also a growth in the informal economy. This process has, with some lag, occurred in all industrialized countries. But it does not explain why employment grew faster and productivity more slowly in the U.S. service sector than it did in most European countries.

Employment, labor costs, and wage structures

The employment miracle in the United States is generally put down to a slower growth in real wages and greater labor market flexibility than in Europe. In fact, U.S. real labor costs, including indirect wage costs, grew considerably more slowly than in Europe even during the 1960s. Furthermore, there was no real wage gap opened up in the United States after the first oil shock as there was in Europe, where real labor costs outstripped productivity. Consequently, the profitability of invested capital was drastically reduced and the pressure for rationalization and labor shedding massively increased. For U.S. companies the pressure to wring out every last drop of productivity growth was considerably less and growth was not associated with a labor-saving bias.

The theoretical and empirical debate about the appearance of a real wage problem is still at its height and in no way resolved.[14] Most empirical studies

are based on the whole economy or on the manufacturing industry. The service sector is influenced by production technologies different from those that influence manufacturing, and it is difficult to isolate the impact of the various factors of production and technical progress. Nevertheless, there have of course been some important innovations in the service sector in recent years, such as in information technology, communications, and office automation, that promote productivity growth. All these technologies are available in the United States and have found wider application there than in Europe.

Large parts of the service sector, such as retail, consultancy, education and health, entertainment as well as restaurants and leisure activities, are necessarily related to the individual and are therefore labor intensive. They can offer very different qualities of service, which must be reflected in the wage structure. What does one find when one considers such differences in the quality and wage structure of the service sector professions in the United States and the Federal Republic? Stanback suggests that the complex process of specialization and diversification in the service sector resulted in the wage structure's splitting in two. Accordingly, the service sector contains concentrations of both highly paid and low-paid professions.[15] This divergence has, in fact, intensified during the 1970s.[16] It is most likely that low

14. See Rüdiger Dornbusch et al., "Macroeconomic Prospects and Policies for the European Community," *CEPS Papers*, no. 1 (1983); Jeffrey Sachs, "Real Wages and Unemployment in the OECD Countries," *Brookings Papers on Economic Activity*, no. 1, pp. 255-304 (1983); Deutsches Institut für Wirtschaftsforschung, "Sind die Unterschiede der Beschäftigtenentwicklung in den USA und der Bundesrepublik Deutschland in der Reallohnentwicklung begründet?" *DIW-Woch-*

enbericht, no. 33, pp. 405-13 (1984); Jacques Artus, "The Disequilibrium Real Wage Rate Hypothesis: An Empirical Evaluation," *IMF Staff Papers*, 31(2):249-301 (1984).

15. See Stanback, Jr., et al., *Services*, tabs. 4.2 and 4.4.

16. Robert Lawrence gave for the year 1983 a similar dispersion of weekly wages in the service as well as in the goods-producing sectors, which

wages, high flexibility, and slow growth in wage rates in the consumer-oriented service sector professions contributed to the creation of a significant number of low-quality jobs that were largely taken by relatively uneducated employees.[17]

Analyses of the wage structure by sector and qualification tend to support the view that the equalization of wage levels continued in the Federal Republic of Germany when, in fact, the need to restructure required more labor flexibility and mobility.

A comparative study of the wage structures in six European Community countries showed that the inequalities in total wage costs between various branches of industry—and a few service industries—were least in Germany and the Netherlands.[18] More intensive and detailed studies are needed to clarify whether, over time, the relative stability of the wage structure in Europe really accentuated the employment problem or whether it in fact promoted a basic social consensus and thus the work motivation of the employed population.[19]

Labor market flexibility and new firms

Most European governments see the main cause of employment and unem-

ployment problems of the last ten years to lie in labor market rigidities and the lack of incentives to work. Consequently, greater labor market flexibility is often used as an explanation for the rapid increase in employment in the United States,[20] with the result that it is also concluded that greater flexibility will overcome unemployment.

Labor market flexibility can mean many things: greater adaptation of wages to external shocks and changed conditions of growth; greater regional and professional mobility of the labor force; the absence of barriers to entry to certain professions; greater flexibility in working hours and the supply of part-time employment; different practices in engaging labor and ending employment contracts; different regulations on health and safety at work; different tax and social security laws; provision for vocational and further education; pension rights; and so forth.

There is no systematic comparison of these regulations and institutions that would enable one to determine whether they promote or inhibit the supply and demand for labor. The differences between the United States and European countries are part of a socioeconomic development that can only be changed very slowly. There are sound reasons for defending each of these systems, which have evolved differently for historical reasons.[21] Nevertheless, one can, with some heroic simplification, describe the

seems to be in contrast to the results by Stanback. See *Brookings Review* (Fall 1984).

17. *Employment Outlook* (Organisation for Economic Co-operation and Development [OECD] Sept. 1984).

18. Christopher Saunders and David Marsden, *Pay Inequalities in the European Community* (London: Butterworth, 1981).

19. See Wolfgang Gerstenberger, *Strukturwandel unter verschlechterten Rahmenbedingungen* (Berlin: Duncker & Humblot, 1984), pp. 227 ff.

20. *Employment Outlook* (OECD) (1984).

21. For the United States, see Jane L. Norwood, "Labor Market Contrasts: United States and Europe," *Monthly Labor Review,* pp. 3-7 (Aug. 1983); for Germany, see Wolfgang Sengenberger, "Das amerikanische Beschäftigungssystem—dem deutschen überlegen?" *Wirtschaftsdienst,* 8:400-406 (1984).

U.S. labor market and employment climate as more flexible in various ways and particularly in the private service sector. There have been signs of growing rigidities in the labor markets of many European countries even if this trend is in reaction to a period of increased unemployment and slow economic growth. Everyday experience, such as with the hours shops are open for business and with trade regulation, also enables one to claim that services are more strongly regulated in the Federal Republic than, for example, in the United States. This does not contradict the suspicion that the internal adaptability and flexibility of German industrial plants is greater than that of American plants.[22]

A further example of the greater dynamism of the U.S. economy is the exceptional creation of jobs in small firms and the creation of new firms. Birch has shown that 80 percent of all new jobs created between 1969 and 1976 were created in firms with fewer than 100 employees.[23] Most of these firms were in the service sector. During the recession years of 1981 and 1982 about 1 million new firms were formed, and 2.6 million new jobs were created in the 14 million small firms in the United States during these years.[24] Studies of the Federal Republic have found no hint of a similar dynamism in the form of new firms being established and jobs being created in small and medium-sized enterprises. As early as the 1960s there was a trend toward greater concentration in

the service sector, which had the effect of reducing the number of workplaces.[25]

Demographic factors and working time

One of the major differences between the United States and Europe lies in the divergent growth trends in the potential size of the labor force. (See Table 6.) The U.S. labor force increased at a rate of about 2.2 percent between 1973 and 1983, which was about the same rate as the growth in employment. This growth has only begun to slow in recent years and can be expected to continue to fall in the future. The total labor force in Europe has grown more slowly, at an annual rate of between 0.7 and 0.8 percent, and this growth slowed considerably in 1983.

There are, however, deeper differences. The baby boom began much earlier in the United States and the percentage of women employed has grown far more quickly. In Europe women are much less involved in paid employment. In the United States the number of women working grew at an average annual rate of 3 percent between 1973 and 1983, but in the Federal Republic, the number of working women stagnated. In the United States it is mainly women and young people who have sought and found employment in the service sector or in lower-paid jobs;[26] this naturally caused major social problems for the poorly educated nonwhite population. Illegal immigrants also

22. Sengenberger, "Das amerikanische Beschäftsdienst."

23. David L. Birch, *The Job Generation Process* (Cambridge, MA: Harvard University Press, 1979); *Employment Outlook* (OECD) (1985).

24. Richard Greene, "Tracking Job Growth in Private Industry," *Monthly Labor Review,* pp. 3-9 (Sept. 1982).

25. Ludwig Berekoven, *Der Dienstleistungsmarkt in der Bundesrepublik Deutschland,* Theoretische Fundierung und empirische Analyse, Bd. 1 u. 2 (Göttingen: Vandenhoek & Ruprecht, 1983).

26. Eli Ginzberg, *Good Jobs, Bad Jobs, No Jobs* (Cambridge, MA: Harvard University Press, 1979).

TABLE 6
DEMOGRAPHIC TRENDS AND PARTICIPATION RATES, 1973-83

	1973	1975	1979	1982	1983
Participation rates*					
United States					
Male	86.2	85.4	85.7	84.7	84.7
Female	51.1	53.2	58.9	61.4	61.9
Federal Republic of Germany					
Male	89.1	87.0	84.5	89.2	80.0
Female	49.6	49.6	49.6	49.8	49.6

	1973-75	1975-79	1979-82	1982	1983
Working age population[†]					
United States	1.5	1.7	1.2	1.0	0.8
OECD[‡] Europe	NA[§]	0.8	1.1	1.2	1.1
Federal Republic of Germany	0.1	0.4	1.4	1.3	1.0
Total labor force[†]					
United States	2.3	2.8	1.6	1.4	1.3
OECD[‡] Europe	1.2	0.7	0.8	0.7	0.2
Federal Republic of Germany	−0.6	0.0	0.7	0.3	−0.1

SOURCES: *OECD Economic Outlook* (Sept. 1984); OECD, *Labour Force Statistics* (Paris: OECD, 1984).

*Total labor force divided by the number of people of working age, that is, 15-64 years of age, multiplied by 100.

[†]Annual average rate of growth in percentages.

[‡]OECD = Organization for Economic Cooperation and Development.

[§]Not available.

increased the size of the working population by what was sometimes up to 5 million people each year.

A specific characteristic of the service sector is the relatively high proportion of women employed and the high incidence of part-time employment.

This peculiarity is particularly pronounced in the United States. But statistics of the Organization for Economic Cooperation and Development cannot substantiate the assumption that the rapid growth in service sector employment was linked to an increase in part-time employment. Part-time employment, principally for women, can only explain one in five new jobs created during the period 1973-81.[27] The relative contribution of part-time employment

to the growth in total employment was significantly higher in many European countries, but here there is also doubt about the comparability of figures.

Finally, divergent trends in the length of the working week in the United States and the Federal Republic could explain the differences in service sector employment. But the number of annual working hours per service sector employee has fallen more slowly in the United States, at an annual rate of 0.5 percent, than in the Federal Republic, at 1.3 percent.[28]

PROSPECTS FOR EMPLOYMENT
IN THE 1980s

The service sector of the economy is highly heterogeneous, and the dispari-

27. *Employment Outlook* (OECD) (1983), tab. 20).

28. During the same period the reduction of annual working hours in the manufacturing industry was 0.1 percent for the United States and 0.8 percent for Germany.

ties between trends in employment within a country and between the industrialized countries are as great as the wealth of factors with which they can be explained. There is therefore no simple answer to the question about whether and how the ability to create jobs in the service sector will be continued.

The employment projections of the U.S. Department of Labor[29] envisage a continued rapid rate of growth of 3 percent for service sector job creation in the United States even with real rates of growth. At the same time the working population could grow at a rate of about 2.0 percent a year up to 1995; between 1969 and 1982 the working population grew at an annual rate of 2.7 percent.

The long-term prospects for employment in the Federal Republic of Germany look far more pessimistic. It is generally expected that there will continue to be significant improvements in labor productivity in the service sector through increased automation. Consequently, the dynamic developments in employment in this sector are not expected to contribute to a general improvement in employment. The main constraint here is more often likely to be the limited supply of services rather than the satiation of demand. The rapid growth in private service activities are hindered by a range of factors such as the supply monopoly in communications, public rationalization in education, legal barriers to entry in the shape of labor and competition laws—shop opening hours, prohibition of advertising for certain professions, and so on.

There are, however, no compelling grounds for pessimism in the assessment of employment prospects in the service sector. The demand for consumer-oriented services in the areas of education, health, and care for the aged, as well as culture and entertainment, could be expanded rapidly if these services could be produced more cheaply. One possible way of doing this would be to follow the United States and allow the creation of a dual employment market. It would be wrong to reject this option for Europe out of hand, but the U.S. model could not be carried over to Europe without radical institutional and behavioral changes on the part of consumers, taxpayers, and wage earners.

There is another way of providing more services more efficiently and cheaply. This is by the use of modern information and communications technology.[30] Modern information technology will not be possible in the service sector until the 1990s because a sufficient infrastructure, such as cable systems and satellite broadcasting, will not be established before then. The service society will thus become an information society. The social innovations made possible by informatics and telematics could create new intermediate services for both production and consumption and thus create new employment. Information technology could also enhance the flexibility of industries and thus help to ease the problems of reductions in working hours. Microelectronics will certainly change the production processes and bring about new markets. But we just do not know how large the net employment effects of the third industrial revolution will be. There are both skeptical views as well as optimistic expectations.

Ultimately, our consideration of the employment potential of the service sector leaves us with as many questions as hopes. The U.S. case shows how large

29. *Monthly Labor Review* (Nov. 1983).

30. See Gershuny and Miles, *New Service Economy.*

the potential for increased employment can be, if certain social and institutional conditions are satisfied. The transfer of this model to the European setting must be treated with some circumspection. Improvements in the conditions and the flexibility of the economy could probably create more jobs in the service sector in Europe. The chances for this are that much greater now that the policies aimed at stimulating adjustment are having some success, which in turn allows some economies to adopt less restrictive macroeconomic policies. As is often the case, there is no simple explanation for complex processes such as the divergent trends in employment in the service sector. It is quite possible that the causes of these divergent trends are less economic than social or sociological in nature.

ANNALS, *AAPSS*, **492**, July 1987

Back to Full Employment:
Old Instruments, New Methods

By WILHELM HANKEL

ABSTRACT: The old Keynesian instruments of monetary and fiscal policies aimed at full employment are currently ineffective. But the monetary instrument can be freed by writing off rather than rescheduling the developing-country debts that cannot be paid and by replacing the private U.S. dollar currency system with a system in which debt limits are specified and controlled by the International Monetary Fund and special drawing rights. Fiscal policy also can make an important contribution to national full employment, despite budgetary constraints. This it can do by promoting human capital rather than real capital and by not treating the black economy as a false path from growth but as its continuation and extension into postindustrial times.

Wilhelm Hankel graduated from the Universities of Mainz and Amsterdam. He worked until 1972 as assistant undersecretary for monetary affairs in the federal government in Bonn and served the European Economic Community (Brussels). Since the 1970s he has been teaching at J. W. Goethe University in Frankfurt am Main and has received fellowships from research institutions such as Harvard, Georgetown, Johns Hopkins in Bologna, Italy, and Science Center Berlin in the Federal Republic of Germany.

NOTE: This article is a summary of a book by the same author entitled *Gegenkurs, von der Schuldenkrise zur Vollbeschäftigung* (1984).

MASS unemployment in the industrialized democracies has many causes and these are largely different from those facing the developing countries.

The objective of this article is to show that the causes of the full-employment deficit explain the problem but cannot solve it. Just as medical science can both diagnose and cure illness thanks to modern drugs, so modern social science faces the challenge of not only diagnosing the problems, such as endemic unemployment, but also finding the remedies. Consequently, one must ask what has made the body of the Western monetary and market systems resistant to yesterday's medicines? These questions are addressed in the first and second parts of this article.

Our starting point is, therefore, not the causes of the problems themselves but the analysis of the instruments that are used to address the problems. As a working hypothesis we use a law, identified and developed by J. Tinbergen in the 1950s, according to which a rational policy can only achieve as many goals as it has supporting instruments. This law is not to be understood merely in a formal sense.[1] We shall therefore have to show that some of the old instruments, such as exchange rates and interest rates, are either no longer or only partially available to national policymakers. Other instruments, such as fiscal policy, have become less effective or less suitable for other reasons. This does not mean, however, that they should be picked out and discarded from the policymakers' box of instruments, but that they should be adapted to the current circumstances.

The findings can be summarized as follows: it was not the Keynesian doctrine of full employment that failed but the way it was interpreted and used; nor is it new technology and the associated increases in productivity that have resulted in a dehumanization of work, but the failure of policy to respond to the new potential for leisure.

THE BACKGROUND OF CHANGES
AFFECTING THE FOUNDATIONS
OF KEYNESIANISM

The concept of full employment stems from Keynes's general theory, developed in the 1930s. The theory was based on the assumption that the full utilization of potential employment in the economy—a kind of overall firm—necessitated a sufficient level of general economic demand. This suffered from two inherent difficulties from the very start, one monetary and one technological. With regard to monetary relations, there should be no loss of general demand as a result of external, or international, liquidity traps, or monetary over-saving. With regard to technology there should be no great leaps in labor productivity. Keynes's investment multipliers always assumed that more investment would result in more income and more employment, not less. In other words, there was a positive and more or less linear correlation between the utilization of capital stock and labor. In the ideal case, 1 percent more investment would result in 1 percent more in wage income and employment.

According to both these assumptions, any full employment deficit could be easily financed away like any cyclically induced economic problem by public, or national, intervention in the form of cheap money and an expansionary deficit-financed fiscal policy. This assumed, of course, that the means of pursuing such a policy—namely, monetary, inter-

1. J. Tinbergen, *On the Theory of Economic Policy* (Amsterdam: North-Holland, 1952), esp. chaps. 4 and 5.

est rate, and budgetary instruments—were firmly in the hands of national policymakers and that stability was not disrupted by external factors. This chain of assumptions always raised doubts as to whether this concept was indeed a general theory and policy. Keynes alone, unlike his many followers and opponents, was always aware of the fragility of his assumptions.

Keynes therefore implemented his system of national full employment by calling for the elimination of the disruption by balance-of-payments factors, whether by administrative import or exchange controls or by the floating of exchange rates, with the aim of replacing employment-destroying deflation with the more employment-neutral devaluation. Keynes also called for a double response from fiscal policy. This should overcompensate for any national or international excess monetary savings—liquidity traps—as well as the effects of growth in labor productivity on unemployment by deficit spending and employment programs.

It is easy to see how both the assumptions and prescriptions of the Keynesian policy of full employment are weakened, not to say destroyed, in the crisis of the world economy in the 1980s. The liquidity traps have not only exploded; more important, they have also been internationalized by a worldwide flight into extraterritorial money rather than national capital value, or investment. Monetary wealth exceeds the real wealth creation that sustains and creates employment. Modern technologies have also changed the old dependable investment, income, and employment multipliers into denominators, and the investment in increased capital stock that does still go ahead has become less and less employment intensive. Consequently,

the employment content of investment is decreasing.

What is the position with regard to the Keynesian policy framework? The current accounts of most of the economies dependent on the world economy find themselves in a state of fundamental imbalance, which cannot be redressed by floating exchange rates or, since the second oil shock of 1980, financed away by an ample flow of credit. The domestic fiscal policies of almost all countries—with the recent exception of the United States—are subject to irresistible restrictive pressures. As a result, the countries can neither put an end to excess monetary savings nor contain technology-induced unemployment by public spending and employment programs. We therefore face the paradox of being able to employ Keynesian ideas to explain the current world economic crisis, but not to resolve it, because global changes in the world economy have undermined the foundations of Keynesianism.

Is this conclusion correct? It will only be correct if the Keynesian approach cannot be adapted to the changes brought about by innovations in the world monetary system and radical technological changes. What are the causes of the global extraterritorial liquidity traps, the fact that more and more monetary savings and credit, which should go to finance national and real investment programs, disappear into the black holes of the ubiquitous world money and capital markets that are free of regulatory, supervisory, or political interference? These traps are clearly the result of and the accompaniment of the demise of the Bretton Woods system, which ended with the introduction of floating exchange rates in the spring of 1973. Whether or not there is any connection, the introduction of these rates came just six months before the beginning of the first oil shock. Since the end of the inter-central-bank system centered on the International Monetary Fund, the business of financing countries' negative foreign accounts has now gone over to the private international banking system. The floating of a currency does not lead to a balanced trade account, but to an unlimited and uncontrollable financing of a negative balance of payments without regard to the existing grid of parities of exchange rate relations. This allows a cumulative deficit financing, which has in the meantime grown to billions of U.S. dollars absorbing increasing volumes of credit and savings and which has become illiquid as a result of the world economic crisis.

The crisis of illiquidity in the debtor countries, in particular in Latin America, results in artificial exchange and interest rates, that is, artificial prices for changing and borrowing money. In order to more easily facilitate refinancing as well as the shifting of their exchange and credit risks onto the debtor countries, the international banking community used U.S. dollars in their contracts and denominated their private balance-of-payments credits in U.S. dollars. This inevitably led to a devaluation of all the currencies concerned against the dollar, which thus became strong, at least in its relation to the weaker debtor countries, despite, not because of, Reaganomics and its own debt management. The interest charged has also escalated because the risk of guaranteeing this credit has increased since the beginning of the 1980s, partly as a result of the second oil-price shock.

Extraterritorial banks and markets were dependent on the U.S. money and bank markets to refinance such U.S.-dollar-denominated credits. They therefore exported interest rate increases to the United States itself, but also from the United States to all the other Western industrialized countries. Since then, the use of the monetary instruments of exchange and interest rates in the pursuit of national employment policies has been blocked in all industrialized countries except the United States. Thanks to their hegemonic position as the refinancer of last resort for a world economy drifting toward bankruptcy, the Americans can also accumulate limitless debt, at least externally, but only at the price of their dollar floating as a result of floating international capital expectations, and their interest rate remaining equally high due to indebtedness. The Americans need have no fear of illiquidity leading to bankruptcy because of their position as a world central banker, but they have no influence on their currency, exchange, or interest rates.

As for the technological unemployment in the industrialized countries, this is clearly visible in the increased labor productivity of electronic gremlins such as robots, computers, processors, and other labor saving devices. But what one sees is a jump in the productivity of employed labor—that is, per hour worked or per worker employed—not an increase in productivity for the total available labor force. This is not a statistical puzzle but the heart of the problem of technological unemployment in the highly developed countries. If one relates the increased production and gross domestic product resulting from the new technology not to the labor force still employed but to the total labor force, including the growing numbers of unemployed, two things become evident.

First, it is only the micro productivity of the leading sectors and firms that is growing and not the macro productivity of the economy as a whole.

Second, the effect of increases in micro productivity in releasing resources raises rather than lowers the potential for macro productivity increases. One gains rather than loses scope for employment programs and policies, if one could only finance them by fiscal or other means.

What does this analysis show? It shows that at both national and international levels one is not facing a real crisis but a crisis of financing. We are dealing with a defect in the flow of liquidities, which causes defects in the flow of real resources and not the other way around.

Can one take any comfort from this conclusion? On the one hand, one cannot, in so far as we, sadly, have so little control of money and credit systems that, rather than protect us from real crises, pitch us into them. On the other hand, one can take comfort in the knowledge that one could, it is hoped, find or create ways out of the crisis by mastering the monetary and credit systems devised to serve us. This is precisely the continuing message of Keynesianism, which must be newly interpreted in an effort to increase our mastery of these systems.

CONCLUSIONS: THE NEED FOR NEW
POLICIES RATHER THAN NEW THEORIES

What must be done to tackle this global crisis of employment? It is first necessary to suppress the factors disrupting the global economy, and then have national fiscal policies that are oriented not, like past policies, toward promoting real capital—investment—

but toward the infinitely more valuable human capital of the unused labor force and working hours.

Let us develop the new Keynesianism.

There are two things that need to be done in the world economy: first, the amortization—not rescheduling—of the world debt mortgage; second, the creation of a world monetary order that excludes *ab ovo* every future repetition of the old debt game. J. M. Keynes developed ideas and policy instruments that are still or could again be of value. In the 1929 debate with B. Ohlin about the German transfer problem that preceded the Great Depression, he pointed out that it would be cheaper for all the countries involved, both creditor and debtor countries, to write off the debt rather than press for payment, because the crisis, which would damage everyone concerned, would thereby be avoided.[2] The debtors would have saved the negative resource transfer, from poor to rich, by having a positive current account. The creditor countries would have saved themselves from importing the crisis in the form of dumping by the debtor countries seeking to increase exports. The creditor countries, we now know, would also have saved themselves from the self-induced decommissioning of their monetary instruments, which robbed them of their freedom of action.

The only unanswered question is how to finance this debt write-off, and here the position in 1987 is far better than it was in 1929. There is development aid, and the write-off of the creditor banks' debt is already fully financed, domestically with public help in the form of tax deductions. Together these provide a

2. John M. Keynes and Bertil Ohlin, "The German Transfer Problem, A Discussion," *Economic Journal,* 39:1, 172, 388 (1929).

full and sufficient debt-relief program. For the foreseeable future, development aid will no longer finance new projects but the debt service payments of the developing world. The creditor banks, having the advantage of obtaining their money from liquid development budgets instead of illiquid development countries, participate in the current debt-relief process by shifting adjustments in their internal value onto their debtors as well as by writing off the debt externally.

The developing countries would have the advantage of saving the burden of transfer payments, and they could resume a path of cautious growth. For the creditor countries, there would be the double advantage of avoiding the importation of an economic depression and once again freeing their monetary policy instruments for use in the pursuit of domestic policy objectives. With normal exchange and interest rates they could also reckon on an economic recovery. The creditor banks would have the debts they have not written off refinanced by means of development aid and would thus convert bad risk of foreign debt into good-risk claims on budget-financed development aid. Thus our banking system would and could be free of any fear of collapse or world financial crisis.

One could then use Keynes's *bancor,* or what we know today as the special drawing rights (SDRs), as the basis for the future world monetary order. This would solve three problems with one blow. First, the world economy would at last have a reserve currency secure against devaluation and speculation. This would solve the problem of the unlimited and uncontrollable production, distribution, and valuation of liquidity. Second, countries could pursue inflationary or deflationary policy objectives by devaluing or revaluing

their currencies against the new SDR just as they did in the old, now defunct, adjustable-peg standard of Bretton Woods. Third, the dollar would be relieved of the burden of being a—indeed the primary—world currency and of the burden of financing all the world's debts. The dollar would again become a currency rather than a medium and could thus be revalued or devalued. In such a system, all future excessive world debt would at last be penalized and discouraged by the single supranational global monarch. This would be an International Monetary Fund bound by its own statute and administering SDRs, which can be found in Keynes's still unfulfilled testament, the proposals for an international Clearing Union of 1941-43.[3]

There is an internal and insufficiently considered aspect of the liquidity phenomenon. This is that real capital investment is self-liquidating, but human capital investment, which is equal to personal consumption, costs liquidity! Whether or not this is important, it is recognized by the finance director of every large company, but does not seem to be recognized by those controlling public fiscal policy.

The modern large company prefers real capital investment for a number of reasons. First, for cash-flow reasons, depreciation of earned capital represents the inflow of liquidity to the company, whereas earned personal consumption or wages represents an outflow just like the purchase of any input. Second, from a financial-planning point of view, self-

3. *The Keynes Plan: A: Proposal for an International Currency (or Clearing) Union, 1942. B: Proposals for an International Clearing-Union, 1943,* International Monetary Fund Documents vol. 3, ed. J. K. Horsefield (Washington, DC: International Monetary Fund, 1969).

determined depreciation can be reduced during periods of reduced income and increased during periods of increased income, but externally determined wage rates are always rigid. Marx's law according to which capital costs are fixed while labor costs are variable was already wrong when he pronounced it. Third, earned depreciation strengthens the capital basis and creditworthiness of the company in the form of replacement investment or financial reserves, whereas labor costs weaken both.

Consequently, the different liquidity characteristics of the two factors of production are a decisive factor in the capital substitution of labor. It is not only the cost advantages of new technology that result in its increased use, but also the liquidity advantages of capital investment. These become a more important factor the more cash-flow thinking spreads. This substitution process of labor, or human capital, by real capital is promoted by public fiscal and tax policies. These stimulate depreciation by tax credits but, in contrast, only allow wage costs to be deducted at par from the taxable profits of a company. In this way the liquidity advantage of real capital is indirectly strengthened as is the liquidity disadvantage of human capital, which affects both the continuance of existing labor and the hiring of new. This is a practice that can be observed in all Western industrialized countries.

When trying to achieve a positive employment effect with a given or even shrinking fiscal effort, there is therefore the problem of granting tax credits on human capital rather than on real capital. This can be done by either granting above-par tax exemptions for wage costs when calculating taxable profits or by a general tax bonus for maintaining or

increasing the company's labor force. Such a fiscal policy would also be self-liquidating in macroeconomic terms, because reductions in unemployment would result in savings in social expenditure and because tax revenue would be increased by the higher levels of employment.

Companies would no longer be forced to convert wage and employment income into social support or transfer payments by reducing employment in order to remain competitive or creditworthy. The excess in technological progress could and would be made compatible, or more compatible, with employment. The rates of growth in macro and micro productivity would converge and the unproductive unemployment would be reduced. A second factor would, or could, be the useful reintegration of the black economy into the white economy measured by gross domestic product. There were real—and not only tax—reasons for the growth of the black economies in most Western industrialized countries. There is also the reduction in official hours worked, not least because of increases in micro productivity. Life expectancy has increased because of advances in medicine, and the difference is increasingly being made up by work for oneself.

This black value-added is penalized and discriminated against as illegal, and as an economic crime in most economic and social legislation even though it is economically legitimate. Indeed, the black economy provides an important cyclical support for growth and employment and even monetary policy objectives, because income earned in the black economy—a massive economic reflationary stimulus—mainly benefits the companies that constitute the white economy. The task of converting the black economy into the white economy is also largely the job of public tax and fiscal policies. The use of more indirect than direct taxes would minimize the problem of tax evasion and tax fraud in this fourth sector of all the Western industrialized countries; it would reduce the discrepancy between the tax burden on the white and black sectors of the same economy and thus ease the competitive pressure between the two; and it would also remove from the black economy the stigma of illegality, which it does not deserve.

The final conclusion from all this can be summarized in one sentence. The old Keynesian instruments of monetary and fiscal policies aimed at full employment are currently ineffective, but this ineffectiveness is neither fate nor a natural law. The monetary instrument can be freed by writing off rather than rescheduling the developing-country debts that can-

not be paid and by replacing the private U.S. dollar currency system with a system in which debt limits are specified and controlled by the International Monetary Fund and SDRs.

Fiscal policy can make an important contribution to national full-employment policies despite all the budgetary constraints. This it can do by promoting human capital rather than real capital and by not treating the black economy as a false path from growth but as its continuation and extension into postindustrial times and as the release of the working person who wants to be his or her own employer.

Such a new Keynesian policy mix may appear to be utopian, but reality does not interpret itself. It is only against the background of such possibilities that one can define the contours, the timetable, and the direction of what is necessity.

ANNALS, *AAPSS*, **492**, July 1987

Intervening on the Supply Side of the Labor Market

By LOUIS EMMERIJ

ABSTRACT: Several policy measures that have been proposed to unclog the labor markets in advanced industrial countries, such as early retirement, extension of compulsory education, shorter working weeks, or work sharing, are ineffective. Therefore a more comprehensive approach is required to reduce the amount of time that individuals spend in the labor market during their life span. Such an approach would aim at combining or alternating periods of education, work, and retirement throughout a person's adult life. Elements of the approach are recurrent education, flexibility of labor supply in accordance with the need of the labor market, discriminatory application for the sake of income distribution, and harmonization of the social security system. The scheme could be financed by money now invested in social security schemes of all kinds as well as out of existing educational budgets.

Louis Emmerij graduated in international economics from Columbia University in 1961. In 1961-62 he was with the Institut d'études économiques et sociales, University of Paris, before joining the Directorate of Scientific Affairs of the Organization for Economic Cooperation and Development (OECD). Between 1971 and 1976 he was director of the World Employment Program of the International Labor Organization before becoming director of the Institute of Social Studies in The Hague. In January 1986 he returned to Paris to take up his present post as president of the OECD Development Center.

UNTIL recently, when we spoke about the employment problem what we meant in actual fact was a Third World employment problem. Since the end of the 1970s, however, the employment problem has become universal. Unemployment in Europe stands at over 12 percent with deviations to over 15 percent in the case of the Netherlands and Spain, and to lower and more or less normal percentages in the case of Sweden and Austria, for example.

The developing countries discovered during the 1960s that economic growth alone was not sufficient to improve employment and income distribution. In Europe today the same phenomenon can be observed, namely, that it is extremely difficult to get back to full employment by means of economic growth alone.

The overriding objective of financial and economic policy today in Europe is to return as quickly as possible to a reasonable and sustained rate of economic growth. The current financial and economic orthodoxy in Europe puts a heavy emphasis on the role of the private sector, on flexibility of the labor market, on privatization, on doing away with distortions, and so on and so forth. The most important policy points on which the current orthodoxy rests can be summarized as follows:

1. The public sector has become too large and has a paralyzing impact on the private sector.

2. It also has a negative influence on inflation in that it has stimulated rather than dampened the latter.

3. Labor costs have become too high.

4. Consequently, and because of certain excesses in the welfare state, European enterprise has lost a lot of its competitiveness. Moreover, high labor costs have done away with many incentives for good entrepreneurship and hard work.

5. Because of all this, the European economy has had great difficulty in adapting sufficiently and with the necessary speed to changes in the world economic structure.

The current orthodoxy, therefore, concentrates heavily on increasing the efficiency of market signals as a guide to an improved allocation of resources. In practice, this is the kind of strategy that is often introduced during a period of crisis when economic stabilization and the adjustment of imbalances are of high priority, and, consequently, measures to improve relative prices usually are accompanied by measures to control the rate of increase in the general level of prices. Emphasis, then, is placed on monetary and fiscal policies and on financial reforms. Employment, it is assumed, will begin to improve once economic recovery has started and economic growth is assured.

Today, in 1987, it is gradually dawning on many policymakers in European countries that economic growth alone will not be able to bring us back to full employment within a humanly tolerable and politically acceptable period of time. In such circumstances the idea of full employment must be dropped, or a more employment-intensive growth path must be introduced, or a set of complementary employment measures must be designed that will be implemented simultaneously, with the economic and financial policies directed to economic recovery. This article will focus mainly on complementary employment policies, including the reduction of working time. But let me say immediately that I consider most of the discussion, as it is being conducted today, to be rather absurd. Indeed, not enough consideration is given to the totally different situation that will exist in the European labor market ten to fifteen years from now, no lessons are being drawn from history, and insufficient attention is given to the need to invest in human capital.

COMPLEMENTARY EMPLOYMENT POLICIES FOCUSING ON REDUCTION IN WORKING TIME

Although there is less talk about reductions of working time today as compared to a few years ago, such policies are still considered to be of great relevance in the present difficult employment situation in Europe. Five traditional policies have been proposed, which we shall quickly review in this part of the article. I believe that all these policies are flawed and I will therefore propose later in this article an unorthodox policy that I believe to be more effectively geared to the present and future situation.

Early retirement

Although there is a lot of talk about reducing the retirement age from 65 to 63, 61, and even lower, it is quite clear that such a measure would not amount to anything substantive with regard to creating additional employment opportunities. In the Netherlands, for instance, more than half of the people in the age group 63-64 already draw on social insurance funds for those declared unfit for work. Of the remaining number of elderly workers, more than half occupy places that are bound to be abolished in due course for reasons of rationalization and streamlining.

All in all, perhaps 20 to 25 percent of the jobs presently occupied by older workers will be vacated; they can and will be filled by younger workers. Moreover, early retirement is somewhat of a contradiction *in terminis*. More and more people in our day and age in most industrialized countries feel fit and well for much longer than was formerly the case. In this context, it is interesting to note that retirement age in the United States has been postponed till 70.

The conclusion must be that this measure may be fairly simple to introduce, but that it is not very effective toward solving the unemployment problem.

Extension of compulsory education

More or less the same reasoning applies for extending compulsory education as for early retirement schemes. A measure to extend compulsory education until, say, 18 is rather defensive because it strives to keep young people from entering the labor market. But far more than half the young people in the age group 16-17 already attend school. Of the others, not all enter the labor market straightaway. Again, therefore, the actual percentage that is prevented from entering the labor market is approximately 20 to 25 percent. These young people are detained at school more or less against their will.

It might perhaps be said that to keep youngsters from lower social circles longer in school serves an important sociocultural end, by bettering their chances to improve their educational backgrounds. But this aim can be achieved in other ways, as will be shown later.

It should be borne in mind that keeping young people in school against their inclinations will result in poorer qualitative results, will draw heavily on a country's education budget, and may cause the youth to look at school with a lasting distaste.

Longer holidays

The alternative of longer holidays is only mentioned here for completeness's sake, because unless holidays become very much longer—and then we shall really have a situation of paid educational leave—such a measure would hardly achieve tangible results in employment terms. Moreover, it has its disadvantages, ranging from shops having to be kept closed for much longer periods to even stronger stimulation of mass tourism and this while we are just beginning to realize that such things do not make us any happier. In the end, nothing would be achieved by such a measure, unless it is turned into paid education leave, as set out later.

Shorter working weeks

Shorter working weeks will probably not achieve tangible results in the middle or long term. Employment or unemployment tends to remain constant whether the working week is of 48, 40, or 35 hours. In the past, employers have strongly opposed a reduction of working time, but time and again we have seen that ultimate results were not too bad owing to the adaptability of people and to the improvement of labor productivity by the introduction of technological innovations.

Trade unions now go to the other extreme in thinking that more jobs can thus be created. In my opinion, this is just about as naive as the employers' stand. In no time technology and productivity would catch up with the new situation and we should be faced once more with the necessity of finding other ways and means of shortening working hours. Moreover, scarce know-how and skills will become even scarcer, and men and women alike will be at their wits' end because shorter working hours away from the house will mean more time spent there, creating additional chores.

Fewer working hours per day—a five-hour working day

Working fewer hours each day implies not so much that additional jobs will be created as that the available quantity of work will be divided among more individuals, with all the negative income consequences.

In fact, it implies a shift from the present situation of one occupant per job to a situation of two occupants per job. These two will together earn at least as much as the one person before and together may well have greater productivity. Another consequence is that more persons—foremost among them women who work at home—will be able to do paid work away from home. It is therefore hardly to be wondered at that women's lib movements, in particular, favor this idea: not only will paid work be divided, but so will unpaid—house—work. It also means, however, that everyone will be more or less obliged to seek a partner, not only to share life with but also in order to enjoy full income!

Markets will develop in which single people advertise for partners of similar professional level and interests. Although this does not have to be bad in itself, it does carry some dictatorial aspects unless one thinks in terms of a more subtle and differentiated approach. But this would have consequences for the effectiveness of fewer daily working hours. For example, if greater flexibility enabled one individual to do two jobs, the effects of fewer working hours per day would be completely annihilated or even reversed. In such circumstances many individuals would probably tend to work ten hours a day instead of five.

Summarizing, the proposal implies that two people will have to work in order to earn one average income; otherwise the whole system would have reverse effects on the employment situation and on the economy as a whole.

PROPOSAL FOR A FLEXIBLE MIX OF WORK, EDUCATION OR TRAINING, AND LEISURE

We believe that a different and more comprehensive approach is required to reduce the amount of time that individuals spend in the labor market during their life spans.[1] Such an approach would not be limited to relatively unimportant measures of labor market policy, but would consist of a more global package, including educational policies, labor market policies, and social policies, combined with economic restructuring and development cooperation policies.

It is our opinion that a social and cultural policy package should be proposed, in addition to purely economic proposals. The foremost characteristic of the new package is that it would combine a progressive policy with leaving the greatest possible initiative to the individual, who would thus have more control over shaping his or her career

1. For a more detailed treatment of what follows, see Louis J. Emmerij and Joop Clobus, *Volledige werkgelegenheid door creatief verlof— Naar een maatschappij van de vrije keuze* [Full employment through creative leave—towards a society of free choice] (Deventer, Netherlands: Kluwer, 1978).

and life pattern than is the case at present. Such a global approach must also be able to deal with the rationing of labor, but as a by-product rather than as its major, or even sole, objective. What would be the contours of such a global approach to the unemployment problem in industrialized countries?

The life of an individual is divided into three parts, separated in most countries by watertight partitions:

—the period spent at school and, for the more fortunate, at university;
—active life, whether spent on the labor market or not, whether remunerated or not; and
—the post-retirement period.

These periods follow one another sequentially. We go to school at an early age and remain there until 16 or 18 years old, depending on the country, and, in the case of university students, very often up to the age of 25 or even older.

Then we enter the period of so-called active life until the age of 60 or 65, when we are kindly but firmly asked to go out into retirement. It is very difficult—particularly in most European countries—to reverse the sequence of these three events.

The essence of our proposal is to transform this rigid sequential system into a more flexible recurrent system, in which it will be possible to combine or alternate periods of education, work, and retirement throughout a person's adult life.

The idea of recurrent education, which cuts through the first two periods of life, was launched toward the end of the 1960s and has been discussed ever since. The complementary idea of retirement à la carte has been discussed less frequently, but it is the logical extension and the mirror image of recurrent education because it cuts across the second and third periods. Individuals could even be given the opportunity to combine all three periods by, for example, taking at age 30 a period of six months of anticipated retirement in order to continue or resume further education. Although this sounds extremely straightforward and simple, in reality it amounts to a social and cultural change of the first order.

Before going into somewhat more detail, it is important to stress the advantages of such an approach for the various partners, social and individual, in our countries.

In the first place, this much more flexible approach would enable an equally flexible labor market policy to be introduced that would have advantages both for employers and for workers. The employers would obtain a labor force that could be more easily and more quickly retrained in line with technological changes. The workers would have easier and more frequent chances to reorient themselves.

The educational system as it exists at present is extremely rigid and has long time lags. These were two of the reasons why in the 1950s and 1960s forecasts of occupational and educational structures of the labor force became fashionable. These were long-term forecasts due to the long gestation periods inherent in the educational production process. Indeed, it takes approximately six years to complete each of the main levels of the educational system. Hence, the school will react very slowly to changes in technology, which, in turn, have implications for the required skill structure of the labor force.

Experience has shown that it is nigh impossible to make more or less reliable long-term forecasts of the occupational and educational structures of the labor force. It is therefore much more realistic and desirable to shorten the gestation periods because, by doing so, the educational system will become more easily adaptable. In other words, the relationship between school and work will become closer, more effective, and more beneficial to all parties.

In the second place, there is a specific advantage to the individual in terms of being able to better realize his or her full potential.

We all know that motivation occurs at very different moments in a person's life and not necessarily at those points in time required by the sequential education system. Educational opportunities and achievements will definitely be enhanced if individuals can go back to school when they are motivated to do so instead of being pushed by parents or by other persons in authority to remain in school. These people are right, of course, because in the present setup it is difficult to return to school once one has dropped out.

What is true for educational opportunities is equally true for occupational and income opportunities. In the global approach that we favor, individuals have more than one occasion to orient or reorient themselves in the labor market. We go even further and offer individuals the possibility of taking a period of anticipatory retirement earlier in life, during which they do not necessarily have to return to school but can do other things for which they are strongly motivated at that particular time of their lives.

In the third place, its flexibility also makes our approach an effective anticyclical weapon. At times when a particularly strong but temporary economic storm flays our countries, more people could be encouraged to withdraw for a while from the labor force in order to benefit from recurrent education or from a sabbatical period.

In the fourth place, and this is also an antistructural weapon, we shall have on the average fewer people in the labor market at each point in time than is presently the case because—and again on the average—people will spend more time in the first and third blocks of their life as compared to the second. In this way, total labor supply will diminish.

The approach we advocate is thus on the one hand a generalization of traditional trade union demands for shorter working hours, more holidays, and earlier retirement and, on the other hand, a generalization of the more recent proposals with respect to part-time work, the sharing of jobs, and the rationing of labor supply in general.

Our global approach thus kills several birds with one stone; the economic structural limits will for once be consistent with the sociocultural objectives of the individual. Instead of a diminishing majority that works harder and harder and an increasing minority that is expelled shamefully from the labor market, we are proposing that available work be rationed more intelligently and more comprehensively than has been suggested so far.

Let us look at the various dimensions intervening on the supply side of our approach in a little more detail.

First, there is the necessity of introducing a system of recurrent education after the compulsory schooling period. There are almost as many definitions of recurrent education as there are people who believe they know what they are talking about! For many it is a second-chance network parallel to the full-time formal education system. This is def-

initely not the case. Recurrent education, as we understand it, is a comprehensive and flexible post-compulsory educational system that combines the present formal educational branches and the various types of adult education. Recurrent education therefore does not necessarily imply creating additional types of education and training, but the integration of existing types into one harmonious whole. In order to speak about recurrent education, four conditions must be met:

1. The education system must be able to receive people from all age groups.

2. It must be one integrated education and training system, as indicated earlier.

3. It must offer educational units of variable and flexible duration that can be used as building blocks for, and stepping stones toward, obtaining a diploma or degree.

4. It must have exit possibilities at different levels that are all to be awarded with a diploma or degree.

A few words on each of these four points.

On the first point, it is to be expected that most youngsters who decide at the age of 17 or 18 to postpone the continuation of their studies for a while will resume their schooling between their twentieth and thirtieth birthdays. This makes sense from an individual and therefore private rate-of-return point of view. It also makes sense from the macroeconomic and therefore social rate-of-return viewpoint. Were people to decide to start their university education at, say, 55 they could not expect to receive important material returns in terms of income during the rest of their lifetime—nor could society. It is to be expected that as people grow older, they will prefer to take up stretches of anticipatory retirement in order to do other things than to return to school.

The second point is important because in our approach individuals must be able to travel along alternative educational paths and still achieve the same educational goal. People must have the opportunity to obtain the same credits by spending, say, 52 long weekends at school as by attending a full-time education program during a period of three to four months. This flexibility must be built into the recurrent system, otherwise it cannot cope with the much greater variety of students and circumstances of today's situation.

This is much more easily said than done—hence the third point, namely, to introduce educational units that in relatively short time periods can provide a well-rounded part of a given educational career. The student or participant can thus build up credits in a flexible manner and does not lose them; they contribute to the total credits necessary to obtain a particular diploma or degree.

The fourth and last point refers to the necessity for recurrent education to have exit possibilities at different levels so that we do not fall into the all-or-nothing trap of current educational systems.

In summary the educational characteristics of our approach are the following:

—to hold as many options open for as long a period as possible;

—to transfer to a later age the emphasis on pursuing higher levels of education in order to interrupt the rat race of spending more and more years of education in the existing sequential system, even when there is no real desire to do so; and

—to integrate formal and nonformal types of education.

The second dimension of our approach is the labor-market-policy component. Our proposal will have positive effects on the structural, cyclical, and individual levels of labor market policy.

On the structural plane, our approach will be instrumental in creating a better linkage between the changing skills required, on the one hand, and the educational and training supply delivered by our recurrent educational system, on the other. There is no doubt that one of the more important structural problems that we face in our industrialized countries, namely, the growing mismatch between skills required and qualifications supplied, will be effectively countered by our proposals.

On the cyclical plane, the government, through appropriate incentives, can stimulate relatively more people to leave the labor force temporarily during an ebb tide of the economic situation. But more precise targets can be attained. For instance, the government could well direct such measures to a specific sector of the economy or to specific groups of workers in the labor force. This could be done by giving higher financial rewards to people working in that sector or in that specific group—higher rewards to withdraw for a given period of time into education or training. In other words, paid educational leave need not necessarily be the same from one group to another, from one sector to another, or from one period of time to another.

On the individual plane, the advantages of our proposals for individuals to reenter the labor market or to change within it are obvious and reflect those mentioned under the structural and cyclical components.

There is, however, one additional point that needs to be emphasized. This refers to the possibility for the individual to obtain an orientation period in the labor market after terminating his or her compulsory schooling and before starting recurrent education and training. During this period youngsters who have not yet firmly decided on their professional career will have the possibility of sniffing at various job opportunities. This would replace the training periods of today—training periods that are very often neither education, nor training, nor work, but fall between all these stools.

A third dimension of our package is related to income distribution. What would be the implications of the system of recurrent education and leave for the income distribution of our countries? The perverse effects on tertiary income distribution of additional educational and other facilities have frequently been noted. Indeed, in most cases education is provided at strongly reduced prices through government subsidies, which come from taxes paid by all. On the other hand, we know that those who attain higher levels of education frequently come from the higher social classes. Such a situation is a clear example of how the poor subsidize the rich. This is one illustration of perverse effects' providing not only education, but also health and other facilities at subsidized prices.

We must therefore take care that paid educational leave is granted as a matter of priority to those who have not been able to benefit optimally from educational facilities when young. In other words, a positive discrimination must be introduced in order to counter the perverse effects.

Still on the subject of income distribution, Jan Tinbergen has drawn on time series from the Netherlands to show that education has expanded faster than warranted on purely economic and technological grounds. This apparent educational oversupply has resulted in a narrowing of income disparities between people with different levels of educational attainment.[2] If his conclusions are correct and can be generalized to situations in other countries, it would follow that our proposals could have further positive implications for income distribution while at the same time maintaining a somewhat better balance between the demand for skills and the supply of qualifications.

Another implication—and this is a fourth dimension of our proposal—would be to create a better work climate. The genuine possibility that people would occasionally have to withdraw from the labor force is likely to diminish the number of those who declare themselves sick or otherwise unfit for work. Absenteeism due to sickness is a growing problem in most countries. Very often it is due to the fact that people work for too long a period under great stress. The safety valve provided by voluntary withdrawal could make a big difference.

Moreover, people who withdraw voluntarily from the labor force are in a very different psychological situation from those who are forcefully expelled. Pressure on health facilities can therefore be expected to diminish, implying a considerable saving of money in the health and welfare sectors—money that can be used toward financing our proposals. Finally, our policy package will

2. Jan Tinbergen, *Income Distribution: Analyses and Policies* (Amsterdam: North-Holland, 1975).

almost necessarily imply the harmonization of the entire social security system. This also means that the great variety of pension schemes now in existence must be integrated in such a way that people are no longer confronted with bureaucratic problems when moving from one firm to another, or from one job to another, with respect to rights to retirement benefits.

THE FINANCING OF
PAID EDUCATIONAL LEAVE

Many may be inclined to think that the approach that has been set out is a very positive way to cause unemployment to disappear by redefining the concept of full employment. On the other hand, the costs involved might be such as to render its realization unlikely, particularly if large numbers of people were to be involved during the initial stages of introduction of paid educational leave, as should indeed be the case. This would be judging too fast, however. Part of the trick—and this is where it ceases to be a trick—is to use the money now invested in social security schemes of all kinds to finance our proposal concerning recurrent education and leave.

Those who will benefit from our approach will consist of two groups: first, the youngsters who, after having finished compulsory education, continue immediately with what will then be recurrent education; and second, those who, after having worked for a certain period of time, withdraw voluntarily into a period of paid leave.

The financing of these groups will come from different sources. The cost of the first is now carried by the ministry of education's budget, combined with tax and other facilities granted to the par-

ents involved. In our approach, the financial resources, insofar as they come from different budgets, will need to be centralized.

In practice, this will amount to the granting of a student salary and to the abolition of present tax and other facilities.

During periods of paid leave, the incomes of those in the second category must come from the amounts that are now paid by social security facilities to people who are involuntarily expelled from the labor market. We refer to those of the unemployed who are declared to be unfit for work and to some of those who are sick and who, through health insurance schemes, can be viewed as being disguised as unemployed.

One can easily calculate the magnitudes involved, regarding people who fall under unemployment benefits, unfit-for-work benefits, and sickness insurance, respectively, but who should in reality be classified as structurally unemployed. In other words, the groups that one must separate from the rest consist of people who are either openly unemployed or unemployed in a more or less disguised manner, and who find themselves in those categories because of the structural unemployment problem in the industrialized world.

The essence of such calculations is to estimate the number of people who can withdraw voluntarily into paid educational leave at any point in time without additional costs being incurred by society, as compared to the present expenses involved in unemployment and social security schemes of all kinds to ensure the incomes of those who are either openly or covertly unemployed.

Instead of spending billions of monetary units for negative reasons—expelling people from their working environment or forcing young people to remain at school while the majority would prefer to do something else before eventually returning to the educational system—we propose that the same amount of money should be used for positive reasons. Our approach creates a new form of income maintenance for periods of inactivity. The difference is that involuntary inactivity for some—normally the weaker groups of society—is replaced by periods of voluntary non-working for all.

Clearly, there are a certain number of problems, but there are also possibilities. First of all, one might wonder whether it is realistic and, indeed, responsible to use funds that are typically meant to remedy cyclical difficulties for the solution of structural problems. But I have already explained that social security moneys are more and more used to alleviate or to hide structural unemployment problems. The statement that these funds are used mainly for cyclical purposes is thus already becoming less true. We are witnessing the fact that social security funds are increasingly used to face up to a structural unemployment situation that threatens to last throughout the 1980s and well into the 1990s. This being so, it would be more honest to recognize this fact and to separate out those funds that are to be used for cyclical purposes from the rest.

A second problem, or possibility, is that concerning the introduction of incentives and disincentives for certain groups in society to take up—or not take up—education leave. Any policy measures on the supply side of the labor market must be sufficiently flexible and even reversible in the event that in the 1990s we face a totally different situation in the labor market. In other words, we are concerned with the general problem of how to ensure that the right number of people, having the right composition, withdraw voluntarily from the labor market at any point in time.

Overall, the total number of people involved might be influenced by changing the percentage of income to be paid. Instead of a payment during the leave period of, say, 80 percent of the latest income, the payment could be increased to 85, 90, or even 100 percent in order to make it more attractive for certain people in certain sectors and in certain regions to take up the opportunity. The payments could be differentiated—for example, by proposing a higher percentage for people who want to go into educational courses that are in high demand in the labor market than for those who want to go elsewhere.

Finally, there is the problem of how to start the whole scheme, assuming that all other obstacles have been cleared. If the proposal is to be any of real benefit to the employment problem, it is essential that people who are now in productive employment decide at the outset to take up educational leave. But that is not all. Not only must we have many guinea pigs but their jobs must be taken by people who are now unemployed. Only in this way can we in due course replace structural unemployment by educational or creative leave. Otherwise we shall be faced with an accumulation of both structural unemployment and educational leave. The proposal would then break down. Therefore we have a matching problem on our hands: how to make sure that those who withdraw voluntarily into educational leave have more or less the same qualifications as those who are at present unemployed. In this connection it is clear that we must start by convincing those workers with the lowest educational and training backgrounds to take their educational leave first. This will kill two birds with one stone: first, these are the people for whom educational leave is relatively the most useful; second, it is in this category that we find the bulk of the unemployed. In other words, the matching problem in this situation would be much easier than in any other and also more productive. The question of how the guinea pigs and all those who take advantage of educational leave thereafter can ever be reinserted into the labor market is very easy to answer. Once the operation has started, some group of people will be away from the labor market at any point in time. There will be an ever changing rotating group. By the time the guinea pigs return from their educational leave, another group will have just gone into voluntary retirement. Their places will therefore be vacated and will be refilled by the guinea pigs and so on and so forth.

CONCLUDING REMARKS

What has been proposed in this article amounts to profound changes in the social and cultural domains of society with a view to achieving a better balance between remunerative work and other aspects of human life. If these changes can be brought about, the employment problem could also largely be solved. Moreover, in the face of lower rates of economic growth and continuing upward trends in technology and labor productivity, we must move from a defensive to a constructive attitude.

The proposed policy package combines a progressive policy with restoration to the individual of a maximum of initiatives.

It has been shown that the proposed changes can be financed from existing public funds by changing their purpose and destination. Only a few, if any, additional funds will be required.

The proposed changes will be equitable, partly because of the built-in positive-discriminatory component. Equality of educational opportunities for everyone will be boosted and income distribution will consequently become less skewed. Weaker groups in society, who are now becoming more and more vulnerable, will become stronger as they are given additional opportunities to return to education and other forms of self-improvement.

The proposed measures will also be efficient because they will boost labor productivity and improve the working climate. They will also increase the flexibility of the labor market and facilitate adjustments to technological changes.

Obviously, at the level of enterprise and organizations, personnel policies must be adapted to face the situation in which more people will be on the payroll than actually on the shop floor because a certain percentage will, at any point in time, be on paid leave. This requires organizational adaptations that, however, are not totally new. In principle, the required adaptations do not differ much from the measures that must be taken by firms facing a relatively high level of absence because of sickness. However, there is a difference in favor of paid leave, because the latter can be planned, whereas sickness is more difficult to foresee.

The proposed policy package will also imply an important adaptation of the welfare state in favor of giving individuals more initiative and scope to shape their own life patterns and moving away from central government-imposed fixed patterns where these are not strictly necessary.

ANNALS, *AAPSS*, **492,** July 1987

The Politics of Full Employment
in Western Democracies

By MANFRED G. SCHMIDT

ABSTRACT: While the majority of the countries of the Organization for Economic Cooperation and Development have been plagued by mass unemployment in the 1970s and 1980s, rates of unemployment have remained low in Austria, Japan, Norway, Sweden, and Switzerland. The basic question addressed in this article is the extent to which structural-economic and political variables account for the full-employment record of these nations. It will be argued that these countries, due to a variety of political processes, institutions, strategies, and policies, have managed to maintain too much employment, relative to the structural-economic circumstances that have prevailed in their national economies.

Manfred G. Schmidt is professor of political science at the Free University in Berlin. He received his doctorate in political science at the University of Tübingen in 1975 and his Habilitation *at the University of Konstanz in 1981. His* Habilitationsschrift *on* Wohlfahrt-staatliche Politik unter bürgerlichen und sozialdemokratischen Regierungen *was awarded the Stein-Rokkan Prize for Comparative Social Research in 1981. He is the author of several books and numerous articles in professional journals in the field of comparative studies of politics and policy.*

WHILE the economic recessions of the 1970s and 1980s resulted in high levels of unemployment in the majority of the nations of the Organization for Economic Cooperation and Development (OECD), rates of unemployment remained at a low level in Austria, Japan, Norway, Sweden, and Switzerland. Moreover, the full-employment countries managed to maintain high or moderately high total employment growth rates and high labor force participation ratios, with the exception of Switzerland. Why has the labor market performance in these countries been better than in other OECD nations? This is the basic question that will be addressed in this article.

International differences in rates of unemployment, it can be argued, are attributable to differences in the nature and the number of economic-structural obstacles to full employment. Thus, for example, efforts to maintain full employment are facilitated by low growth rates in labor supply, high growth of the gross domestic product (GDP) and low productivity growth, and a low degree of trade dependency, to mention just a few factors. In contrast to this, governments that are confronted with high labor supply growth rates, weak GDP growth and high productivity growth, heavy external dependence of the economy, wage rigidity, and the presence of industries with heavy adjustment problems will find it far more difficult to control unemployment effectively.[1]

However, it does not necessarily follow from this that economic-structural obstacles to full-employment pol-

icy, or favorable conditions for full-employment strategies, actually result in increasing levels of unemployment or in full employment. Structural-economic circumstances present problems, but they do not dictate a particular solution. The nature of particular solutions is largely contingent upon the impact of factors that intervene in the complex relationship between structural-economic circumstances and labor market outcomes. Among the intervening factors, three—political processes, strategies of collective actors, and policies—deserve to receive major attention. Empirical analysis of the data that were collected in my research project on economic and social policy in OECD countries serves to illustrate this point.[2] Table 1 arrays data on rates of unemployment and on a simple additive index of structural-economic obstacles to full-employment policy in 15 OECD nations (see Table 1).

One of the most intriguing findings of the data consists of the weakness of the statistical association between rates of unemployment and the index of structural obstacles to full-employment policy. Relative to the nature and number of economic-structural problems, the full-employment nations, except Japan,

1. See, for example, Organisation for Economic Co-operation and Development (OECD), *Employment Growth and Structural Change* (Paris: OECD); *OECD Economic Outlook*, no. 35, pp. 40-47 (1985).

2. Labor market data for this article were taken from OECD, *OECD Labour Force Statistics* (Paris: OECD, annually); *OECD Employment Outlook* (1985); OECD, *OECD Economic Outlook—Historical Statistics, 1960-1982* (Paris: OECD, 1984). Political data were taken from Manfred G. Schmidt, "The Welfare State and the Economy in Periods of Economic Recession," *European Journal of Political Research*, 11(1):1-27 (Mar. 1983); David R. Cameron, "Social Democracy, Corporatism, Labor Quiescence, and the Representation of Economic Interests in Advanced Capitalist Societies," in *Order and Conflict in Contemporary Capitalism*, ed. John H. Goldthorpe (Oxford: Clarendon Press, 1984), pp. 143-78; Klaus von Beyme, *Parteien in westlichen Demokratien* (Munich: Pipers, 1984).

TABLE 1
RATES OF UNEMPLOYMENT AND ECONOMIC-STRUCTURAL OBSTACLES TO FULL EMPLOYMENT POLICY IN 15 OECD NATIONS

Country	Index of Economic-Structural Obstacles to Full Employment*	Type of Obstacle†	Average Rate of Unemployment, 1974-82		Change in Average Rate of Unemployment§	
			Actual Value (percentage)	Residual‡	Actual Value (percentage)	Residual‖
Australia	3	LS, W, CI	5.4	1.1	3.4	1.3
Austria	4	D, GAP, I, CI	2.1	-2.6	0.6	-1.6
Belgium	4	D, GAP, I, CI	8.2	3.5	5.7	3.5
Canada	4	D, LS, U, CI	7.7	3.0	2.3	0.1
Finland	3	GAP, W, CI	4.7	0.3	2.1	0.0
France	4	GAP, W, CI, I	5.4	0.7	2.9	0.7
Germany	5	D, G, GAP, I, CI	3.6	-1.4	2.6	0.1
Italy	6	D, I, LS, U, W, CI	7.2	1.6	1.5	-0.9
Japan	2	I, CI	2.0	-1.7	0.8	-1.2
Netherlands	4	D, G, LS, CI	6.2	1.5	4.7	2.5
Norway	3	LS, W, CI	2.1	-2.2	0.4	-1.6
Sweden	4	D, G, W, CI	2.1	-2.6	-0.1	-2.3
Switzerland	6	D, G, GAP, I, W, CI	0.4	-5.0	0.3	-2.1
United Kingdom	7	D, G, GAP, I, U, W, CI	6.9	1.1	3.4	0.9
United States	4	G, LS, U, CI	7.1	2.4	2.5	0.3

SOURCES: Organisation for Economic Co-operation and Development (OECD), *OECD Economic Outlook-Historical Statistics, 1960-1982* (Paris: OECD, 1984); OECD, *Labour Force Statistics 1962-1982* (Paris: OECD, 1984).

*Additive index of the total number of economic-structural obstacles to full employment. (See, for details, the list of indicators in fn. 2 to this table.) The borderline between cases that were classified as "obstacles" or "else" was empirically defined via the arithmetic mean of the 15 OECD nations for which comparable labor market indicators were available. Thus, for example, gross domestic product (GDP) growth rates below the average growth rate of 2.1 percent were counted as an obstacle to full employment. The critical thresholds of the other indicators are as follows: export dependence > 20 percent; GDP-productivity-gap differentiation < 1.7. Moreover, the existence of crisis industries was regarded as an obstacle to full employment.

†CI = existence of crisis industries; D = export dependence, that is, exports as a percentage of GDP in 1977; G = average annual growth rates of real GDP, 1974-82; GAP = GDP-productivity-gap, that is, average annual growth rates in GDP per persons employed, 1974-82; I = employment in industrial sector as a percentage of total employment, 1973; LS = labor supply, that is, average annual growth rates in total labor force, 1974-82; U = average rate of unemployment, 1968-73; W = wage differentiation in manufacturing sector, that is, ratio of wages paid in highest-wage and lowest-wage branches in manufacturing industries, 1978 (ISIC Major Division 3, at 3-digit level). Data were taken from the International Labor Organization.

‡Computed from the regression equation $Y = 3.18 + .372 (X)$, $R^2 = .038$. Y = average rate of unemployment, 1974-82; X = number of obstacles to full employment. Negative signs indicate levels of unemployment that are too low, relative to the number of obstacles to full employment.

§Average rate of unemployment, 1974-82, minus average rate of unemployment, 1968-73.

‖Computed from the regression equation $Y = 1.81 + .093 (X)$, $R^2 = .005$. Y = average rate of unemployment, 1974-82, minus average rate of unemployment, 1968-73; X = number of obstacles to full employment. Negative signs indicate that the level of and the increase in the rate of unemployment are too low, relative to the number of obstacles to full employment.

were by no means in a better position than the nations that were plagued by mass unemployment. Austria, Norway, Sweden, Switzerland, and also Japan have managed to maintain too much full employment, relative to the strength of pressure that was generated by structural-economic characteristics of these nations. Conversely, the rates of unemployment in the majority of the mass-unemployment countries have been too high, relative to structural-economic circumstances.[3] It is this differential responsiveness of rates of unemployment to structural-economic problems that requires explanation. Following recent political-institutionalist contributions to the comparative study of public policy and macroeconomic performance,[4] I will argue that the variation in

3. Similar results—not reported here—can be obtained for separate regressions of single economic-structural indicators on rates of unemployment.

4. See, for example, David R. Cameron, "The Expansion of the Public Economy," *American Political Science Review*, 72(4):1243-61 (Dec. 1978); Francis G. Castles, ed., *The Impact of Parties. Politics and Policies in Democratic Capitalist States* (Newbury Park, CA: Sage, 1982); Jens Alber, *Vom Armenhaus zum Wohlfahrtsstaat: Analysen zur Entwicklung der Sozialversicherung in Westeuropa* (New York: Campus, 1982); Manfred G. Schmidt, *Wohlfahrtsstaatliche Politik unter bürgerlichen und sozialdemokratischen Regierungen: Ein internationaler Vergleich* (New York: Campus, 1982); idem, "Welfare State"; Cameron, "Social Democracy"; Gerhard Lehmbruch, "Concertation and the Structure of Corporatist Networks," in *Order and Conflict*, ed. Goldthorpe, pp. 60-80; Fritz W. Scharpf, "Economic and Institutional Constraints of Full-Employment Strategies: Sweden, Austria, and West Germany, 1973-1982," in ibid., pp. 257-90; Peter J. Katzenstein, *Corporatism and Change: Austria, Switzerland, and the Politics of Industry* (Ithaca, NY: Cornell University Press, 1984); Leon N. Lindberg and Charles S. Maier, eds., *The Political Economy of Inflation and Economic Recessions* (Washington, DC: Brookings Institution, 1985).

rates of unemployment, controlling for economic-structural circumstances, can, to a fairly large extent, be accounted for by an explanation that rests on political determinants of labor markets.

POLITICAL ASPECTS OF LABOR MARKETS: THE LABOR-DOMINATED ROAD TO FULL EMPLOYMENT

With respect to economic-structural problems—such as heavy external dependence, and the presence of crisis industries and institutional rigidities that, it is commonly argued, prevent the labor market from clearing—Austria, Sweden, and Norway were not in a dramatically better position than were countries in which unemployment strongly increased (see Table 1). Despite this, the rates of unemployment in these countries remained low. Why?

It is my contention that an understanding of full employment in these countries must largely be premised on a political explanation.[5] Austria, Norway, and Sweden may be regarded as repre-

5. This section is based on OECD, *OECD Economic Surveys: Austria* (Paris: OECD, annually); idem, *OECD Economic Surveys: Norway* (Paris: OECD, annually); idem, *OECD Economic Surveys: Sweden* (Paris: OECD, annually); and on numerous contributions to the study of economic policy and labor market policy in these nations. See, for example, Franz Butschek, *Vollbeschäftigung in der Krise: Die österreichische Erfahrung 1974 bis 1979* (Vienna: Wirtschaftsverlag Dr. Orak, 1981); Günter Schmid, "Arbeitsmarktpolitik in Schweden und in der Bundesrepublik," in *Aktive Arbeitsmarktpolitik*, ed. Fritz W. Scharpf et al. (New York: Campus, 1982), pp. 29-62; Katzenstein, *Corporatism and Change;* Scharpf, "Economic and Institutional Constraints"; Manfred G. Schmidt, "The Politics of Unemployment: Rates of Unemployment and Labour Market Policy," *West European Politics,* 7(3):5-24 (July 1984); Gösta Esping-Andersen, *Politics against Markets* (Princeton, NJ: Princeton University Press, 1985).

senting the major examples of a labor-dominated full-employment policy process. In these nations, trade unions are highly organized, politically united, and ideologically moderate. Moreover, they have participated in tripartite corporatist arrangements over a long period and have consequently been successful in institutionalizing their power. Measured by indicators of working-class mobilization and Social Democratic parties' participation in government, the Austrian, Norwegian, and Swedish labor movements are exceptionally strong. In these countries, a balance of class forces has been characteristic of the structure of industrial relations, the distribution of power in parliament, and the prevailing ideological hegemony. Ideologically, solidaristic Social Democratic values are strongly emphasized on the part of the electorate and on the part of the majority of the political elites. Relationships between unions, employers, and the state tend to be based on the principles of compromise and equal exchange—or, at least, on an institutionalized stalemate between collective actors too powerful to be coerced into acquiescence—and these principles also influence the timing and the content of economic and labor market policy. To a large extent, full employment in these countries is an aspect of the prevailing political orthodoxy. Thus the political strategy of whatever party is in office aims at maintaining high levels of employment.

Institutional conditions, such as the relative high degree of policy coordination across policy areas and the low degree of autonomy on the part of the central bank, have facilitated the formation and implementation of fiscal-monetary-incomes policy mixes oriented toward full employment. The instru-ments that were adopted for the purpose of maintaining high levels of employment varied from country to country.

Among the major characteristics of Norwegian full-employment policy, the long tradition of, and the expertise in, global demand management and fine-tuning the economy deserve to receive major attention. The Norwegian authorities have continued to attach the highest priority to the maintenance of full employment and have been more or less successful in offsetting recessionary tendencies emanating from abroad by sharply raising levels of domestic demand, expanding employment opportunities in the public sector, introducing or extending flexible industrial policy measures, and maintaining a protectionist shelter for rural areas and regions with a stronger primary sector.

In Sweden, a wide range of selective or active labor market policy measures have been used to combat unemployment, while coordination of fiscal, monetary, and wage policy has been weaker than in Austria. Swedish labor market policy was estimated to have reduced the potential rate of unemployment by more than four percentage points per year. In addition, the extraordinarily strong increase in employment in the public sector more than offset employment losses in the private market economy.

In contrast to Sweden, the employment policy approach that the Austrian authorities, supported by the trade unions and employers' associations, chose in the 1970s emphasized the importance of a capitalist growth policy, based in a highly developed coordination of expansionary fiscal policy, moderately expansionary monetary policy, incomes policy, and wage restraint and complemented by short-term work measures and bans on overtime work and labor-hoarding practices in the private sector and, in particular, in the nationalized industries. In contrast to Norway and Sweden, the control of labor supply played an important role in the Austrian full-employment policy. Early-retirement schemes for older workers and, in particular, restrictive foreign labor policy carried a larger part of the burden involved in the management of the economic crisis. With full support from the powerful trade unions, the foreign labor force's share of total employment was reduced from 8.7 percent in 1973 to 5.3 percent in 1983.

As far as the division of responsibility for the maintenance of full employment in Austria, Norway, and Sweden is concerned, the public sector carried a major part of the burden that the economic problems of the 1970s generated. By international comparison, the growth of employment in the public sector in these countries has been very strong. Thus the Austrian, the Norwegian, and the Swedish road to full employment rests largely on an active interventionist role of the state and on job-creating capacities of the public sector. It is the Social Democratization of the state and of the civil society in these countries that has generated determined efforts to maintain full employment.

POLITICAL ASPECTS OF
LABOR MARKETS: THE
CONSERVATIVE-REFORMIST
ROAD TO FULL EMPLOYMENT

Similar outcomes may have different causes. It has not universally been the case that the maintenance of full employment in the 1970s and 1980s mirrors a labor-dominated policy process. Full employment can also result from a policy process that is dominated by conser-

vative-reformist tendencies such as that in Japan and Switzerland.

The Japanese case

When the Japanese economy entered the recession of the 1970s the efforts to maintain high levels of employment were facilitated by a variety of structural characteristics of the economy, such as less external dependence and high levels of wage differentiation and wage flexibility.[6] In addition, growth in real GDP continued to be higher than elsewhere in the OECD area, and this has facilitated growth in employment. However, relative to excessively high growth in the 1950s and 1960s, a striking feature of the Japanese labor market performance in the 1970s and early 1980s has been its "apparent relative immunity to weaker growth of the economy."[7]

It is my contention that an explanation of the relative immunity to historically weaker growth must be based largely on the private-public policy mix in Japan. While full employment in Austria, Norway, and Sweden is based on the ideological and political power of labor and its corporatist and state interventionist correlates, the Japanese case of full employment rests on the dominance of nonsocialist tendencies, the weakness and incohesiveness of the Left, a weak and strongly decentralized trade union movement, and the existence of a strong bilateral relationship between the state bureaucracy and the business community. With respect to employment, we are confronted with a dual economy.

6. This section is based on OECD, *OECD Economic Surveys: Japan* (Paris: OECD, annually) and on numerous studies on the Japanese labor market.
7. OECD, *OECD Economic Surveys: Japan* (1983), p. 36.

The weaker sector of this economy carries a major part of the burden involved in managing economic recessions. The modern sector of this economy is strongly influenced by semi- and precapitalistic rules of conduct for leadership and cooperation, which have been transmitted from the past and have been successfully amalgamated with a "creative conservatism"[8] among policymakers. Determined efforts to promote economic growth at all costs, including the devaluation of the yen in the mid-1970s, elimination of excess capacity in structurally depressed industries, and incentives given to the modernization of the industrial structure, coincide with the commitment to maintain high levels of employment on the part of the government and the business community. Japanese authorities were willing to go along with the most advanced European practice with respect to maintaining full employment by means of expansionary demand management, increases in public indebtedness, selective aid to industry and individual firms, and selective labor market policy but drew the line at expanding public sector employment and assistance to depressed areas and industries.

Low rates of unemployment in Japan have also been due to a variety of private labor market policy measures. Labor-hoarding practices, lifetime employment systems, cuts in overtime work, and extensive reallocation of workers within broad internal labor markets of larger companies tended to stabilize employment at least in the short run. Thus, for example, the Japanese economy was estimated to retain a surprising amount of excess labor—some 6 percent

of the total labor force—at the expense of productivity.[9] In addition, flexible adjustments of income to productivity levels, the acceptance of mobility requirements, and the willingness of wage earners to forgo wage increases or even to take wage cuts have strongly facilitated the rapid "positive adjustment"[10] of the Japanese economy.

Last but not least, it should be emphasized that the Japanese unemployment statistics tend to underestimate the underlying weakness in the Japanese labor market. Thus, for example, unemployment statistics do not fully mirror the high cyclical sensitivity of labor supply. According to estimates, the rates of unemployment among female workers are not at some 2 percent but, in reality, almost twice as high as the figures that are originally published.

It is thus in a threefold sense that the Japanese policy of full employment differs from the labor-dominated road to full employment of Scandinavian or Austrian origin. First, there is a wide range of differences in the underlying political structure of full-employment policy. Second, the Japanese full-employment record rests almost exclusively on the rapid expansion of employment in the market sector. Buoyant recruitment of labor in the private market economy is partly attributable to private labor market policy on the part of large firms, but it mainly reflects the considerable support that the market economy receives from public policy. Third, the Japanese labor market performance, defined in terms of conventional labor market indicators, is some-

8. T. J. Pempel, *Policy and Politics in Japan: Creative Conservatism* (Philadelphia: Temple University Press, 1982).

9. Koji Taira, "Japan's Unemployment: Economic Miracle or Statistical Artifact?" *Monthly Labor Review*, 106(7):36 (July 1983).

10. OECD, *Positive Adjustment Policies: Managing Structural Change* (Paris: OECD, 1983).

what weaker than is the performance of the Norwegian and Swedish labor markets. Thus, for example, the growth in total employment and the growth in labor force participation ratios in the period between 1973 and 1982 were weaker in Japan than they were in Sweden and Norway. Moreover, hidden unemployment in Japan seems to be larger than in other full-employment countries, except Switzerland. In this respect, the Japanese case of full employment partly resembles the Swiss road to full employment.

The Swiss road to
full employment

Measured by levels of open unemployment, the Swiss labor market's record is exceptionally good. From the end of the 1930s till the early 1980s unemployment has been virtually close to zero. It was not before 1984 that the rate of unemployment reached an all-time high of 1.0 percent. The Swiss full-employment record does not readily lend itself to the explanations and generalizations that have been prevalent in the literature on political and economic determinants of rates of unemployment so far.[11] The unions and the Social Democratic Party are weak, but wages are high. Although wages are high, the rate of inflation is low. And although price increases are exceptionally moderate, and although monetary policy follows a restrictive monetaristic policy stance, and despite the absence of fully developed demand management, full employment is among the most conspicuous characteristic of the Swiss labor market.

11. For a study of the Swiss case, see Manfred G. Schmidt, *Der schweizerische Weg zur Vollbeschäftigung* (Frankfurt: Campus, 1985).

Moreover, the low rate of unemployment in Switzerland is not amenable to a structural explanation. Although a number of factors, such as the absence of large-scale basic industries with heavy adjustment problems, proved themselves to be a major asset in Swiss economic policy, efforts to maintain full employment were confronted with major structural problems, such as heavy external dependence of the economy, concentration of employment in the industrial sector, and major adjustment problems on the part of the clock and jewelry industry and the construction and building industries. In addition, the dramatic decrease in GDP volume in the mid-1970s, itself largely due to an extremely tough stabilization policy, contributed to the economic malaise. However, the rate of unemployment remained at an exceptionally low level.

Why is the Swiss rate of unemployment low? In periods of economic recession, full employment in Switzerland consists of a balance between the rapid decline in the demand for labor and a rapid downward adjustment in the supply of labor. This contrasts sharply with the labor market performance of other full-employment countries. The Swiss notion of full employment is of a selective nature. In political terms the Swiss road to full employment rests on a conservative-reformist model of social partnership between unions, employers, and the state that is dominated by nonsocialist tendencies. However, the norms and the style of conflict resolution that guide the decision-making process are strongly influenced by consociational techniques, concerns about the political integration of labor, and strategies that attempt to maintain the high level of consensus that has emerged in Switzerland since the mid-1930s. The priority that is given to the maintenance of job security for nationals—Swiss labor and foreign workers with a permanent residence permit—is an aspect of the political exchange between government, unions, and employers' associations.

In terms of policy, full employment in Switzerland is based on a policy mix. The mix comprises market-oriented, liberal policies and a limited role of the state in demand management, on the one hand, and on the other hand, an active, directing, and interventionist role of the state in sectors that are of strategic importance in the efforts to maintain job security for nationals. Among the major examples of the latter role are the control of foreign labor supply and the protectionist umbrella placed over rural areas.

In addition, low rates of unemployment in periods of economic crisis are attributable to high cyclical sensitivity to labor supply on the part of Swiss female workers. As far as the dismissal and recruitment of labor are concerned, Swiss entrepreneurs have considerable room for maneuver. This is basically due to the weak legal protection of job security for disadvantaged labor market groups, and it also mirrors the fact that the control of foreign labor supply and the retreat of female workers from the labor market are regarded as politically, socially, and culturally acceptable. In addition, the control of labor supply was complemented by a wide variety of selective labor market policy schemes, such as extensive utilization of short-term work allowances, reforms of the apprenticeship system, and measures that were targeted to economically weak regions.

Although the Swiss public authorities have restricted the applicability of full employment in periods of economic recessions to nationals, in particular to male nationals, the policy stance that was adopted differs from the course of action that was chosen in many other countries. The priority that was given to the control of inflationary pressure resulted in a dramatic decrease in the level of total employment in the mid-1970s, but the conscious effort to maintain low levels of unemployment in the domestic labor market sharply separates Switzerland from a large number of other OECD countries in which the economic recessions of the 1970s and 1980s had a fairly direct and strong impact on the rate of unemployment. However, the Swiss road to full employment also separates the *Eidgenossenschaft* ("Swiss Confederation") from the full-employment concept of Scandinavian and Austrian origin. The latter countries' labor market performance can be regarded as real full employment. In contrast to this, the Swiss case constitutes a unique pattern of selective full employment.

CONCLUSION

I have argued that there have been two roads to full employment or near full employment in the 1970s and 1980s. In political terms, full employment is first and foremost the outcome of a labor-dominated policy process of the kind found in Austria, Norway, and Sweden. The strong and conscious efforts to maintain full employment in these countries is largely due to the institutionalized power of the labor movement. The power of labor and the willingness on the part of the public authorities to pursue full-employment-oriented policies proved themselves to be sufficiently strong to keep the rate of unemployment far below the average level of unemployment in the OECD countries. However, full employment, in the sense of low rates of open unemployment, can also result from a policy process that is dominated by conservative-reformist tendencies, such as that in Switzerland and in Japan. Low rates of unemployment in the latter group of countries are largely attributable to a variety of strategies on the part of political elites that are characterized by paternalistic traditions and techniques of consensus building and preventive crisis management.

While the outcomes, defined in terms of rates of registered unemployment, are similar, the labor-dominated road to full employment differs from the conservative-reformist one in a number of respects. The labor-dominated road involves a rapid expansion in the number of full-time and part-time jobs in the public sector. In contrast to this, the conservative-reformist road to full employment is based on strong growth rates in employment in the private market economy, as in Japan, or on the rapid adjustment of labor supply to the decrease in the demand for labor, as in Switzerland, and on low growth rates in public sector employment. Moreover, the labor-dominated full-employment countries have been more successful than nations that are characterized by a conservative-reformist approach to full employment: the overall labor market performance, defined in terms of rates of unemployment, total employment growth, and level and change of labor force participation ratios, was better in the labor-dominated nations, in particular in Sweden and in Norway, than in the conservative-reformist countries. The difference may partly be attributable to differences in the nature of structural problems, to which the full-employment countries found themselves exposed. For

example, the Swiss policymakers were in a more difficult situation vis-à-vis structural-economic problems than the governments in Japan, Austria, Norway, and Sweden (see Table 1). However, the bulk of the difference between the two groups of full-employment countries, and the bulk of the difference between the full-employment countries and nations that were plagued by mass unemployment,[12] can largely be explained by differences in the distribution of power, differences in the interaction between the state and the economy, and differences in the willingness to pursue a policy of real full employment.

One of the messages that can be derived from the analysis is this: in contrast to the 1930s, when the world-wide recession resulted in dramatic increases in the rate of unemployment in Western democracies, and when the authoritarian regimes in Japan and in Germany were the earliest examples of successful efforts to regain full employment, the labor market performance in Austria, Norway, Sweden, Japan, and Switzerland in the 1970s and 1980s suggests that democratic regimes are, in

12. Mass unemployment was only implicitly covered in this article. I have argued elsewhere that the emergence of mass unemployment in the OECD countries in the 1970s is associated with and, by inference, is attributable to a variety of political circumstances, such as the absence of a longer history of full employment, unstructured confrontation between labor and capital, dominance of nonsocialist and non-paternalistic-reformist parties in government, politically weak unions or unions that are organizationally and ideologically incohesive, absence of cross-sectoral patterns of policy coordination, high priority of control of inflationary pressure, and a high degree of autonomy on the part of the central bank. See Manfred G. Schmidt, "The Politics of Labour Market Policy," in *Managing Mixed Economies*, ed. Franz Lehner, Francis G. Castles, and Manfred G. Schmidt (Berlin: DeGruyter, forthcoming).

principle, capable of maintaining full employment, or near-full employment, within the context of adverse economic circumstances.[13]

Another message that one can derive from the analysis is this: the nature and number of economic-structural obstacles to full-employment policy are important factors in any effort that is geared toward explaining international differences in unemployment rates, but the major part of the cross-national variation mirrors the impact that the distribution of political power among collective actors, political ideology, strategies, and institutions has on the timing and the content of economic and labor market policy. Thus the key to an understanding of international differences in labor market imbalances is to be found in the political aspects of full employment and mass unemployment.

13. See, for example, Peter A. Gourevitch, "Breaking with Orthodoxy: The Politics of Economic Policy Responses to the Depression of the 1930's," *International Organization*, 38(1):95-130 (Winter 1984).

ANNALS, *AAPSS*, **492**, July 1987

Toward Global Action

By BERTRAM GROSS

ABSTRACT: Despite the world's rising unemployment and underemployment, the United Nations has deserted its earlier commitments to full employment. This reflects the attitudes of most member states. In turn, economists have failed to measure the full labor surplus, analyze it globally, or update earlier full-employment concepts. Fortunately, new quality-of-life employment proposals in the U.S. Congress provide a political impetus for improved data analysis and policymaking in the United States. Its sponsors also urge regional and global fact-finding conferences under U.N. auspices. This would require new-style expert appraisals. Such appraisals might well indicate that joblessness, underemployment, and job insecurity (1) affect the majority of people in every region of the world; (2) have enormous economic and social consequences; (3) undermine the purchasing power and productivity needed to reverse economic stagnation and prevent collapse; and (4) are used to justify arms escalation as a way of providing jobs.

Bertram Gross was executive secretary of President Truman's Council of Economic Advisors and key draftsman of the bills leading to the Employment Act of 1946 and the Full Employment and Balanced Growth Act of 1978. He is now Distinguished Professor Emeritus, Hunter College, City University of New York; visiting professor in peace and conflict studies, University of California, Berkeley; and professor at large, Saint Mary's College, Moraga, California. Among his books are Friendly Fascism *and* Social Intelligence for America's Future, *based on issues of* The Annals *of the American Academy of Political and Social Science (May and September 1967).*

THE full employment pledge in the United Nations Charter marks a historic phase in the evolution of the modern conception of the functions and responsibilities of the democratic state. . . . It reflects the fundamental importance of the promotion of full employment . . . first, as a condition of economic and social progress . . . and secondly, as a necessary prerequisite for the maintenance and smooth working of an international economic system."[1]

As World War II ended the Great Depression of 1929-39, many people in Western Europe and America feared that victory in war would be followed by another depression. To prevent such a calamity, President Franklin Roosevelt's planning board proposed a postwar economic bill of rights, based on the right to a job at fair wages, in "a jural world order outlawing imperialism, old or new-fashioned." In January 1944, Roosevelt embodied most of these ideas in an economic-bill-of-rights message to Congress.[2] A little later Sir William Beveridge proposed full employment as a postwar goal for Britain. Full employment soon became "a flag around which every one could rally."[3] In the United States the flag was unfurled in a full-employment bill that tried to translate rhetorical pledges into statutory obligations. This measure was strongly opposed by those parts of the business community that saw, accurately, that while full employment would provide larger mar-

kets for their products it would also strengthen labor and weaken corporate power. The bill was finally passed as the Employment Act of 1946. In essence, this law committed the federal government not to full employment but to preventing mass depression.[4]

In 1945, while this debate was unfolding in the United States, Article 55 of the U.N. Charter, over objections from U.S. conservatives, committed its members to promote full employment. In 1948 the United Nations' Universal Declaration of Human Rights strengthened this commitment; as stated in Article 23: "Everyone has the right to work, to free choice of employment, to just and favorable conditions of work and to protection against unemployment." The 1949 U.N. Group of Experts proposed policies to make these rights a reality.

For a while the flag kept waving. But throughout the following decades, the idea of a right, or entitlement, was abandoned in most capitalist countries outside of Scandinavia. In place of a commitment to full employment, governments pacify the jobless through unemployment compensation, welfare payments, and training for jobs that do not exist. They tend to ignore the employment-expansion roles of fiscal and monetary policy and of specific programs in such vital areas as health, education, housing, conservation, mass transportation, and public works and services. Tiny job-creation efforts tend to concentrate on such small and weak constituencies as the youth, at the expense of the nonyoung; the narrowly

1. U.N. Group of Experts, *National and International Measures for Full Employment*, E 1584 (New York: United Nations, 1949). The members of the group were John Maurice Clark, Nicholas Kaldor, Arthur Smithies, Pierre Uri, and E. Ronald Walker.

2. State-of-the-union message, 20 Jan. 1944.

3. Herbert Stein, *The Fiscal Revolution in America* (Chicago: University of Chicago Press, 1969), p. 171.

4. Bertram M. Gross and Jeffrey D. Straussman, "'Full' Employment Growthmanship and the Growth of the Labor Supply," *The Annals* of the American Academy of Political and Social Science (Mar. 1975).

defined poor, usually excluding the employed poor and the jobless nonpoor; or localistic action that moves employment from one region to another. Meanwhile, the concept of full employment has widely been redefined, as will be discussed in the next section. "Frictional unemployment" has been widely replaced by "natural unemployment."

In turn, policies to help developing countries often provide greater help to transnational corporations. Foreign aid may tax the poor in rich countries to aid and enrich the rich in poor countries. The impressive rhetoric of growth, development, and basic needs is often used in a manner that distracts from the healthy growth and development that could use un- and underemployed labor in meeting basic needs through useful employment. The reality of interdependence among nations is ignored, as discussions of developing countries proceed on the bland assumption that high goals can be obtained without structural changes within both developed and developing societies.

The subject of full employment has not yet been fully addressed by the Organization for Economic Cooperation and Development. Under statist socialism, where people are guaranteed a job, unemployment takes the form of hidden underemployment; in bloated bureaucracies people receive wages that they do not really earn. While market socialist efforts to reduce padded payrolls bring some of this hidden unemployment into the open, the Council for Mutual Economic Assistance follows the example of the Organization for Economic Cooperation and Development in dodging the subject. In the Third World, the Committee of 77 and the nonaligned movement touch on it cautiously. In his 1983 report to the nonaligned movement,

Fidel Castro gingerly proclaimed that "880 million jobs in the underdeveloped countries" are needed by the year 2000.[5] But he confined himself to the old-style Third World pattern of trade and aid. He studiously avoided any discussion of economic rights or planning for full employment, a subject on which Third World regimes are deeply divided. The latest nonaligned meeting concentrated on the debt crisis and stayed even further away from the other issues involved in creating useful employment.

As a combined result of these national and transnational orientations, full-employment commitments have been ignominiously deserted by the U.N. Secretariat. Most U.N. agencies, even those originally set up to promote full employment, now keep secret both the United Nations' full-employment commitments and the realities of unemployment and underemployment. Some actively support transnational corporate actions that sharpen the hushed-up crisis. Nor have many signatories to the United Nations' more recent Covenant on Economic and Social Rights been very ardent in support of the full-employment commitments formally restated in the covenant.

HIDING LABOR SUPPLY AND SURPLUS

The notion of measuring the labor supply, or the unused position of labor supply as a residual, was abandoned [in the 1940 U.S. Census]. . . . There was no demand for a measure of total supply as such, probably because labor supply seemed abundant for all possible demands.[6]

5. Fidel Castro, "The World Economic and Social Crisis" (Report to the Seventh Summit Conference of Non-Aligned Countries, Havana, 1983).

6. Gertrude Bancroft, *The American Labor*

The current definition of unemployment captures only the tip of the iceberg of potential workers; it is itself part of a grand cover-up of the shortage of jobs.[7]

Although statistics do not lie, liars can use both statistics and statisticians. Some of the most effective misinformation is provided by honest statisticians who apply concepts that serve the interests of the dominant forces in society. Indeed, the propensity of many social scientists—not only statisticians—is to prefer, as Kurt Rothschild once pointed out, being precisely wrong rather than vaguely right.

During the Great Depression battles raged around the world on how to measure the unemployment "iceberg." In Europe and England, unions reported on their unemployed members and unemployment insurance offices reported on the people receiving benefits. In the United States, with few unions and no social insurance, the field was wide open. One highly respected economist from the Brookings Institution estimated unemployment in a historic analysis of America's productive capacity.[8] For 1929, the peak year of pre-depression prosperity, he estimated unemployment at 19 percent. Percent of what? Of the "gainfully occupied"—a concept very close to the total supply of available labor. In 1937, the federal government's National Resources Committee estimated that, on the basis of "full time equivalents," unemployment

during the years 1932-34 averaged 45 percent of the total available labor supply.

But the political demand during the depression, a period of extreme job shortage, was not for a measure based on the total available labor supply. As Gertrude Bancroft later pointed out, "There was no demand for a measure of total supply as such"—or even for a measure of the total labor surplus. Rather, the demand was for data that "would understate the degree of unemployment and thereby vindicate the effectiveness of government programs of job creation."[9] A group of brilliant technicians, including Gertrude Bancroft, met this demand by inventing the "labor force." This artifact included as unemployed only the jobless of 16 years of age and over who were reported as actively seeking paid employment. This excluded millions of jobless who were not in the labor force—people who, although able and willing to work for pay, were not reported as actively seeking it. If a similar method were used to estimate the number of unmarried people, no singles—not even Catholic priests—would be unmarried unless reported as actively seeking a spouse. The "labor force" also excluded many other groups: people working only an hour or two, who were classified as employed; those receiving public assistance or special job training; those in institutions, which were often a haven for the jobless; those under 16; and, until recently, those working in the armed services.

Ironically, the labor force concept was first used in the 1940 census, just as World War II was unfolding and the

Force (New York: John Wiley, 1958), pp. 185-88.

7. Frank F. Furstenberg, Jr., and Charles A. Thrall, "Counting the Jobless: The Impact of Job Rationing on the Measure of Unemployment," The Annals of the American Academy of Political and Social Science (Mar. 1975).

8. Edwin G. Nourse, America's Capacity to Produce (Washington, DC: Brookings Institution, 1942).

9. Stanley Moses, "Labor Supply Concepts: The Political Economy of Conceptual Change," The Annals of the American Academy of Political and Social Science (Mar. 1975).

United States would soon have to mobilize its unmeasured labor reserves. Eight million people not in the labor force were quickly drawn into it. But with victory, the specter of massive joblessness returned. Postwar policies sent women back into the home, older people into retirement, young people to tertiary education, and many ethnic minorities into ghettos. The labor force concept came into its own, with many commissions and agencies involved in technical improvements. The U.N. statistical offices labored mightily to apply the concept in as many countries as possible. They succeeded beyond all expectation—except in socialist countries, where there was no demand for any measure of labor wasted through the underemployment of paid labor. Their greatest success was in developing countries, where the best economists knew it was nonsense—since it could not cope with massive underemployment—but where the leaders relished statistics that would understate the horror of their vast populations.

In earlier years, full employment was often defined as a situation in which there are job opportunities for everyone able and willing to work for pay. This was close to Sir William Beveridge's original definition: a situation in which more employers seek workers than people seek employment. So for a while, the essence of full-employment planning was to set goals for the number of people to be employed—as, for example, in President Roosevelt's famous goal of 60 million postwar civilian jobs. Later, as more conventional minds prevailed, the idea of employment goals was buried. A new approach became dominant: measuring full employment by the amount of frictional—and then natural—unemployment. In the United States this measure tended to rise over the decades.

In the 1940s, tolerable full employment was 2-3 percent unemployment; in the 1950s, 3-4 percent; in the 1960s, 3-5 percent; in the 1970s, 4-6 percent; in the 1980s, 6-8 percent. In the 1990s it could be 9-10 percent, and the figure for the year 2000 could rise to 10-12 percent.

Generally, rising rates of unemployment were publicly justified by the entry of more women, younger people, and ethnic minorities into the labor force and by the presumed need for more unemployment and recessions to control inflation by preventing wage increases or, when inflation had already been reduced, to raise profit rates by repressing wage rates and fringe benefits. Behind all these justifications, however, lay a more sober definition of full employment, as often lamented by Representative Augustus Hawkins, chair of the House Labor and Education Committee: the highest level of unemployment that is politically tolerable.

To some degree, larger or smaller, all of the previous observations apply to First World countries, particularly England and nations in Western Europe. In most of these countries, the U.S. statistical method of underestimating the number of jobless has long been followed, although a few have used their own devices in hushing the subject. But the biggest cover-up—partly based on ostrich-style statistics—is found in Third World countries. Anyone slightly familiar with Asia, West Asia—anachronistically called the Middle East—Africa, Latin America, and the Caribbean knows that each of these areas is plagued by staggering job shortages. Moreover, each suffers from all the many forms of underemployment—farmers and farm workers who are jobless nine months of the year, urban peddlers thronging the streets all day long and making but an occasional sale, college graduates working at poverty wages in jobs far below their skill level, office and factory workers who stretch out two hours of work to fill an entire day so that they will not work themselves out of a job.

Back in the 1950s the U.S. labor force concept—never intended for application to Third World countries—was imposed on them by U.N. experts seeking worldwide uniformity in statistical concepts. This laudable goal might have been achieved if they had tried to develop generally applicable concepts of labor supply and labor surplus. Yet labor experts around the world tended to accept unemployment reports based on the labor force concept. Thus the *1985 Report on the World Social Situation* reports that "the numbers openly unemployed have swelled."[10] From 1973 to 1980, "open unemployment" rose 175 percent in Egypt, 180 percent in Indonesia and Thailand, 140 percent in India, and 100 percent in Brazil. The report also states that such figures "convey little of the immediate crisis or of the longer term prospects." One justification is the lack of reliable estimates on underemployment and the informal, or underground, sectors. Another—often stated privately but not publicly—is that serious work to develop estimates of the full labor surplus might suggest the need for fundamental restructuring of development policies.

QUALITY-OF-LIFE EMPLOYMENT: A NEW APPROACH

Employment is a basic right, a right which protects the freedom of all to participate in the economic life of society.[11]

In the United States, 67 members of the Congress have taken an important step toward updating earlier full-employment goals. Their proposed quality-of-life action act would require the president to submit to Congress every year a short- and long-term program for quality-of-life employment. It also mandates certain principles that might be used in coping with—and measuring—the labor surplus in other countries as well as the United States.

The first principles transcend necessary technicalities and rise to the level of economic rights. The old "right to a job" is replaced by the "right to earn a living," a formulation that suggests much more than merely being on a payroll. Also, the measure recognizes the right of those unable to work for pay or find a suitable job to "an adequate standard of living that rises with the wealth and productivity of the society."

Second, the quality-of-life action act puts job and income rights in the context of comprehensive quality-of-life action. It links such action with "environmental protection, better opportunities for small business and family farmers, civil rights and liberties, and personal and national security."

Third, it mandates the creation of millions of more jobs by lowering the hours of paid work without lowering take-home income. This would help compensate for the labor-displacing impact of increased labor productivity, while also increasing opportunities for the voluntary leisure needed for fuller participation in decision making in the household, workplace, neighborhood, and nation. -

Fourth, in place of the old Keynesian idea that any growth is O.K., it calls for

10. United Nations, Secretariat, Department of International and Social Affairs, *1985 Report on the World Social Situation,* E/CN.51985/2 (New York: United Nations, 1985).

11. U.S. Catholic Bishops, *Economic Justice*

for All (Washington, DC: National Conference of Catholic Bishops, 1986).

a focused "industrial policy" in tune with the new service society. Industry is to be revived through planning for more and better goods in transport, public works, housing, and materials recycling. More and better services are to be encouraged in child care, education, training, health, basic science, and repair facilities. This policy puts real teeth into recent neoliberal proposals. It aims at the more meaningful work that yields needed goods and services and challenges the creativity of both employees and employers.

Fifth, the act mandates large-scale federal aid for local public works, community renewal, economic development, and environmental protection. Localities would develop high-priority, short-term projects with the perspective of quality-of-life goals through the year 2000. These would be backed up by openly debated assessments of unmet needs, labor-availability surveys, and the mobilization of funds from both private and public sources. The emphasis on vigorous participation by all private sectors—unions, the unemployed, neighborhood groups, religious organizations, and smaller as well as larger businesses—could go a long way toward eliminating what Samuel Bowles and Herbert Gintis call "the political wasteland between the individual and the state."[12]

Sixth, without authorizing a single new dollar in appropriations, the act requires a total reconstruction of the U.S. budget's present expenditures of over $1 trillion. Money is to be mobilized not only by reducing wasteful or unnecessary military spending and eliminating the many tax loopholes untouched by the 1986 tax law, but also by using pension funds to initiate development bank investment in urban and rural

areas. Federal budget processes are to be modernized by subordinating them to full-employment goals. Provision is also made for long-overdue reforms to squeeze some of the mystery and nonsense out of federal budgeting: a federal capital budget, a national wealth inventory, net outlay budgeting, total impact studies, and use of both constant and current dollars in debt and deficit estimates.

Seventh, the act mandates a Conversion Planning Fund to be financed by 1 percent of all military spending. Unlike other conversion proposals, it is not limited to conversion from military employment, which has been expanding. Dealing also with conversion from steel, auto, and other civilian industries that have been declining, it focuses on projects for expanded economic activity wherever more or better goods and services are needed.

Eighth, the act mandates policies to stem the flight of capital and jobs to other countries. Aid to the International Monetary Fund or World Bank is to be contingent on their reversing present austerity policies and working to raise the wages and incomes of the poor in Third World countries. Also under the act, any direct or indirect assistance would be withdrawn from American companies or foreign countries that keep foreign wages down by denying collective bargaining rights or persecuting labor unions. This adds a new dimension to present debates on free versus fair trade.

Finally, the act calls for fact-finding conferences—both global and regional—on uncovering the magnitudes of the immediate crisis and the longer-term prospects with respect to the world's waste of labor resources. Continued improvements in the United Nations' world social-situation reports could help in this effort.

12. *Democracy and Capitalism* (New York: Basic Books, 1986).

THE JOBLESS: A MAJORITY ISSUE

Franklin Roosevelt once said, "We have learned that we must live as men, and not as ostriches."[13]

Before the introduction of the quality-of-life action act, many labor, minority, and research organizations in the United States used official unemployment estimates to prove that official unemployment was a serious minority problem. They showed that unemployment has generally been higher than the average for women maintaining families; for black, Hispanic, and Native American men; for all teenagers; and particularly for minority teenagers. They pointed out that all the average figures are higher in urban ghettos and in those depression regions hit by plant closings, declining industries, agricultural foreclosures, or rural stagnation. Occasionally, they supported local studies that used the official definitions more carefully than the federal data collectors did. Thus a door-to-door survey in Youngstown, Ohio, by a university center for urban studies revealed 29.3 percent unemployment in this depressed area as against the federal report of only 15.2 percent.[14] They also used some of the data collected by the government but never included in the government's reports on total unemployment. Thus the American Federation of Labor and Congress of Industrial Organizations has regularly added two categories to the category of officially unemployed: part-timers seeking full-time work, and the discouraged outside the labor force. The Council on International and Public Affairs has regularly left out the first of these two categories but has included the discouraged and also added job wanters not in the labor force. It has also demonstrated that the large increase in service employment—often hailed by Europeans as the American miracle—has been mainly in the lowest-paying sectors and often at wages below the poverty level.[15] Such facts help explain why, despite the enormous wealth of the United States, an estimated 35 to 40 million people live in poverty.

More recently, however, the sponsors of the quality-of-life action act have gone much further. Pulling their heads out of the sand completely, they have started to deal with the full labor supply and the full labor surplus. In doing this, they demonstrate that joblessness is a majority issue. They now

—use all three sets of government unemployment data not included in the official unemployment statistics, namely, part-time employees seeking full-time work, the discouraged jobless, and job wanters outside the labor force;

—estimate as probably twice the number of jobless those employees whose wages, working conditions, and job security are undermined by the many jobless people willing to replace them; and

—estimate an average of at least one full or partial dependent for each of the total jobless and those suffering from bad jobs and job insecurity.

This approach is also applicable to the many other countries in which official data underestimate the total number of jobless, ignore the impact of joblessness on wages and job security, and rather blindly take no account whatever

13. State-of-the-union message, 20 Jan. 1944.

14. *Daily Labor Report* (Bureau of National Affairs), 5 Nov. 1984.

15. *The Underbelly of the U.S. Economy: Joblessness and Pauperization of Work in America* (New York: Council on International and Public Affairs, 1986).

of dependents. It has thus far yielded the estimates shown in Table 1 for the United States for 1986.

In urban ghettos and depressed localities, the total proportion of direct victims of joblessness, as defined in Table 1, surely exceeds 71 percent of the population. Throughout the country, moreover, a few million businesspeople suffer from the fact that the jobless and the working poor are bad customers, tenants, and creditors. This is partly measured by the rising rates—particularly among small businesses—of bankruptcy and failure.

There have been no attempts yet, however, to calculate statistical estimates of the full social cost of joblessness, bad jobs, job insecurity, and the various forms of underemployment. The most obvious impacts are reductions in self-respect, skills, and physical and mental health. The consequences include more alcoholism, drug abuse, family breakdown, violence in the home and the school, lower-income crime, and suicide. Less obvious is that joblessness and bad jobs are the deepest roots of the poverty and hopelessness that produce high dropout rates in ghetto schools and undermine efforts to cope with the so-called culture of poverty through education and training alone. All this has meant massive anxieties that can be quickly exploited by demagogues. This is one of the reasons that Franklin Roosevelt warned that failure to enact an economic bill of rights could nurture "rightist reaction" and "the spirit of fascism here at home."[16]

GROWTH, PURCHASING POWER,
AND DEPRESSION

Some other statistics are a little easier to develop. Thus the Congressional

Budget Office has estimated that for fiscal year 1987 a 1 percent reduction in the number of the officially unemployed would reduce federal outlays for unemployment insurance, other entitlements, and net interest by $7.0 billion. It would also increase federal tax revenues by $37.3 billion.[17] Conversely, every 1 percent beyond some tolerable minimum means an additional $44.3 billion in the federal deficit. If account were taken of the increased outlays and reduced revenues resulting from total joblessness, underemployment, and job insecurity, this figure of $44.3 billion would certainly be higher.

Wasted labor also reduces economic growth. For over 30 years Leon Keyserling, chair of President Truman's Council of Economic Advisors, has been calculating the annual loss of gross national product resulting from official unemployment. Multiplying the millions of unemployed beyond 4 percent of the labor force by the estimated gross national product per employed worker, he calculates the lost gross national product in any one year. Over the long 1953-84 period he estimated a loss of many trillions of dollars worth of output that could have been used to provide for better health, education, housing, conservation, improved human services, and productive investment in industry.[18]

This approach also has implications for purchasing power. Fuller use of surplus labor through paid employment automatically raises the level of wage income and thus of effective demand. In Asia, West Asia, Africa, and Latin

16. State-of-the-union message, 20 Jan. 1944.

17. Letter to Representative Charles Hayes from Rudolph G. Penner, director, Congressional Budget Office, U.S. Congress, 27 Mar. 1986.

18. U.S. Congress, House Committee on Education and Labor, *Oversight Hearing on the Full Employment and Balanced Growth Act of 1978*, Testimony of Leon H. Keyserling, 99th Cong., 2d sess., 18 Mar. 1986.

TABLE 1
JOBLESSNESS IN THE UNITED STATES, 1986:
A MAJORITY ISSUE (Millions)

1. The jobless	
Job seekers (the official unemployed)	8+*
Part-time employees seeking full-time work	5+
Discouraged jobless (outside the labor force)	1+
Jobless job wanters (outside the labor force)	5+
Approximate total jobless	20
2. The underpaid and insecure (about two or three times the total jobless; rough estimate)	40 to 60
3. Full or partial dependents of the jobless, underpaid, and insecure (average of one dependent per person)	60 to 80
Total direct victims	120 to 160
Percentage of U.S. population of 242 million	50% to 66%

SOURCE: Bertram Gross, "Quality-of-Life Jobs—I: Rethinking Full Employment," *Nation*, 17 Jan. 1987, p. 46.
*Of these, 5 million receive no unemployment compensation.

America, higher levels of domestic demand would go a long way toward facilitating higher levels of domestic output and investment. Yet more employment, it is widely argued, could be inflationary by pushing up wages and labor costs—cost push—or by creating excessive demand—demand pull—or both. Unfortunately, debates on this subject have tended to ignore the complexities of labor costs, productivity, and profitability. It is to be hoped that future fact-finding on the economic consequences of the world's growing labor surplus will recognize that (1) higher wages do not mean higher labor costs if compensated for by increased productivity or absorbed through lower profit rates; (2) higher levels of output—as illustrated by the entire history of mass production—can reduce total costs per unit of output and raise total profits even if profit rates are lower; and (3) reductions in job insecurity can help eliminate work slowdowns motivated by the fear that greater productivity will mean that workers are working themselves out of a job. With such possibilities in mind, Samuel Bowles, David Gordon,

and Thomas Weisskopf have recently advocated "wage-led growth" for the United States.[19] Attention needs to be given to the possible applicability of this concept to Third World countries.

It is also desirable to recognize the risk of inflationary pressures resulting from efforts to expand employment. The response to this risk, state the U.S. Catholic bishops, "must not be to abandon the goal of full employment, but to develop effective policies that keep inflation under control."[20] This could mean coping with inflationary dangers not from excessive wage increases but also from excesses in public or private debt, speculation, hoarding, cartel activity, or monopolistic price fixing.

The waste of labor power and the resulting deficiencies in demand also have implications for the possibility of future economic collapse. This possibility has been widely seen as the outcome of a shaky banking system in which potential default by Third and Second World

19. *Beyond the Wasteland* (Garden City, NJ: Anchor, 1983).
20. U.S. Catholic Bishops, *Economic Justice for All*.

borrowers could exceed the entire capital and assets of the world's largest banks. But this view ignores possible links between the sickness of banking systems and the deeper diseases—often spread by bankers—of economies and societies, namely, untamed business cycles, long-term tendencies toward stagnation, poverty-stricken markets, high interest rates that make default more probable, and austerity policies that may help convert potentially good loans into bad ones by increasing unemployment and underemployment.

EMPLOYMENT THROUGH ARMAMENTS

[Since World War II] about 150 armed conflicts, big and small, have killed about 16 million people, perhaps as many as 20 million.

The total number of men and women currently serving in the regular armed service is estimated at about 29 million in 1983 . . . [excluding] reservists and paramilitary personnel estimated to exceed the regular armed forces.

In the early 1980s . . . roughly 50 million people were employed in meeting the demand for military goods and services.[21]

Toward the end of the eighteenth century Robert Malthus argued that war—along with famine and disease—was one of the best ways to reduce surplus population. As the first economist to introduce the idea of effective demand, he also foreshadowed Keynesian views on government deficits as a way to employ surplus labor. One wonders whether, if he were alive today, he would support the military Keynesianism that has served to reduce both the labor surplus and the population.

The United Nations' *1985 Report on the World Social Situation* presents an impressive array of facts on these matters. After reviewing data on military conflicts, deaths, forces, and spending in different parts of the world, the report also touches on how some countries have become overly dependent on the economic stimulus of armaments. "The effect on individual communities of a drop in military orders can be severe," states the report, "and has indeed provoked strong local opposition and lobbying in the past. In the United States, one might add, the military budget is sold in every state and congressional district as a job-creation program. "We're about to hit another jackpot," President Ronald Reagan boasted recently in Reno, Nevada, in defense of his new Star Wars budget, using a metaphor attuned to the world's slot machine capital. "We pulled the handle and it came up jobs, jobs, jobs." Star Wars, he argued, will open up "whole new fields of technology and industry" that would improve "the quality of life [*sic!*] in America and around the world."[22]

After identifying many effects of military spending, both positive and negative, the U.N. report provides a quick survey of "proposals for reallocating resources to civilian and development use." Most of these proposals, however, relate only to "the relationship between disarmament and development." This orientation tilts too much away from unemployment and underemployment, which often become worse with development, and from the problems of the industrially developed countries. It therefore lacks a global perspective on the challenge of joblessness and job insecurity. Also,

21. United Nations, Department of International and Social Affairs, *1985 Report on the World Social Situation.*

22. "Reagan Asserts 'Star Wars' Will Create Jobs and Better Life," *New York Times,* 31 Oct. 1986.

most of the proposals reported on relate to action after reductions in military spending rather than action to make such reductions feasible. Future U.N. work in this area should focus more broadly on arms control, development, and unemployment, with special attention to planning for healthy civilian alternatives to unnecessary or wasteful military spending.

Book Department

INTERNATIONAL RELATIONS AND POLITICS

BLAIR, BRUCE G. *Strategic Command and Control: Redefining the Nuclear Threat.* Pp. xiv, 341. Washington, DC: Brookings Institution, 1985. $32.95. Paperbound, $12.95.

LEDEEN, MICHAEL. *Grave New World: The Superpower Crisis of the 1980s.* Pp. xii, 244. New York: Oxford University Press, 1985. $17.95.

Although these two policy-oriented books are quite different in many respects, they also have several aspects in common. Most important, both argue that there are serious dangers in the present and foreseeable relationship between the United States and the Soviet Union.

The basic thesis of Blair's book is that because traditional assessments of U.S. and Soviet strategic capabilities have tended to exclude evaluations of command, control, communications, and early warning networks (C³I), they have understated U.S. vulnerabilities. On the basis of a masterfully detailed technical analysis, Blair convincingly demonstrates that U.S. C³I are extremely vulnerable. He then argues that because U.S.

C³I are so vulnerable, there is a significant risk of inadvertent war. Since a Soviet attack on U.S. C³I might cripple the U.S. ability to retaliate, there is a strong incentive for the United States to launch a large-scale retaliatory attack before the character of a Soviet nuclear attack could accurately be assessed, thus foreclosing the possibility of a limited nuclear exchange.

The argument of Ledeen's book is that U.S. and Soviet leadership, albeit for different reasons, have been indecisive and have pursued incoherent policies. This has encouraged smaller states, such as Cuba and Israel, to take the initiative, creating a more complicated, less manageable, and more dangerous world situation. According to Ledeen, the U.S. elite is not prepared to formulate a long-term strategic plan for U.S. foreign policy, and the unbridled, adversarial, and unaccountable mass media seriously interfere with the elite's ability to implement any policy. Soviet incoherence stems from structural crises in the Soviet domestic and alliance systems.

Both Blair and Ledeen reject the rational, unified-state actor premise that so often guides analyses of international relations. Instead, they see fallible human beings and bureaucratic organizations determining state policies and actions. Both books strongly criticize past U.S. policies. Both suggest new courses of action. Blair recommends that more resources should be devoted to improving C³I and that the United States should adopt a "no immediate second use" doctrine. Ledeen hopes for a more enlightened, far-sighted, and steadfast elite and, in his terms, a more responsible mass media.

Each book is flawed. Blair's book contains no mention of the Strategic Defense Initiative, despite its seeming relevance to his topic. The assumption in many of his analyses that even in a limited attack the USSR would target the U.S. C³I is somewhat implausible. Although Blair recognizes the possibility of limited nuclear exchanges, his assessments of damages to the U.S. C³I tend to assume large-scale Soviet attacks. Ledeen's book is poorly organized. The analysis is often based on hearsay evidence, and it contains many controversial judgments.

These flaws notwithstanding, both books merit reading. If their diagnoses are even partially correct, they point to serious situations. If both are right, if strategic weapons are on a hair trigger and international relations have become increasingly unmanageable and unstable, the world is indeed extremely dangerous, much more dangerous than many of us may think.

HAROLD K. JACOBSON
University of Michigan
Ann Arbor

BORNSTEIN, MORRIS. *East-West Technology Transfer: The Transfer of Western Technology to the USSR.* Pp. 190. Paris: Organization for Economic Cooperation and Development, 1985. Paperbound, $9.00.

MONKIEWICZ, JAN and JAN MACIEJEWICZ. *Technology Export from the Socialist Countries.* Pp. x, 170. Boulder, CO: Westview Press, 1986. Paperbound, $19.50.

Recent years have witnessed the appearance of numerous volumes on East-West technology transfer. One might well question what the two slim volumes under review can contribute to the rapidly expanding literature on East-West trade and technology transfer. Yet each book makes a valuable addition to our understanding of this complex subject.

Morris Bornstein's volume, produced under the auspices of the Organization for Economic Cooperation and Development, is a remarkably comprehensive and concise examination of the major issues related to East-West technology transfer. In just 140 pages of text Bornstein analyzes the technological level of the Soviet economy, the organizations involved in making Soviet technology policy, problems of assimilation of Western technology, financing arrangements, credits, countertrade, as well as the various modes of technology transfer. Perhaps the most detailed and thoroughly documented chapters assess the impact of Western technology on the Soviet economy. Bornstein summarizes the findings of numerous case studies of the chemical, motor vehicle, machine tool, energy, and forest products industries and concludes that although the total impact of Western technology on the Soviet economy is relatively small, in some sectors imported turnkey plants produce sizable shares of particular products, such as polyester fiber, passenger cars and trucks, numerically controlled machine tools, large-diameter pipe for gas pipelines, and drill bits.

Although Bornstein covers a vast and complex array of issues in a minimum of space, his analysis is sophisticated, thoroughly documented, and supported by the latest trade statistics of the Organization for Economic Cooperation and Development. The work provides the most up-to-date, complete, and comprehensive survey of East-West trade and technology transfer available.

The vast majority of the literature on East-West technology transfer neglects transfers from the East and transfers within the Council on Mutual Economic Assistance (CMEA). The contribution by Monkiewicz, of Warsaw Technical University, and Macie-jewicz, of the Institute of Planning and Statistics in Warsaw, seeks to fill that void; however, it is only partially successful. Monkiewicz and Maciejewicz note that the extent of technology exports from CMEA member states is relatively small and that such exports primarily involve sales to other CMEA members and Third World countries. Their attempts to assess the comparative technological level of East European industry by examining the percentage of gross national product devoted to research and develop-ment, patents registered, and export equip-ment prices, however, seriously overstate the performance of CMEA members. Apart from problems in their analysis of macrolevel phenomena, their microlevel case studies of Polish and Czech technology exports provide useful substance for the specialist.

GORDON B. SMITH
University of South Carolina
Columbia

COX, ANDREW, PAUL FURLONG, and EDWARD PAGE. *Power in Capitalist Society: Theory, Explanations and Cases.* Pp. viii, 235. New York: St. Martin's Press, 1985. $27.50.

MUNKIRS, JOHN R. *The Transformation of American Capitalism: From Competitive Market Structures to Centralized Private Sector Planning.* Pp. x, 235. Armonk, NY: M.E. Sharpe, 1985.

Insightful and wide-ranging, *Power in Capitalist Society* juxtaposes the major-power theories in an effort to assess their heuristic value and practical relevance.

Cox, Furlong, and Page's substantive contribution begins with a lucid consideration of Marxism, both in its original and revision-ist versions. Their thematic focus is on voluntarism, that is, the extent to which economic structure dictates political out-comes. Although not explicitly subscribing to any Marxist paradigm, their analysis is weighted heavily against the orthodox instru-

mental Marxism propounded by Soviet and some European analysts and toward the neorevisionist position that "it is the balance of political forces which shapes state inter-vention in any society." Relying primarily on the writings of fellow Briton Bob Jessop, Cox and his coauthors regard the state as a bellwether responsive to those movements most capable of exerting pressure at decisive points in the political process. Consequently, they also reject the interim position advocated by Ralph Miliband, who contends that while the complex social structure of advanced capitalism affords the state relative autonomy, the continuation of private ownership "in the last analysis" constrains any transformative tendencies within the system.

The chapter on elite theory is somewhat less provocative, in large part reflecting the relative incoherence of elitism itself. Begin-ning with Pareto and culminating in the studies of certain recent American sociolo-gists, elite writings have often been marked by conceptual flaccidity and methodological ineptitude. Positioned on a middle ground between a more analytically rigorous Marxism and a more normatively congenial pluralism, elite theorists have generally focused on the personal characteristics of power holders or, alternatively, on what Cox, Furlong, and Page rather vaguely term "socio-political determination." At the same time, elitism has also been internally divided between its European proponents, with their emphasis on the amorality and inevitability of rule by a few, and the school's more recent American branch, which has sought to reconcile demo-cratic values with the existence of a plurality of elites. Cox and his coauthors do a com-petent job in delineating these distinctions, but somehow their discussion as a whole lacks a certain clarity and vitality.

In contrast, the chapter on pluralism constitutes the book's high point, not least because it correctly targets pluralism's essen-tial feature. Contrary to popular misconcep-tion, this is not the contention that the American political system is equally acces-sible to all, but rather that democratic politics incorporates a much wider range of actors than is allowed by either Marxist or elitist theorists.

Cox, Furlong, and Page follow up their abstract analysis by a set of case studies in which the various power theories are applied to specific public policy questions. Their treatment of the military-industrial complex is particularly stimulating. While each theory is shown to have some relevance to this all-important issue, the degree of insight they provide varies considerably. Thus while pluralism is given high marks for its descriptive specificity, it is rated relatively low in analytical sophistication or prescriptive credibility. In particular, the pluralist contention that significant reform can be achieved through the ballot box is viewed as simplistic given the structural roots of military-industrial influence.

In conclusion, *Power in Capitalist Society* can serve as a valuable summary reference in upper-level political science or political sociology courses. Although sometimes turgid, it is based on extensive secondary research and benefits greatly from a commitment to pluralism of the intellectual variety. As Cox and his coauthors note in their brief concluding chapter, "Each theory, while providing useful insights into the way capitalist societies are structured and changed, is not on its own capable of fully explaining the complex reality of power."

The Transformation of American Capitalism is an ambitious study detailing the U.S. economy's monopolistic structure, but largely lacking the type of insight into power relations provided by the first book reviewed here. Writing in the populist tradition pioneered by J. R. Commons, Munkirs attempts to show how major financial institutions—termed the "Central Planning Core"—have gained ever greater control over individual corporations and, indeed, over entire industrial sectors. The importance of interlocking boards of directors, on which the Central Planning Core is prominently represented, is emphasized as a key factor in ensuring that major firms are bound together and integrated into a single system of production and distribution.

Although Munkirs provides valuable evidence on how the monopoly issue has either been ignored or "ritualized" by political leaders, he does not appear to understand why those leaders have been so obdurately unresponsive to the dangers posed by centralization of economic power. In particular, he neglects to consider that the state itself may be an integrated component of the very monopolistic structure he himself so rightly deplores.

DAVID H. KATZ

Michigan State University
East Lansing

DANIEL, DONALD C. *Anti-Submarine Warfare and Superpower Strategic Stability.* Pp. xii, 222. Champaign: University of Illinois Press, 1986. $32.50.

Arms controls, parity or superiority in weaponry, of course, are a vital aspect of the relationship between the Soviet Union and the United States. The current debate in the United States concerning the Strategic Defense Initiative, or Star Wars, various other weapons systems, the military budget generally, and the unthinkable catastrophe overshadowing the possibility of employing such instruments of destruction reflect apprehensions ranging from the most technical and specific to the apocalyptic.

Anti-Submarine Warfare and Superpower Strategic Stability contributes to our knowledge and understanding in a specific area while also addressing the broader issues of deterrence and stability.

Donald C. Daniel's book is a detailed, technical description, explanation, and discussion of detection devices—acoustic, nonacoustic indicators, and so forth—their deployment as well as other aspects of antisubmarine warfare. Included is a precise assessment of U.S. and Soviet research and deployment of such sensors. Strategic thinking relative to submarine and antisubmarine warfare is also carefully addressed. This is an important strength of the work. Submarine developments—in the numbers, types, age, vulnerability to various detection modes, and the like—are included in Daniel's considerations.

This thoroughly researched work includes several tables, developed by Daniel, summarizing characteristics, strengths, and weaknesses of various U.S. and Soviet sensors, submarines, and weapons systems. These are well done and quite useful.

For general readers, the book is flawed by the extensive use of many acronyms that, unfortunately, have now become an integral part of the military/weapons specialized vocabulary. However, within these parameters, the work is readable and very well organized.

Daniel's general assessments and conclusions are thoughtful and relatively encouraging. His is not the panicky view so often encountered in arms-related literature.

Of particular interest is the general discussion of the U.S.-USSR war potential, as related only to submarines. In this area, the question of stability in that relationship is crucial. Daniel finds, here, U.S. superiority in some areas and, in general, no immediate likelihood of drastic, destabilizing developments during the next decade.

DON LeFAVE

Yuba College
Marysville
California

FORBES, H. D. *Nationalism, Ethnocentrism, and Personality: Social Science & Critical Theory.* Pp. x, 255. Chicago: University of Chicago Press, 1985. $27.50.

The first part of this book begins with a detailed restatement of the theory found in *The Authoritarian Personality* (1950), as well as a commendable review of the critiques of the 1950 book. The second and third parts—empirical and theoretical—challenge the contemporary consensus about ethnocentrism and authoritarianism. Forbes argues that both supporters and critics of *The*

Authoritarian Personality have missed the point, that what is obvious in the United States is not obvious elsewhere, that nationalism has different connotations in different nations. He agrees that in the United States conservatism does involve ethnocentrism, belligerent patriotism, and rejection of many minorities, and he notes that in U.S. literature nationalism means essentially anticommunism. But he also correctly notes that studies inspired by the 1950 book have generally criticized right-wing fascism but not left-wing fascism, and have questioned American nationalism but endorsed "nationalism of the various peoples in revolt." Forbes notes that *The Authoritarian Personality* hypothesis that individual differences in prejudice are mostly due to different personalities is now generally rejected, and he turns his attention to the modified version of the hypothesis that authoritarianism is one source of ethnocentrism. His goal is to test the modified personality hypothesis in a different setting: Canada. He analyzes self-administered questionnaires given to 1825 seniors in Canadian high schools in 1968. Forbes suggests that the contrast is not between ethnocentrists and humanitarians, but rather between philanthropists and misanthropes, "boosters and knockers." Forbes suggests that the assumed dichotomy between democracy and fascism is too simple and that *The Authoritarian Personality* produces a "rather rosy picture of the democratic equalitarian."

Forbes criticizes the prevailing worship of statistics and the failure to explore alternative theories adequately, admires Horkheimer and Adorno but suggests that they shared the U.S. belief that democracy was superior to all other forms of government, and concludes that *The Authoritarian Personality* "illustrates intellectual provincialism."

Forbes notes the narrowness of his sample, but also notes that he included both French-Canadian and English-Canadian students in a period of intense consciousness about nationalism in Canada, presents supplemental data, and presents strong arguments against "the idea that our results would have been completely different if somewhat older and more sophisticated respondents had been chosen."

Forbes has succeeded in his goal and raises important questions that deserve more in-depth examination. Some of his findings are disturbing on the surface, but ultimate progress demands more complex and probing analyses of a philosophical nature. Forbes has produced a commendable book that should encourage more attention to the study of nationalism and ethnocentrism.

ABRAHAM D. LAVENDER

Florida International University
Miami

JOHNSON, R. W. *Shootdown: Flight 007 and the American Connection.* Pp. xvi, 335. New York: Viking, 1986. $18.95.

In the predawn hours of 1 September 1983, a South Korean airliner en route to Seoul from Anchorage—Korean Airline (KAL) flight 007—was shot down off Sakhalin Island by a Soviet fighter, killing all 269 passengers and crew on board. The news of the shootdown produced a widespread reaction of horror and indignation at such a wanton disregard for human life by the Soviet Union. Granting that 007 had intruded into Soviet airspace, many wondered what kind of society or regime would have to make a point of defending its territorial sovereignty by shooting down a passenger plane with women and children in it. Tragic as it was, the 007 incident thus was a huge propaganda bonanza for the Reagan administration, which had said all along that a more vigilant military posture was needed to deal with such an "evil empire."

Almost from the beginning, however, nagging questions about the incident emerged that could not be satisfactorily answered, and the refusal of the Reagan administration to disclose pertinent information only fueled a growing suspicion that fateful flight 007 might indeed have been involved in a U.S. intelligence operation as alleged by the Soviet

government. Once the navigational-error hypothesis was ruled out as probably bordering on impossibility in light not only of the super-reliable three-layered backup system of the Inertial Navigation System, but also of other incriminating evidence of KAL 007's flight behavior, the troublesome question that remained was, Why did 007 deliberately intrude into Soviet airspace in the area widely known to be sensitive to the Soviet air defense?

Dismissing the saving of fuel as an entirely implausible explanation for the errant KAL flight, Johnson develops an elaborate hypothesis of conspiracy among the top-level members of the Reagan administration, specifically William Clark and William Casey, and the KAL 007 crew. The mission plan for fateful flight 007, according to this book, perhaps the most comprehensive book to date on the incident, must have been to test Soviet radar responses to a deep and prolonged penetration of the Soviet airspace over Kamchatka and Sakhalin. Only a civilian airliner feigning navigational error could make such a penetration with the least risk of being shot down.

Shootdown is a deeply disturbing book, for it makes such an unthinkable proposition not only thinkable but downright irresistible even to those of us who are usually disdainful of conspiracy theory in politics and wish to believe that the deliberate risking of innocent lives for intelligence purposes is simply out of character with a decent democracy such as the United States. The sheer brilliance and analytical thoroughness of a proper Briton and Oxford University scholar whose personal and intellectual integrity cannot be questioned make it very difficult to dismiss this book as an example of an overly inquisitive mind probing into the darkest reaches of wicked imagination.

SUNG HO KIM

Ohio University
Athens

MOUZELIS, NICOS P. *Politics in the Semi-Periphery: Early Parliamentarism and Late Industrialism in the Balkans and Latin America.* Pp. xix, 284. New York: St. Martin's Press, 1986. $32.50.

Amalgamating political economics—quasi Marxism—and political sociology domination—Weberian—types for comparative, cross-regional, historically oriented study of politics and bureaucracy of "societies geographically distant and culturally dissimilar" is an ambitious undertaking. Nicos P. Mouzelis, building upon his previous research in organization theory and Greek politics, is only partially successful in the task of comparing selected "semi-periphery" nations.

Mouzelis's subjects are the Balkans and Latin America, primarily Argentina, Chile, and Greece and secondarily Bulgaria, Yugoslavia, and Brazil. Having obtained independence in the nineteenth century from patrimonial empires, they adopted parliamentary political systems. Mouzelis postulates that each state had oligarchical controls restricting popular participation but highly statist "incorporative" orientations co-opting middle and lower classes into "dependent-vertical" relationships. Incorporative patterns, especially after 1929, rested upon bureaucratic clientelistic patronage of populism under charismatic, patrimonial leaders co-opting lower classes. Contrasted to Western "integrative" politics, these patterns hindered growth of unions and intermediate structures not designed by state authorities, something reinforced—dramatically in Argentina, Chile, and Greece—by relatively late but impressive industrialization and urbanization, which undermined rural influence. They became "semi-peripheral," not Third World peripheral.

Centralized states were paramount when industrial working classes evolved. Public employment and "national arenas," including armies, markets, and cities, expanded. Still, these political-economic developments politicized increasing numbers, undercutting government "incorporative-exclusionist controls" and challenging the autonomy of military establishments. Throughout, controllers of bureaucracy were not driven by class or economic imperatives but were protecting their own and state interests, which gave them domination and power for co-optation and developing state-sponsored capitalism.

When military bureaucracies assumed power in Argentina (1966), Greece (1967), and Chile (1973), nations with historic "praetorian tendencies," where military subordination to civilian leaders was always less than in "center" Western "integrative" systems, they were primarily protecting their own status. Influences, including "managerial ethos"—stimulated by American training and President Kennedy's military involvement in national political development there—and forces such as inflation, low productivity, and civilian regime instability, were germane but not paramount. Military bureaucracies continued incorporative statism but failed to generate stability due to prior extensive politicization, lack of viable ideology, and inability to promote mass mobilization.

These are Mouzelis's hypotheses comparing historical similarities of incorporative political domination forms. While he presents interesting national political-administrative histories up to the 1970s, there are difficulties with his comparative analyses. His data too neatly, often quite redundantly, explain away admitted observable differences of regional, economic, cultural, and unique historical factors. This projects inevitability to incorporative evolution not prescient in his comparison or perhaps not accurate vis-à-vis 1980s' developments.

CHARLES A. JOINER

Temple University
Philadelphia
Pennsylvania

ORVIK, NILS, ed. *Semialignment and Western Security.* Pp. 286. New York: St. Martin's Press, 1986. $35.00.

WILLIAMS, PHIL. *The Senate and U.S. Troops in Europe*. Pp. xi, 315. New York: St. Martin's Press, 1985. $25.00.

Semialignment is the condition of being in but, in one way or another, not fully part of an alliance. Noticing that about half of the smaller or middle-range members of the North Atlantic Treaty Organization (NATO) are in or showing signs of this condition, Orvik brought a team together at the Center for International Relations at Queens University, in Ontario, Canada, to study the phenomenon. This book is the product of their efforts, its core being case studies of five states. Carsten Holbraad makes a comprehensive and skillful analysis of Denmark's semialigned tendencies. Constantine Melakopides studies Greece, claiming that its post-1974 semialignment was "inevitable," primarily because of its deep suspicion of a fellow NATO member, Turkey. The chapter on the Netherlands by Ruud Koole and Paul Lucardie focuses almost entirely on the security policy of the Social Democratic Party. Canada attracts two chapters: Christopher Rose gives an informative and critical account of Canada's contributions—or, rather, their lack—to NATO, and Hugh Thorburn traces the growth of anti-NATO feeling in Canada's small New Democratic Party; the rationale for the inclusion of the latter chapter is hard to understand, however. Nils Orvik, in a thorough and wide-ranging chapter, writes very interestingly—although a little bit long-windedly—on Norway.

We are then offered two conclusions! The editor sums up against semialignment, seeing it as irresponsible and perhaps counterproductive. All the other contributors band together to offer a more sympathetic analysis of the policy, suggesting that in some respects it might strengthen the alliance. This is an interesting bonus at the end of what is, on balance, a very worthwhile volume.

Whereas the Orvik book deals with large issues, that by Phil Williams focuses on just one aspect of the Western alliance, but a crucial one: the attitude of the U.S. Senate to the stationing of American troops in Europe.

The initial commitment, following the outbreak of the Korean War, was vigorously challenged by many senators, leading in 1951 to a "debate that has rarely been matched either in its bitterness and vindictiveness or in the excessive claims made by the proponents of presidential power on the one side and the advocates of congressional prerogatives on the other." This the administration won, and for more than a decade the issue lay fallow. But in the early 1960s the size of the American commitment led to restiveness among a handful of senators, including Mike Mansfield. From 1966 to 1970 there was what Williams calls "gentle pressure" on the issue, expressed in a number of resolutions that were never pushed to a vote. But this activity "represented the beginnings of the congressional revolt against the predominance of Cold War policies, and the dominance of what would later be called the 'Imperial Presidency.'" Then in the early 1970s came a series of Mansfield amendments calling for troop reductions, of which that of 1973 represented the peak. On several occasions they threw the Nixon administration into a frenzy. Yet their author, a former professor, had a "gentle style of leadership" and had toward his own proposals an attitude "almost . . . of scholarly detachment." None of the amendments were ultimately successful, but they played a large part in the movement to bring Congress back into the policymaking process. Williams suggests that the issue with which they dealt is far from closed.

Williams takes his readers through the story in a meticulous fashion, but the going never becomes heavy. His book is a splendid scholarly achievement and immediately establishes itself as the authoritative account of this important matter.

ALAN JAMES

University of Keel
Staffordshire
England

ROSE, CLIVE. *Campaigns against Western Defense: NATO's Adversaries and Critics*. Pp. ix, 318. New York: St. Martin's Press, 1985. $27.50.

MONTGOMERY, JOHN D. *Aftermath: Tarnished Outcomes of American Foreign Policy*. Pp. xvii, 200. Dover, MA: Auburn House, 1986. $24.95.

It is worth recalling that not long ago tens of thousands of protestors on both sides of the Atlantic took to the streets to call for an end to the nuclear arms race. Some keen observers at the time were struck by the apparent similarity between the demands in Europe and the United States for a nuclear freeze, if not unilateral disarmament, and the folly of appeasement on the eve of World War II. Soviet attempts to exploit the Western public's fear of nuclear war and desire for peace in order to erode popular support for the North Atlantic alliance is the central concern of Clive Rose's book, *Campaigns against Western Defense*.

The villains, according to Rose, are international Communist-front organizations, such as the World Peace Council, that prey on the naiveté of useful idiots in the West inclined to toe the party line in Moscow's war of words and ideas with the United States and its allies. Rose marshals an array of details to demonstrate that the USSR's political machinations are no less threatening to Western security than its military threat. His analysis unfortunately restates the obvious: the Soviets take their propaganda seriously and will go to great lengths to disinform and manipulate foreign opinion. The crux of the issue in this book is the effectiveness of the fronts and their fellow travelers as weapons of Soviet foreign policy. No better example is the North Atlantic Treaty Organization's 1979 decision to deploy Pershing II and cruise missiles by 1983. Try as the Kremlin did, the Soviets failed to stop the deployment and their various fronts did little to help. Rose, to his credit, suggests that the North Atlantic Treaty Organization's difficulties with the European peace movement had more to do with the alliance's own failure to make a persuasive case for the necessity of nuclear deterrence. Rose would have been better served if he had pursued this theme with as much vigor as he pursued the elusive threat of Soviet rhetorical skulduggery.

Currently a professor at Harvard's Kennedy School of Government, John D. Montgomery is also a policy analyst with nearly four decades of involvement in the implementation of American foreign policy. The purpose of his book is to fathom the reasons why this policy has occasionally failed so miserably in the years since 1945. Montgomery argues that America's good intentions abroad have not been matched by sufficient resources. Moreover, the makers of American foreign policy too often let their can-do spirit overwhelm their sense of prudence and proportion in the commitment of American power and prestige abroad. He concludes with a plea that the United States stop behaving like a superpower and act more like a great power, similar in stature to the other principal nations in the West.

Montgomery fashions five case studies in which he was a participant-observer to support this conclusion: the use of atomic bombs to end the war; experimenting with tactical atomic weapons to reduce the possibility of full-scale war; efforts to reconstruct Japan as a stable, democratic nation; the tragedy of Vietnam; and programs to generate economic independence in former colonial states. Each of these issues is handled with great expertise. Unfortunately, America's responsibilities in contemporary world affairs cannot be wished away. One can only concur with Montgomery's hope that in the future the United States will define its national interests more judiciously than its leaders have done in the past.

PAUL MICHAEL KOZAR
Mount Vernon College
Washington, D.C.

AFRICA, ASIA, AND LATIN AMERICA

ARIAN, ASHER. *Politics in Israel: The Second Generation.* Pp. 290. Chatham, NJ: Chatham House, 1985. $25.00.

This volume explains in detail the interaction of domestic and international factors that shape democracy in contemporary Israel. It is especially useful in demonstrating how political behavior is shaped by the patterns of immigration and settlement that are too little appreciated by outsiders. At the same time, Arian, a twenty-year resident of Israel, is not mesmerized by the alleged uniqueness of the country as he dissects the intricacies of coalition formation and other aspects of hierarchical party politics in the Jewish state. Indeed, the enduring quality of this analysis lies precisely in the careful delineation of legitimacy, identity, integration, and political culture as persistent problems. Arian understands that the "world of Israeli politics often seems confusing to the uninitiated" and seeks to uncover the continental European roots that have shaped the political system in both the first and second generations.

The book's clear organization facilitates comparisons between Israel and other democracies and allows readers to explore in depth particular interests in electoral arrangements or public policy. Those concerned with obtaining an overview will find the chapter on ideology, communication, and socialization most enlightening because it brings together the various strands of Arian's argument and demonstrates why the conventional vocabulary of "the left-right continuum" has scant application in Israel's setting of "attitudinal stability." The strength of style over substance in Israeli politics is well documented, as is the gap between support for "abstract democratic norms" and "practical tolerance."

The wealth of data presented together with the clear articulation of its significance renders this volume essential for any serious student of comparative politics. In addition, Arian's immersion in his topic as both participant and observer gives the work an authority that even the more general reader will appreciate.

LINDA B. MILLER

Wellesley College
Massachusetts

BULLARD, MONTE R. *China's Political-Military Evolution: The Party and the Military in the PRC, 1960-1984.* Pp. xviii, 209. Boulder, CO: Westview Press, 1985. Paperbound, $15.75.

CHAN, ANITA. *Children of Mao: Personality Development and Political Activism in the Red Guard Generation.* Pp. viii, 254. Seattle: University of Washington Press, 1985. $19.95.

EDWARDS, R. RANDLE, LOUIS HENKIN, and ANDREW J. NATHAN. *Human Rights in Contemporary China.* Pp. 193. New York: Columbia University Press, 1986. $25.00.

That China's basic institutions, its legal system, and its political environment are undergoing radical change has been dramatically demonstrated in these three very different books. Each examines a specific aspect of political culture or institutional development in the People's Republic; when taken together they present a powerful portrait of a nation redefining itself.

Monte R. Bullard's *China's Political-Military Evolution* is a monograph that fits the rather classic model of what might be called elitist studies. Of the three works being reviewed it is the closest to its origins as a dissertation in political science. What this means in practical terms is that it is, in its opening sections and in its presentation of the author's analytic insights, the least accessible to an educated lay public. If one is willing to crash through the thicket of jargon and Bullard's tendency toward overly precise—and lengthy—definition, one finds a useful and quite clearly drawn portrait of a military system in the midst of change. One finds as well a useful road map that can guide one through the complexities of party-bureau-cracy-army interaction in post-Maoist China. Bullard, as a career military man and Army China expert, is most comfortable describing bureaucracies and defining the power relation-ships and the system of "interlocking direc-torates" he finds in the People's Republic and does this in an effective manner. Thus his book is useful to the student of military systems and to anyone interested in how political structures and political relationships have evolved in modern China.

Children of Mao permits the reader to move from the mountain of high policy-making and elitist bureaucratic politics to the plain of interpersonal political interaction; Anita Chan's fascinating book allows us to enter the realm of political culture on its most fundamental level. Her work can be seen as an exploration in what I would term political social psychology. The basic ques-tion she asks is a simple one: how were children and teenagers affected by the social-ist revolution in China and by Mao's attempt to maintain the spirit and the power and the impetus of his personal revolution? She answers her question by studying a select number of young people who served as Red Guards. Her sample was a small one, but the individuals she chose were from key urban-class backgrounds and she argues that their experiences were exemplary of those of many others in urban China. She defines four types of activist personalities and in each chapter, after introducing some key trends and tendencies, focuses upon the four individuals who best represent each of her four archetypes. The first chapter introduces Chan's subject and her approach. The second examines the primary school years of her subjects. In the third, adolescence is studied. The fourth covers the Red Guard period, and the fifth focuses upon the waning of the revolution. Chan concludes with a discussion of the process of political socialization. She has given us a well-organized, well-written monograph that has the power of a great panoramic novel; it is a book that leaves one shaken at what has been witnessed.

Louis Henkin, R. Randle Edwards, and Andrew J. Nathan, each a professor at Columbia University, have combined forces to put together a useful set of essays that deals with a third dimension of Chinese political life, that of human or personal rights. *Human Rights in Contemporary China* is the most abstract book of the three being reviewed and is the most broadly based in the coverage of its topic. It is also clearly aimed at an educated lay audience; each essay conveys information with grace and authority but without overwhelming detail or voluminous footnotes. Henkin, a specialist in the problem of human rights, provides the reader with a comparative overview of rights in the United States—his model for a rights-oriented society—and the People's Republic of China. R. Randle Edwards, an expert in the Chinese legal system, deals with the way personal rights are defined in China. Andrew J. Nathan, a political scientist and specialist on the problem of democracy in modern China, first traces the development of polit-ical rights in the various modern Chinese constitutions and then concludes the book with an essay on the sources of Chinese thinking on the issue of political and human rights. Each essay is a distillation of its author's thought on his given subject. Taken together they provide a clear, well-defined introduction to the problem.

Each of these books has its value. The first illuminates elitist politics. The second shows how young people learned to survive in a political environment gone mad. The third shows why thinking of China in Western terms is a dangerous exercise. When taken together, they give us a sense of what the political dimension of modern Chinese life is like.

MURRAY A. RUBINSTEIN
Baruch College
New York City

FUNG, EDMUND S.K. and COLIN MACK-ERRAS. *From Fear to Friendship: Aus-tralia's Policies towards the People's Re-*

---

public of China 1966-1982. Pp. x, 351. Manchester, NH: University of Queensland Press, 1985. $37.50.

Throughout the postwar period China has been a major factor in Australian foreign policy. It was perceived as a threat and feared. Politicians fought elections on the need to contain the influence of Chinese communism. As the title of the book indicates, this fear turned into an open embrace. China was taken up as a friend and ally in the global struggle against the Soviet Union.

The dominant influence in Australia's foreign policy, however, has not been China but the United States. In crucial aspects of its policies toward China, Australia has followed the United States's lead. Thus an important theme embedded in this book is the way Australia's relationship with the United States has limited its freedom of choice in foreign policy. On the question of recognition of the People's Republic of China (PRC), membership of the PRC in the United Nations, and Taiwan, it long adhered to the precepts of successive U.S. administrations. One result has been the lesson that the United States has no compunction about changing policy without informing its allies. Nixon's initiatives in 1972 were a considerable embarrassment to the Australian government of the day.

On some issues Australia did of course exercise independence. It traded extensively with China when the United States did not. Fung and Mackerras demonstrate that Australia adopted a pragmatic approach in this regard. It generally sought to separate issues of trade and politics. Predictably some segments of domestic opinion saw this as duplicity with communism. Nevertheless it became an impetus to Australia's recognition, in 1972, of the PRC.

Though the book is informative, thorough, and comprehensive in scope, it is a pedestrian narrative with no vivifying insights. It would have been a more forceful book had Fund and Mackerras done more to draw out and probe some of the themes it contains. In particular there is a disappointing absence of any adequate sense of the political processes that shaped Australia's policies. There is more about what happened and when than precisely why it did or whether it was really important. Mackerras writes, with genuine interest, about the development of cultural relations, but have they contributed much to the substantive issues of the relationship?

It is a book that will serve more as an introduction to Australia's China policies during a particular period than as a source of interpretive argument. Perhaps this is the inevitable result of setting out with a time frame rather than a set of incisive questions.

PAUL KEAL

Australian National University
Canberra

GALBIATI, FERNANDO. P'eng P'ai and the Hai-Lu-Feng Soviet. Pp. vi, 484. Palo Alto, CA: Stanford University Press, 1985. $45.00.

The role of the peasantry in a communist revolution is a controversial issue. It has been debated among scholars and revolutionaries. One of the characteristics of Chinese communism during the Mao Zedong era is the crucial role played by the peasants. The theoretical foundation of this practice is often attributed to Mao for his successful adaptation of the Marxist doctrine to the Chinese milieu. Thus Mao's supporters claim that Mao has made a major contribution to the communist movement in the Third World. Then there is the argument about the originality of Mao's theory because many communist leaders before Mao, including Lenin, also discussed the potential role of the peasantry in a communist revolution.

If Mao is not the first leader to emphasize the role of the peasantry in the international communist movement, certainly most people, including most of the Chinese communists, believe that Mao is the first Chinese communist leader to do so in the Chinese communist revolution. The book P'eng P'ai and the Hai-Lu-Feng Soviet by Fernando Galbiati even challenges this popular assumption. Galbiati argues convincingly that P'eng P'ai, not Mao Zedong, was the first Chinese leader to stress the importance of the peasants in the Chinese revolution and it was P'eng who established the first rural people's soviet—the Hai-Lu-Feng Soviet, in China. He further contends that Mao was influenced by P'eng's peasant movement in east Kwantung Province.

The book is divided into three parts with a total of 11 chapters. It provides a detailed description and analysis of the life and times of P'eng P'ai and the geographical, political, economic, and social conditions of the Hai-Lu-Feng area in east Kwantung. It is an insightful microstudy of the peasant movement in a two-county area in the 1920s. The book is based on many original sources. It links P'eng's peasant union movement in Haifeng and Lufeng to the larger perspective of political development in Kwangtung Province, the Chinese Communist Party (CCP), the Kuomintang (KMT), the KMT-CCP united front, and the policy of the Comintern toward China. Chapter 10 gives an account of the operations and problems of the Hai-Lu-Feng Soviet, which was crushed by KMT forces. The book has more data on Haifeng than on Lufeng. Galbiati points out the problem of "peasant mentality" and the strength and weakness of the peasantry in a communist revolution. P'eng's Hai-Lu-Feng Soviet was a prototype of later Chinese communist developments.

The book contains too many trivial details and quotations. It is tedious and repetitive in some places. A more systematic analysis of P'eng's ideology based on his writings would have made this book more significant in our study of P'eng and the policy of the CCP toward the peasants in its early years. Galbiati's book has broken some new ground, and it is an important contribution to the literature on Chinese communism.

GEORGE P. JAN

University of Toledo
Ohio

HARRIS, LILLIAN CRAIG and ROBERT L. WORDEN, eds. *China and the Third World: Champion or Challenger?* Pp. xvii, 174. Dover, MA: Auburn House, 1986. $29.00.

CHANG, PAO-MIN. *The Sino-Vietnamese Territorial Dispute.* Pp. viii, 119. New York: Praeger, 1985. $29.95. Paperbound, $9.95.

Here are two new works on a single subject, China's changing relations with the Third World. One is a broad, global overview; the other, a narrow monograph treating only one of three key issues in China's relations with a single state.

China and the Third World is the broader and yet the weaker of the two. With an introduction by Harris and Worden and seven essays "written independently" by as many scholars, it covers a considerable range of perspectives on China's foreign relations, not only with the Third World but, inevitably, with the powers as well. The weakness of the book lies in its arrangement. The introduction tells the reader what to expect of whom, and the following essays seem already familiar as they are read. In addition, some redundancy in seven perspectives on the same topic is perhaps to be expected, but the degree of it here is simply tiring. More active editing might have spared the reader some of this. The discrete essays are interesting and well argued, but as a whole they tend to dull and diminish each other. Since the book has no real conclusion, it is difficult to know what the chief purpose of the project was; as it stands now, it seems to have been to demonstrate that if you turn seven scholars onto a topic you will emerge with seven perspectives. Many readers, of course, will have discovered that from their first semester of teaching.

The Sino-Vietnamese Territorial Dispute, on the other hand, is a sharply focused monograph and a lively exploration into one of the major problem areas in China's Third World relations. Treating only the territorial dispute, while noting the equal importance of the ethnic Chinese and the Kampuchean issues, Chang describes both the historical antecedents of the dispute and the recent drifting into armed conflict over the issues. After careful analysis of those issues, he sees no easy resolution, but rather continued conflict in the future. Within his narrowly defined limits, Chang offers an exemplary study of a vexing China problem.

R. KENT LANCASTER
Goucher College
Baltimore
Maryland

LAITIN, DAVID D. *Hegemony and Culture: Politics and Religious Change among the Yoruba.* Pp. xiii, 252. Chicago: University of Chicago Press, 1986. $30.00. Paperbound, $13.95.

This small book deals with several very large issues. Laitin, a political scientist, uses data from field research in Nigeria to question both the "social systems theory" of Clifford Geertz and the "rational choice theory" of Abner Cohen. Laitin argues that neither of these theories explains his data as well as the theory of "hegemonic control" associated with Antonio Gramsci.

The situation that provoked the comparison and evaluation of these theories was encountered by Laitin among the Yoruba, an ethnic-tribal group of southwestern Nigeria. Although approximately half of the Yoruba are now Christian and half Muslim, religious affiliation seems to have very little relevance as far as political action is concerned. Political conflicts are often intense among the Yoruba, but Christians and Muslims join causes and take positions on the basis of values other than religious ones. This seemed to Laitin to be an anomalous situation, and he is concerned with explaining what he perceives as the "unnatural toleration" of one religious group by the other.

Since Laitin conceives of social systems theory as stressing the integration and congruence of cultural subsystems, he holds that the Yaruba data do not fit the model because the religious subsystem is seemingly unrelated to the political subsystem. On the other

hand, rational choice theory is said to be inadequate because it does not explain the origin of the values that hold people together in cohesive groups. Laitin prefers a hegemonic theory, which holds that certain cultural subsystems become dominant in a society and come to be most significant in directing action. Among the Yoruba, the dominant values center on derivation from ancestral cities. When aligning themselves for political action, the Yoruba stress loyalty to an ancestral city above all else, and in spite of extensive shuffling of the population, it is place of origin that forms the ultimate basis for political affiliation. Although the basic values behind this orientation were clearly present in precolonial times, Laitin argues that the British had an important role in their development as dominant values, since in setting up their system of indirect rule, the British gave chiefs and cities a significance they had never had before. Thus a hegemonic political system is seen as having had a crucial role in the development of a hegemonic value system.

Most of Laitin's conclusions are based on secondary sources, since his field research was relatively limited. He spent a year in the city of Ile-Ife, where he regularly attended an Anglican church and a mosque, and in addition to interacting informally with members of the congregations, he conducted formal interviews—through an interpreter—with 35 Christians and 35 Muslims, all elite males. Although the data collected by Laitin provide a rather narrow base for the kinds of generalizations he makes about political attitudes, he is able to cite several other studies that corroborate his findings.

The most serious criticism of this work relates to the basic assumption with which Laitin began, namely, that since religion is often associated with political conflict in his own society, the same relationship should exist in all societies. Not only is this assumption ethnocentric; it also led to a distortion of the research situation. Laitin regularly challenged his informants to explain to him why there was no hostility between Christians and Muslims, thereby requiring that they look at the situation from his perspective, not their own. Since Laitin's focus was on understanding Yoruba values, this was clearly not the best way to proceed.

Even granting these criticisms, however, Laitin's book is an excellent study of political behavior among the Yoruba. It is clearly written and scholarly, includes a candid discussion of methodology, and presents a stimulating combination of theory and data.

SETH LEACOCK

University of Connecticut
Storrs

PAYNE, ANTHONY, PAUL SUTTON, and TONY THORNDIKE. *Grenada: Revolution and Invasion.* Pp. xi, 233. New York: St. Martin's Press, 1986. Paperbound, $11.95.

VALENTA, JIRI and HERBERT J. ELLISON, eds. *Grenada and Soviet/Cuban Policy: Internal Crisis and U.S./OECD Intervention.* Pp. xxii, 512. Boulder, CO: Westview Press, 1986. $38.50. Paperbound, $20.00.

The two books under review were written before the files of the Grenada Archive became open to scholars at the U.S. National Archives. These files, which tell us a great deal about the inner workings of any socialist country in the world, yield information that makes obsolete a considerable portion of both books.

The Payne, Sutton, and Thorndike book, originally published in 1984, is written in earnest anger over the U.S. military intervention in Grenada. Payne, Sutton, and Thorndike had read only a few of the internal documents of the Grenada Archive and, as a result, they have generally taken the People's Revolutionary Government (PRG) at its own word, always a mistake in political analysis. They do not generally censure any excesses of the PRG but, rather, try to understand them as attempts by sincere young men to establish socialism in their small island nation. For instance, the elimi-

nation of all the oppositional press is not viewed with any particular alarm and the closing of *Grenada Voice* is passed over by the bland statement that its appearance "could not but appear to the PRG to be part of a CIA plot." On a very superficial reading of only a few scattered sources, they also see the PRG as having "genuine" economic successes; more thorough investigations show a much less rosy picture and that economic difficulties were an important cause for the political difficulties of the regime. (Frederic L. Pryor, *Revolutionary Grenada: A Study of Political Economy* [New York: Praeger, 1986.]) This book does contain some useful factual materials about U.S. Caribbean policy in general and the military intervention in particular, but much of the authors' analyses of these materials is as tendentious as their views about what happened in Grenada. A much better book on Grenada, *Grenada: Politics, Economics and Society* (Boulder, CO: Lynne Rienner, 1985), was published some months later by Tony Thorndike alone, who does not excuse the PRG any longer because by this time he no longer considers it to have really been socialist.

The Valenta-Ellison volume is a set of 1984 conference papers that were already published in a preliminary version edited by Valenta and Ellison, *Soviet/Cuban Strategy in the Third World after Grenada* (Washington, DC: Kennan Institute for Advanced Russian Studies, Woodrow Wilson International Center, 1984). It starts with a first-rate paper by Jiri and Virginia Valenta that had appeared in *Problems of Communism* and that was based on extensive interviewing in Grenada. Most of the remaining papers were written by people with no particular expertise on Grenada; for the most part their analyses are conventional. Fortunately, some of the weaker papers in the conference volume were not reprinted. The book is supplemented with 230 pages of Grenada documents, most of which have previously been published. (U.S., Department of State and Department of Defense, *Grenada Documents: An Overview and Selection,* ed. Michael Ledeen and Herbert Romerstein, processed [Washington,

DC, 1984]; Paul Seabury and Walter A. McDougall, eds., *The Grenada Papers* [San Francisco: Institute for Contemporary Studies Press, 1984]. Still earlier the United States Information Agency had published several volumes of *Documents Pertaining to Relations between Grenada, the U.S.S.R., and Cuba* [Washington, DC, n.d.], but these are difficult to obtain and few libraries seem to have them.)

A majority of the papers deal with foreign policy implications of the intervention, especially its impact on countries in various parts of the world. A considerable amount of the discussion on Grenada is repetitive because each author seems to refer to the same documents. Future scholars may also have difficulties in tracing down the originals of these documents since the authors generally use the log numbers, rather than the cataloging numbers employed in the Grenada Archive. Except for the Valenta and Valenta paper, the reader learns little about Grenada itself. Some—but not all—of the papers seem to view the PRG as part of a nefarious plot by the Soviet Union. The documents in the Grenada Archive suggest a much different interpretation, namely, that the Soviets did not know what to do with Grenada, that they gave Grenada relatively little aid, and that their refusal to grant Grenada an emergency loan in the summer of 1983 led to the unraveling of the entire government. Some of the papers also suggest that the murder of the prime minister, Maurice Bishop, was the result of a leftist plot by the "hard-liner" Bernard Coard, an interpretation also made by both Ronald Reagan and Fidel Castro. Again the archival materials plus testimony emerging from the trial of the accused murderers suggest a much more complicated picture.

Given the fact that almost all of this study has already been published in one form or another, albeit in a less polished state, one must ask, Was this book really necessary?

FREDERIC L. PRYOR

Swarthmore College
Pennsylvania

SELLA, AMNON and YAEL YISHAI. *Israel: The Peaceful Belligerent, 1967-79.* Pp. ix, 218. New York: St. Martin's Press, 1986. $27.50.

Amnon Sella and Yael Yishai have written an important book explaining how Israel and Egypt achieved a contractual peace agreement in 1979. Arguing that the territories conquered in the June war of 1967 enabled Israel for the first time to bargain for a peace on acceptable terms, the book's thesis appears straightforward, even obvious. But appearances, in this case, are deceptive. Keeping in mind the dramatically different outcomes of wars in 1967 and 1973, Sella and Yishai's formulation that these two wars became the means to peace is remarkable for its originality and comprehensiveness. The account not only contains fresh empirical information, but also offers a thoroughly new view of Israel's success in negotiating for recognition and a treaty of peace.

Sella and Yishai distinguish between the various domestic and international factors stimulating peace initiatives without ignoring the very real and considerable obstacles to peace embedded in decades of wars and confrontations. Drawing on a wide range of documents, secondary literature, and survey research material, the book's most distinctive contribution is to show how the burden of peace is borne by Israelis along with many other burdens. Sella and Yishai put it this way:

The unorganised public played a dominant role in the mobilisation process. Changes occurred in the civic arena: Israelis took to the streets and demonstrated for or against a given policy. They went on strikes more often, demanding higher wages and incomes. Close scrutiny of the demonstrations reveals, however, that they were concerned with a variety of interests and issues and were not focused on the question of peace. They were moreover mostly non-violent and no threat to legitimacy.

For Israeli voters, then, the peace issue is not always central. Nor, understandably, is it always a priority on the political agenda of elected officials.

Sella and Yishai's study seems exemplary for its political science sophistication and for its sensitivity to the nuances of Israeli political life. Without devaluing their bravery or diminishing their vision, it can be said that Anwar el-Sadat and Menachem Begin did not, alone, make peace. They operated, as political actors, in a context in which the policy of effecting peaceful ties between Israel and Egypt became increasingly plausible. *Israel: The Peaceful Belligerent* elaborates the contours of the Israeli context and in so doing provides a compelling analysis.

DONNA ROBINSON DIVINE
Smith College
Northampton
Massachusetts

TSOU, TANG. *The Cultural Revolution and Post-Mao Reforms: A Historical Perspective.* Pp. xiv, 351. Chicago: University of Chicago Press, 1986. $29.95.

This collection of articles on the Chinese political system by Tang Tsou is not for the casual reader. It is especially valuable to scholars with a more intimate background in modern Chinese history and with an appreciation of theories of political and social science. Tsou has selected eight of his essays, published over the years from 1968 to 1983, to explain Chinese political behavior. Some historical background is included, but the main exegeses relate to the events and changes during and after the Cultural Revolution.

One of the major themes regards the changes in the form of the state from an authoritarian traditional Chinese system at the end of the nineteenth century to varying degrees of "totalitarianness," to use Tsou's term. Tsou uses the definition of "totalitarian" to measure the extent of penetration of political power into civil society and the economic system. He argues that the total collapse of China's traditional political system left a vacuum that permitted the introduction of a communist system, which, initially, could have been considered moderate.

This communist system then began to break down when radical and unpopular programs were introduced. Having survived the Korean War—a winning war is a great unifier—the 3-Anti and 5-Anti movements, and agriculture reform, the system was strained by the Great Leap Forward and expansion of the communes. The people's resistance engendered panic in the leadership, which, viewing the disintegration of the system, then resorted to increasingly greater control leading eventually to the Cultural Revolution.

The Cultural Revolution differed from most revolutions in which elites united with the people to oppose the existing system. The Cultural Revolution was characterized by Mao Zedong attempting to rally the people to oppose the elites. He was supported by the ultra-leftists—the anti-party Gang of Four—who controlled, or at least dominated, the most influential official Chinese periodicals.

In Tsou's view, Chinese Marxism is separated into three phases: Mao Zedong's Thought, from 1927 to 1955-57; movement to the left, from 1955-57 to 1978; and movement to the right, from 1978 to the present. Mao Zedong's Thought on Marxism includes especially the sinification of Marxism, the two most significant contributions of which are: military power versus economic power—political power grows from the barrel of a gun; and material Marxism versus abstract Marxism—Marxism must be tailored to fit the circumstances in which it is applied.

The 1955-57-to-1978 movement to the left encompasses the Great Leap Forward and commune expansion, commencement of the cult of personality of Mao Zedong and the Cultural Revolution, and the movement toward "feudal-totalitarianism."

The phase from 1978 to the present is characterized by a retreat from totalitarianism encouraged by improved U.S.-Chinese relations.

The post-Mao reforms have resulted in a much more broadly based authority. No longer is a cult of personality likely, not even of a present leader such as Hu Yaobang or Deng Xiaoping. The changes in the responsibility system in agriculture have led to increases in private plots and free markets and have resulted in a dramatic increase in agricultural production. In both education and industry, responsibility and leadership have been shifted from the party and government to managers and superintendents in the field.

This compilation of Tsou's essays presents analyses of the most important phases and events in recent Chinese politics in terms of social science theories. Its contribution to the understanding and interpretation of Chinese political evolution is of the greatest value to all specialists in Chinese affairs.

JAMES D. JORDAN

Alexandria
Virginia

TURLEY, WILLIAM S. *The Second Indochina War: A Short Political and Military History, 1954-1975.* Pp. xvii, 234. Boulder, CO: Westview Press, 1986. $24.95.

William Turley's account of the Vietnam war—he touches only briefly on the wars in Cambodia and Laos—is comforting in its familiarity to those of us who lived through it, yet bracing in its freshness. Orthodoxy is not challenged, but rather qualified, and propaganda deftly dissipated with reference to recently available documents and Turley's interviews with leading participants of both sides. The narrative is sober and briskly paced.

However, engaged readers may find their passionately held beliefs dealt with rather too dispassionately. Academics might ask for more exegesis, particularly on whether and when Hanoi deliberately planned military actions primarily to influence decision makers in Washington rather than to demoralize the Southern regime or liberate a piece of territory.

Turley finds the Southern insurgency demonstrably manned and led by the North although supported by some Southerners; the U.S. and Army of the Republic of Vietnam military pacification efforts by and large successful if not very efficient; and the celebrated Tet Offensive a severe defeat acknowledged by the North that left the South stronger than it had been since the war began. The outcome of the war was never certain, but, equally, the narrowness, corruption, and dependency of the Southern elites in contrast to the determination and discipline of their Northern adversaries made it unlikely that continuing U.S. military aid could do more than stave off defeat year after year, which the American political system could not, and did not, tolerate. No surprises here; Turley steers to the mainstream with a steady hand, and the reader is drawn willingly in his wake.

Turley's conclusion on the lessons of the war, and their price, is at once obvious and thought provoking, and the reader hopes Turley will in the future expand not only on the lessons for the United States today, but also for other challengers, other insurgents, and other client regimes. Nevertheless the book's succinct narrative, footnotes, maps, chronology, and bibliographic essay make it a reliable and useful history and an admirable summary of a complex event.

Turley is associate professor of political science at Southern Illinois University.

STEVE HOADLEY

University of Auckland
New Zealand

EUROPE

BELOFF, NORA. *Tito's Flawed Legacy: Yugoslavia and the West since 1939.* Pp. 287. Boulder, CO: Westview Press, 1985. $23.00.

TERZUOLO, ERIC R. *Red Adriatic: The Communist Parties of Italy and Yugoslavia.* Pp. xi, 255. Boulder, CO: Westview Press, 1985. Paperbound, $21.50.

Neither time nor documentation has brought consensus about Yugoslav socialism.

At its best, Western scholarship captures the subjects's complexity and ambiguity. Prognoses about the regime remain tied to judgments about political authenticity. Did the wartime communist resistance forge an enduring multinational regime? How effectively can self-management and nonalignment resolve Yugoslavia's crisis of ideological identity? These books suggest indirectly why the controversy is not likely to be resolved. Eric Terzuolo deals with the question of relations between Italian and Yugoslav communists. Nora Beloff promises a "reassessment" of the entire Yugoslav communist experience. Both authors devote more than half of their work to the period before Yugoslavia's expulsion from the Cominform in 1948, and both have a good command of the sources. Neither author is entirely successful.

Terzuolo's narrative of interparty relations ranges from delicate problems of postwar boundaries and the Slovenes in Italy through Togliatti's "hesitancy" in supporting the Cominform Resolution, and the rise of communist polycentrism. One wishes for better attention to the impact of Yugoslav domestic developments in shaping attitudes toward the Italian Communist Party, but Terzuolo explains how shared interests of both parties toward the Soviet Union impel cooperation. Both parties needed autonomy as a precondition for adaptation to their societies, and they responded to political imperatives from within them. Many will find that the book offers a dimension to the image of Yugoslav political authenticity despite the relative emphasis on the Italian side.

Nora Beloff offers a different image of Yugoslavia. Like all Marxist regimes, the country lives an ignoble lie that runs from Tito's efforts to keep Churchill and Roosevelt "seriously misinformed" about wartime conditions to the "pickled falsehoods" still current in official Yugoslavia and the West. Instead of autonomy, the foreign position of the regime is one of double subordination, "underpinned ideologically by the East and economically by the West." Only the West is cheated. Some parts of this image are well

known, such as the shallow "partisan myth," the massacre of noncommunist resistance forces, and the continuing abuse of human rights. The image nonetheless begs many questions.

Would Beloff's account be different if she had been better treated by the authorities? Why does criticism of Yugoslavia and its intellectuals erupt periodically from Moscow? Why do many Yugoslavs continue to express a strong preference for self-management and nonalignment despite the regime's abundant shortcomings?

The books are reminders that Yugoslavia is a political anomaly that is obscured by anticommunist polemics as much as by the superficial platitudes of regime spokespersons. Yugoslav and Italian communists have in fact transcended many of the dysfunctions that attend Soviet Marxism, and in the judgment of many, the programs are politically congruent with their societies. That is no guarantee of success, nor even relevance. In the 1980s, we are likely to see more, rather than less, of the conflicting images in these books as all political prescriptions—not the least those of communism—experience greater strain.

ZACHERY T. IRWIN
Pennsylvania State University
University Park

DIBB, PAUL. *The Soviet Union: The Incomplete Superpower.* Pp. xxi, 293. Champaign: University of Illinois Press, 1986. $29.95.

WHITING, KENNETH R. *Soviet Air Power.* Pp. xi, 264. Boulder, CO: Westview Press, 1986. $28.50.

Although there is no shortage of attempts to analyze the Soviet Union and to measure its actual power in the international arena, few of these achieve the fine balance that pervades Dibb's study. Drawing on long experience in both academic work and intelligence analysis, he neatly avoids the pitfalls of methodological fanaticism and sheer impressionism to produce a finely tuned assessment of Soviet strengths and weaknesses. In particular, he remains consistently alive to divergences between actualities and the perceptions of them that so often make Soviet conduct and pronouncements puzzling to outsiders.

The book is divided into two main sections, one examining the domestic scene and the other, somewhat longer segment focusing on global aspirations, capabilities, and vulnerabilities. Interestingly, Dibb treats both the Soviet multinational state and its multinational empire under the domestic rubric, in effect reviving the distinction between Foreign Office and Colonial Office. There is, of course, some merit in treating the administration of a client-state system as a domestic problem analogous to the nationality problem within Soviet borders. Both involve much restiveness, and both have been mishandled by the Soviet regime. But by folding the two problems together, Dibb tends to understate the difference that sovereignty—conditional as it may be—still makes, and thus obscures the reasons why the empire is so much more fragile than the state.

What is more important, however, is that he underscores the seriousness of both of these Soviet vulnerabilities, adding a trenchant analysis of the economy's poor performance to round out the portrayal of besetting domestic difficulties. He succeeds admirably in showing how troubled the Soviet leadership has to be, but without suggesting either that the maladies could prove fatal or that such an outcome might be desirable.

On the global plane, since his subject is the assessment of Soviet power, Dibb's treatment focuses largely on military and strategic issues, secondarily on the Soviet Union's position in the international economy. In common with most treatments of military calculations in the context of nuclear capability, this section conveys an unsettling aura of artificiality, since we all know, as do the Soviet leaders, how fallible the assumptions of strategic planning would likely turn out in the event of a nuclear conflagration. Yet that

is in the nature of Dibb's subject and, to his great credit, this portion of his analysis might serve as required reading for those Western officials and citizens who still rely on the stale formula of an evil empire bent on world conquest. Instead we see, under Dibb's guidance, a gigantic state, whose power in the world is almost exclusively military, forced to maintain that power at the expense of a weak economy, the further stagnation of which would in turn threaten its military power, which, in any case, Dibb urges us not to exaggerate. That is what is meant by "incomplete superpower."

Whiting's book might almost be seen as an extended footnote to Dibb's assessment, an examination of Soviet military strength in the air. Filled with technical detail on aircraft, military organization, and strategic planning, this compendium probably would not count as recreational reading for most of us. But it brings a large quantity of data together in coherent form and is especially interesting in its placement of air power as a factor in each of the world areas where the Soviet Union seeks to exert a major influence.

LYMAN H. LEGTERS

University of Washington
Seattle

DOUGLAS, ROY. *World Crisis and British Decline, 1929-1956.* Pp. viii, 293. New York: St. Martin's Press, 1986. $29.95.

In 1929, the British Empire, comprising about a quarter of the globe and an equivalent percentage of the world's population, exercised an influence of first standing in the counsels of international relations. Approximately 25 years later, in 1956, London was "ordered out" of Suez by the United States and, to a lesser extent, the USSR, confirming British decline from great-power status. What were the causes of that decline? Roy Douglas, a reader at the University of Surrey and author of several works on Britain, seeks to advance an answer in his *World Crisis and British Decline.*

He contends that, while a number of global crises contributed to the decline, those crises exhibit close causal relationship to the Great Depression. The latter, the argument goes, sponsored economic nationalism, which, in turn, induced policies such as the Smoot-Hawley tariffs in the United States, French financial pressures on Germany, and uncharacteristic protectionism in the United Kingdom. The differential impacts of those policies varied from the movement toward autarky and unrest in various areas of the British Empire to expanded aggression by Japan and the rise of Hitler in Germany. The last development caused World War II and, with it, an unprecedented depleting of Britain's material resources. Concomitantly, London became unable to replace an outdated navy with the defense requirements of a nuclear age.

Douglas identifies other factors contributing to Britain's decline: its retention of old industrial equipment as well as archaic attitudes toward labor and capital while, contrastingly, other states were "building afresh to meet [the] requirements of the second half of the twentieth century." Such factors, however, were collateral.

The study is absorbing, but, to be persuasive, needs to show more organic links between the Great Depression and the consequences that are claimed to have issued from it. Further, matters varying from labor unrest in the Caribbean to the impact of nationalist sentiments within the British Empire—especially India—and the reverberating effect of the worst single military defeat—at "the hands of Asians"—in Singapore should be more thoroughly discussed.

The work is dispassionate, well organized, and global in focus, thus truly reflecting the worldwide interests of the British Empire. While challenging the theses of many a scholar, the material remains accessible to the average reader; and scholars in global politics, international relations, or twentieth-century political history should find it very useful.

WINSTON E. LANGLEY
University of Massachusetts
Boston

GILLINGHAM, JOHN R. *Industry and Politics in the Third Reich: Ruhr Coal, Hitler and Europe.* Pp. xii, 183. New York: Columbia University Press, 1985. $20.00.

WEBER, R.G.S. *The German Student Corps in the Third Reich.* Pp. xi, 209. New York: St. Martin's Press, 1986. $27.50.

In these well-researched, scholarly studies, Gillingham and Weber have examined two specific examples of the Nazi attempt to implement the policy of *Gleichschaltung* throughout German society. Their findings also further affirm the established conclusion that in many respects the Nazi regime was its own worst enemy, suffering from lack of direction, overlapping administrative bureaus, minimal planning, and lack of expertise. The organized disorganization that allowed all power to be kept in Hitler's hands becomes evident.

Both the Ruhr coal industry and the German student corps proved difficult, indeed impossible, to bring fully into line with the new Nazi order. Yet in both cases this was not due to any sense of ideological opposition to nazism or Nazi ambitions for Germany. Rather, it stemmed from a conservative resistance to change, a hostility toward Nazi attempts to alter traditional rights, privileges, or modes of operation.

John Gillingham's business history of the Ruhr collieries during the Nazi period provides an example of an industry that refused to modernize. Failing to adjust to new moves into synthetics, it refused to respond to stimuli provided by the Nazi regime aimed at developing expanded production capabilities that would look beyond immediate market demand for coal and coke. When war broke out and demand for coal greatly increased, the mines were unable even to maintain existing production levels.

Gillingham also discusses the tremendous impact, both direct and indirect, of the massive Allied bombing raids of 1943-44. Not only did they severely damage mines and transportation systems; they also engendered massive absenteeism and deterioration of morale, as miners sought new housing and minimal security for their bombed-out families. The use of recruited and conscripted foreign labor, as well as Russian prisoners of war, is discussed and evaluated, though mainly from a productivity viewpoint.

Particularly useful is Gillingham's examination of the international agreements between coal producers in Belgium, the Netherlands, France, and Germany, both before and during the war. In fact, the Nazi New Order in Europe broke down old barriers and allowed private firms and banks to organize international groupings and arrangements more easily than had been possible before. Gillingham asserts that it was assumed that many of these would remain permanent, whatever the outcome of the war. He demonstrates convincingly that the ultimate successful creation of the European Coal and Steel Community was due in great part to a continuum of developments that can be traced back well into the pre-World War II period.

R.G.S. Weber's examination of the Nazi relationship with the famed dueling corps of the German universities, while providing much new information, is only a mixed success. Weber sketches a useful historical background of the German fencing fraternities. But when he reaches the focal point of his study, he allows himself to become enmeshed in small details and a multitude of acronyms. There is also no consideration of the place of the fraternity federations in the larger university structure during the Nazi period, nor of the possible interrelationship between Nazi efforts to bring the student corps into line and concomitant attempts to Nazify the whole higher-education system.

While most of the student federations eventually, if reluctantly, accepted Nazi control, one of the two largest federations, the Kosener Senioren-Conventen Verband (KSCV), remained actively hostile, and ultimately dissolved itself in October 1935 rather than accept Nazi regulations. In part the resistance stemmed from the KSCV historical tradition of noninvolvement in politics, plus a reluctance to expel the handful of Jewish members of alumni chapters. But the major opposition was to Nazi attempts to do away with the traditional student honor code

and the dueling that resulted from it. In particular, there was bitter resentment at the banning of the *Mensur*, the obligatory fencing duel required of all candidates for membership in one of the fraternities. Possibly, all this justifies Weber's conclusion that the student corps served as a breeding ground for development of anti-Nazi elements in Germany. Yet the evidence he presents indicates clearly that their opposition was minimally ideological; rather, it originated primarily from allegiance to a dueling tradition and an aristocratic honor code that in many ways engendered the elitist arrogance that helped make Nazi doctrines acceptable in Germany. The traditions and activities of the dueling fraternities, still alive in Germany today, are not ones that merit positive evaluation in terms of the values and attitudes most people regard highly.

PAUL C. HELMREICH

Wheaton College
Norton
Massachusetts

GLOVER, MICHAEL. *The Fight for the Channel Ports, Calais to Brest (1940): A Study in Confusion.* Pp. xv, 269. Boulder, CO: Westview Press, 1985. $25.00.

Michael Glover, with *The Fight for the Channel Ports,* continues his solid contribution to the recording of British military history, a task he began in 1963 with *Wellington's Peninsular Victories.* Few people who study the events of World War II will ever forget the name Dunkirk, a French port where the British were forced to evacuate most of their expeditionary force (BEF) in May 1940. What is little known and what is the subject of *The Fight for the Channel Ports* is that for 18 days after Dunkirk, the BEF outside the Dunkirk perimeter retreated to western France for evacuation from such ports as Calais, Le Havre, Cherbourg, and Brest. By 18 June, the Royal Navy had evacuated 144,171 men. More than 20,000 remained on the Continent.

As one reads this amazing and, at most times, very detailed account of how the British and French resisted the German onslaught, it becomes evident that the scenario for disaster was in place long before the Germans started their push through Belgium on 10 May. In fact, this dilemma was created when, during the BEF buildup in France in 1939-40, the decision was made to place the BEF under French command. This led to critical national defense problems, confronting first Chamberlain and then his successor, Churchill. How long would Britain defend French soil, remembering at all times that once the Germans took the coastal areas in France, the Netherlands, and Belgium, they could use these for staging air raids on Britain? Eventually the Luftwaffe operated from bases in all three countries. Nevertheless, Churchill, throughout May and June, struggled with a major political problem: at what stage could he make a strategic withdrawal, and still save face with the French, to save his troops and materials to fight war another day? Churchill understood that Britain could not sacrifice its men, its fighter command, or its bomber command for the sake of the French alone and was aware that once France had fallen, the Germans were likely to invade Great Britain.

Compounding this problem were key leadership changes. On 10 May, Churchill replaced Chamberlain as prime minister in Great Britain. On 20 May, French General Maxime Weygand replaced General Maurice Gamelin, the latter being relieved for incompetence. So while the German panzer divisions under Generals Guderian and Rommel were bearing down from the east, the Allied military command and political structures were in disarray.

If one wants a single thesis of *The Fight for the Channel Ports,* a passage in the epilogue so states:

Had the B.E.F. been twice as large as it was in May, 1940, there would have been little he [Gamelin] could have done to alter the outcome of the campaign. By his faulty dispositions and the inadequacy of his command system, Gamelin had insured France's defeat *before the first German*

soldier marched into the Ardennes [Editor's emphasis]. Even the Germans who, by March, 1940, had appreciated many of Gamelin's errors, were astonished by the ease and completeness of their victory. Had the *Wehrmacht* had any conception of what they were about to achieve they would have prepared plans, at least in outline, for the next stage of the war—a decisive blow against England. They had done nothing of the kind.

One final point. I would encourage the reader to read the prologue, epilogue, then chapters 1 and 9, in that order, to receive a clear background for the detailed account of the battles recorded within chapters 2 through 8. Chapters 2 through 8 contain the detailed accounts of Dunkirk and its immediate aftermath. Glover handles the interface between battle reports and field maps better than most. However, constant reference to maps in the front of the book does have a minor disruptive and distractive effect on the reader.

In conclusion, I found *The Fight for the Channel Ports* an awe-inspiring book and suggest it be kept close at hand as an excellent military reference book.

RICHARD E. JOHE
Winston-Salem
North Carolina

UNITED STATES

ARNOLD, PERI E. *Making the Managerial Presidency: Comprehensive Reorganization Planning, 1905-80.* Pp. xiv, 374. Princeton, NJ: Princeton University Press, 1986. $37.50.

Studies of comprehensive reorganization of the executive branch of the national government are usually dry and tedious. Peri Arnold, however, has treated this subject with judicious balance and historical sweep and has raised significant questions about the value of such efforts. His chronological and analytical study about reorganization attempts even becomes engrossing when he examines the plans of Johnson, Nixon, and Carter.

Arnold traces his subject from the perspective of public administration, political science, and politics. We follow the process from the efficiency/economy perspective of Taft to the policy analysis/policy evaluation approach of the 1960s.

The major lesson of this survey, which covers the period 1905-80, is that recurrent reorganization planning seeks a more effective presidential management of the executive branch, even though different purposes and organization solutions are suggested. By the 1970s, presidents tended to regard the burdens of managing the executive branch as insurmountable—the tools were simply inadequate. The political pressures for decentralization have outweighed the effects of administrative reform. Reform has been initiated by both Congress and president; their perspectives and motives have varied. Nixon attempted to increase presidential influence in order to achieve greater policy control while Carter saw reorganization as a means of making government more understandable to ordinary citizens and more responsive to their needs.

Arnold traces comprehensive reorganization from Teddy Roosevelt through Carter. There were eleven major planning entities. Assessment of the goals, membership, organization, and success or failure of each is provided. Sources include archival records, interviews, and the public record.

Despite differences in their form and recommendations, there is a thread of continuity in reorganization. Johnson was not notably more successful than Nixon in achieving his organizational changes. Reform plans are compared in terms of their public visibility—low to high—and independence of the president—low to high.

Arnold not only meticulously describes the outcomes of reform; he also raises important questions with regard to the whole process: why does comprehensive reorganization planning occur so frequently, and what are the different formats that have been adopted? He provides a statistical exercise that compares reform efforts and the rate of change in government expenditure. Economy has not been a direct purpose of reform since 1953.

Reorganization planning—such as that by Nixon and Johnson—has often been a response to distrust of permanent government. Arnold finds that such planning viewed in terms of institutional and individual benefits does not fit the interplay of incentives and benefits present in the planning. Comprehensive reorganization was a political project of extraordinary importance even though the recommendations were fought over and then ignored. None of the plans has enabled presidents to manage the executive branch fully. Hence the managerial conception of the presidency is untenable. The managerial presidency then becomes a trap, offering greater capacity and influence to presidents, but generating unrealistic expectations. This does not mean that presidents should abandon such efforts, since administration is central to the modern presidency and to the implementation of policy. All in all, it is a fascinating exploration of one aspect of the paradoxes of presidential power.

JAMES R. KERR

Southern Illinois University
Edwardsville

AU, WILLIAM A. *The Cross, the Flag, and the Bomb: American Catholics Debate War and Peace, 1960-1983.* Pp. xvii, 278. Westport, CT: Greenwood Press, 1985. $29.95.

William Au presents a detailed exposition of American Catholic thinking on war, focusing on the period from 1960 through the issuance of the bishops' pastoral letter, "The Challenge of Peace: God's Promise and Our Response," in 1983. Au begins with a clear analysis of the state of the question in 1960, showing the Catholic Association for International Peace (CAIP) and the Catholic Worker reflecting the polarities in Catholic thought. The CAIP represented the realist position, articulated by Reinhold Niebuhr, Hans Morgenthau, and Catholic thinkers such as John Courtney Murray, S.J., and William O'Brien. The Catholic Worker, principally Dorothy Day, embodied a pacifist position. Au sees the CAIP's moral assessment of war as being defined within the framework of the necessity of thwarting communism. The Catholic Worker, which did not share that sense of the moral superiority of the West, opted for an absolute critique of the use of force. Au argues persuasively that it was "their differing judgements on the moral quality of American society" that "constituted the major dividing line" in the Catholic debate on war and peace over the ensuing two decades.

That debate grew more vigorous with America's deepening involvement in Vietnam, followed by the burgeoning concern over nuclear weapons policy. Au carefully delineates the evolution of positions in this debate, concluding with a fine analysis of the emergence of the bishops' pastoral through its various drafts. Au's study documents, as well, the clear shift in Catholic thinking over this period away from the CAIP realist position to one much closer to the Catholic Worker perspective.

Au's focus is the realm of ideas: books, articles, and pastoral letters. Although he subtitles his work *American Catholics Debate War and Peace,* the American Catholics he deals with are bishops and priests, theologians and political theoreticians. There is no attempt to assess how this quarter-century debate affected the masses of American Catholics. How was it incorporated in Church teaching; how, if at all, did the perceptions of American Catholics shift? William Au has done a fine job of probing American Catholic debate on the issues of war and peace. What is needed is a companion work that assesses the impact of those ideas on that quarter of the American population that makes up the membership of the Catholic Church.

JOHN O'SULLIVAN
Florida Atlantic University
Boca Raton

KOMER, ROBERT W. *Bureaucracy at War: US Performance in the Vietnam Conflict.* Pp. xviii, 174. Boulder, CO: Westview Press, 1986. $20.85.

KOLKO, GABRIEL. *Anatomy of a War: Vietnam, the United States and the Modern Historical Experience.* Pp. xvi, 628. New York: Pantheon Books, 1985. No price.

Both of these books are rooted in the events of the Vietnam war period in that their authors have undertaken subsequent research in order to develop and substantiate points of view that they acquired at the time: Komer was an official in charge of so-called pacification between 1966 and 1968 and later a RAND analyst; Kolko was an antiwar activist and leading critic of post-World War II American foreign policy. Inevitably their points of view are diametrically opposed, even though some of their criticisms of U.S. policies overlap. They also differ in the form of their approach, Komer adopting a political science approach whereas Kolko is above all a historian.

Komer's book belongs to the lessons-of-Vietnam school of writing, seeking to establish a critique of American performance in Vietnam as opposed to analyzing the causes of involvement. Many of his observations are very perceptive—although by this stage not always original. But too often they hinge on the notion that Vietnam was atypical, which implies that in some other Asian country the American bureaucratic and military machine would have done better. This is open to question, as Kolko demonstrates. What is dangerous, in both cases, is the assumption that the eventual collapse of South Vietnam in 1974-75 was due primarily, if not entirely, to American mistakes in the 1960s rather than to the failure of American will during the 1970s. Komer, more than Kolko, fails to trace the course of the actual fighting. In his eagerness to emphasize the value of pacification—when done properly—he fails to see that for much of the time the Vietnam war was, after all, a military conflict.

By contrast, Kolko does pursue the stages of the conflict, analyzing each in its own terms. Some of the themes he explores are extremely interesting and pertinent—notably, the financial and economic dimensions of

U.S. policy and the dilemmas that arose from trying to prevent the Vietnam commitment from distorting American global strategy. In 1967-68, the gold war was probably as important as events in Southeast Asia in determining President Johnson's critical decisions of March 1968, and, for that matter, more important than the antiwar movement to which Kolko belonged. Despite his sympathy with Hanoi, however, Kolko does not repeat the propaganda myths of the side he supported at the time; he offers a hard-hitting analysis of Hanoi's avowed attempt to reunify Vietnam through whatever means were most appropriate during each phase. Nevertheless in the end Kolko is a Marxist-Leninist for whom the triumph of the revolution over imperialism was both inevitable and a good thing. Many who will gain from the perceptiveness of his analysis will find it difficult to accept his assessment of the ultimate significance of the war and his refusal to take seriously even the possibility that a substantial part of the population of Vietnam—or any other Third World country—might legitimately have preferred to live under a non-Communist regime indefinitely.

R. B. SMITH

University of London
England

POLLARD, ROBERT A. *Economic Security and the Origins of the Cold War, 1945-1950.* Pp. 378. New York: Columbia University Press, 1985. $32.50.

Robert A. Pollard, formerly a research associate at the Woodrow Wilson Center and now with the United States Foreign Service, offers a fresh analysis of American foreign policy in the seminal five-year period following World War II. His carefully researched study focuses on the Truman administration's determination to substitute traditional peacetime isolation for a vigorous plan to build a postwar world in which the mutual economic dependence of the industrial nations would militate against future wars. It is the most balanced account yet of the American policy of economic security, a reasoned alternative to the revisionist historians' interpretations that have dominated for nearly two decades.

After 1945, the United States enjoyed unparalleled economic power and accepted unprecedented responsibility for rebuilding the war-ravaged nations of Europe and Asia. Pollard illustrates that Harry S Truman, Dean Acheson, William L. Clayton, and other key leaders shared a common view that the causes of World War II lay with the autarkic, self-contained economic systems and economic rivalries that led to depression during the 1930s. They sought to avoid similar conditions by encouraging a free trade system that would bind the industrial powers together as interdependent economies. This policy of economic interdependence, they believed, would bring prosperity and security not only to the United States but to the world.

Pollard reviews the major American foreign policy developments from the Bretton Woods Conference to the Korean War. He examines the Marshall Plan, the crises in Western Europe and Germany, the reconstruction of Japan, the establishment of the North Atlantic Treaty Organization, and relations with the Soviet Union that led eventually to the policy of military containment. In addition, he demonstrates that the economic security strategy was a success: the Marshall Plan did restore European production and facilitate political cooperation between West Germany and its former enemies; Japan was reconstructed as a politically stable state the economy of which was linked to the Western democracies; and Western economic growth did make possible an enduring alliance between the United States, Japan, and most of Europe. It was only the 1949 victory of the Communists in China and the outbreak of the Korean War in 1950 that ended the successful substitution of economic for military power to achieve American security interests.

Revisionist scholars such as Joyce and Gabriel Kolko, William Appleman Williams,

Thomas G. Paterson, Fred L. Block, and others have emphasized that the Truman administration made extensive use of trade policy and foreign aid for political purposes, particularly to contain communism. Pollard generally agrees with their emphasis on the ideological and economic foundations of American foreign policy. He disagrees, however, with those who argue that the United States sought to restructure the world simply so American business could trade and profit without restrictions and to preclude the Left from power. He emphasizes that American foreign policy objectives were not necessarily achieved at the expense of other countries and that the United States did not oppose only the Left; the Truman administration opposed all forms of economic nationalism, moving as vigorously against commercial discrimination by the British as by the Soviets. Pollard finds that American leaders were willing to sacrifice short-term national advantage to long-term gains in stability and security. Their policy of economic security certainly aided American capitalism, but it was not designed for that narrow purpose. It was designed to foster global prosperity and, thereby, to promote United States security.

This is a balanced, thoughtful study. It makes a convincing case that the Truman administration was more successful than any subsequent administration in executing foreign economic policy. Pollard demonstrates that the postwar leaders were correct in their view that the foundation of American security is a healthy and interdependent world economy. Conditions have changed since the 1940s, of course, and the United States no longer has the economic dominance that it had in 1945-50. Nonetheless, we must not undervalue the role of economic interdependence in upholding the Western alliance and American national security. In this regard, Pollard sees today's challenge as being less from the Soviet military than from internal economic ills among the Western nations.

ROBERT DETWEILER

California State University
San Bernardino

SMOLLA, RODNEY A. *Suing the Press: Libel, the Media, & Power*. Pp. viii, 277. New York: Oxford University Press, 1986. $18.95.

Smolla's book capitalizes on the public interest in libel law sparked by Carol Burnett, Ariel Sharon, William Westmoreland, and other political and entertainment luminaries who have recently pursued well-publicized cases against the press. This focus on celebrity plaintiffs is at once a strength and a weakness: it enables Smolla to illustrate developments in libel law by explicating dramatic, inherently interesting cases; however, it also leaves one wondering whether the book paints a representative picture of libel litigation today.

Smolla links his selection of cases—most dealing with libel, but with some on obscenity and privacy—by arguing that they show how cultural changes underlie shifts in libel law. *New York Times* v. *Sullivan,* which required public officials to prove actual malice, was an offshoot of and stimulus to 1960s' activism; recent Supreme Court decisions and the spate of suits by business leaders and others against the press underscore concern about protecting reputations and reining in runaway media. One bit of telling evidence Smolla notes is the frequency with which juries misunderstand or ignore the high standard of the actual malice rule and find against media defendants. Despite the plausible connection that exists between cultural milieu and anti-media litigation, the book could profit from more thorough attention to the history of press practices, popular reaction to them, and the course of libel law. Along these lines, *Protecting the Best Men: An Interpretive History of the Law of Libel* by Norman L. Rosenberg, which appeared at about the same time as Smolla's book, provides a more satisfying historical foundation.

Although Smolla devotes much space to the colorful facts of well-known libel cases, he carefully weaves in his analysis of key legal developments. A seeming retreat from the actual malice doctrine has altered the balance between protecting reputation and promoting uninhibited discussion. One up-shot is that plaintiffs now use libel suits for disputes that cannot be resolved by litigation, Smolla laments. Such cases as *Westmoreland* v. *CBS, Sharon* v. *Time,* and *William Tavoulareas* v. *Washington Post* involved clashes of ideology and interpretation more than disputes about facts. Compounding the problem for the press is the scrutiny of news-production practices that litigation brings. Few news organizations emerge unscathed from the rigorous discovery process that accompanies most suits, and, unfortunately, many journalists resort to arrogant proclamations about freedom of the press to justify their actions. Given popular attitudes toward the press, Smolla observes, media self-righteousness backfires in jury decisions.

Smolla's decision to focus on suits brought by well-known plaintiffs makes for engaging reading and provides ample opportunity to develop his ideas about the state of libel law. Unfortunately, this emphasis prevents the book from providing a complete view of libel law today. Smolla notes the work of the Libel Defense Resource Center and Stanford law professor Marc Franklin in tracking nationwide trends in litigation, but he discusses it only in passing. More attention to run-of-the-mill libel suits would show how cases involving prominent plaintiffs have affected developments everywhere—if indeed they have, as Smolla suggests. *Suing the Press,* therefore, provides a lively, though not perfectly balanced, status report on libel and related media law.

RICHARD B. KIELBOWICZ
University of Washington
Seattle

WILSON, CHRISTOPHER P. *The Labor of Words: Literary Professionalism in the Progressive Era.* Pp. xviii, 239. Athens: University of Georgia Press, 1985. $24.00.

In *The Labor of Words*, Christopher P. Wilson examines the rise of journalism as a profession during the Progressive Era in the United States. His main interest is in a cultural analysis of the new values and social structures that journalism both reflected and created. The effect of the market economy at the end of the nineteenth century turned a genteel, elite, literary, and personalized occupation into an organized, mass-oriented, editor-dominated system of specialized routine, with higher pay and status. Newspaper, magazine, and book writers were faced with new roles in a new structure.

One of the very good things about Wilson's book is his ability to connect systemwide contradictions and individual ambiguities. The first four chapters describe the larger structural changes in journalistic publishing, and the last four present case studies of four popular writers of the day, each of whom contend with these changes in particular yet patterned ways.

The new power of publishers and editors to dominate the writing process through office organization and assignment meant control both of subject and of style—"popular naturalism." In the name of independence from party politics and of democratic service control both of subject and of style—popular to a mass readership, men such as S. S. McClure, William Randolph Hearst, and Frank Doubleday created a system that seemed to promise writers independence and a position from which to change society but in fact absorbed both the writers and their products in new and more thorough ways.

The new system Wilson describes is the context for his closer look at the careers of Jack London, Upton Sinclair, David Graham Phillips, and Lincoln Steffens. In each case, the writer's idiosyncratic conception of his role evolved, was modified, and finally clashed with the new work system and its ethos of professionalism. For each the result was a painful recognition that he was part of the very system he aimed to change.

Wilson is most effective when he is writing about the interplay between economic forces, social structures, and personal desires and values, as in his analysis of Sinclair's *The Jungle,* where editorial control, rhetorical strategies, and packaging are sorted out with shrewdness and discrimination.

Less successful are Wilson's comments on style, specifically naturalism. Despite numerous generalizations, there is little careful analysis of tone and language worthy of the level of the book's other arguments. When Wilson remarks, to pick out one example, that "reporting, in turn, set the tone for other writers," we need to know exactly what the tone was and to see the influence at work. Yet when we turn to the particular writers in the latter half of the book, the discussion of style is short, rather obvious, and never carefully tied to the earlier generalities.

Wilson's own writing is serviceable but given to dissertation mannerisms. Also, the general reader will occasionally wish that dates were more often provided as we jump from the early chapters to the later ones. Overall, though, Wilson's book is worth reading by the nonspecialist as it traces the beginnings of a system that, later extended through radio and television, now affects us all.

TOM SCANLAN

University of Minnesota
St. Paul

SOCIOLOGY

DANZIGER, SHELDON H. and DANIEL H. WEINBERG, eds. *Fighting Poverty: What Works and What Doesn't.* Pp. viii, 418. Cambridge, MA: Harvard University Press, 1986. $27.50.

ROCHEFORT, DAVID A. *American Social Welfare Policy: Dynamics of Formulation and Change.* Pp. xii, 206. Boulder, CO: Westview Press, 1986. Paperbound, $22.00.

Assessing the dramatic growth in governmental efforts to ameliorate poverty in the United States during the last twenty years is the focus of these two very different volumes. That this trend has been checked to some degree in recent years underscores the need to undertake the kind of evaluation to which these works contribute.

Fighting Poverty is a meaty anthology that includes essays by many well-known social scientists who study the economics, politics, and sociology of American poverty, including such individuals as Robert Haveman, Nathan Glazer, Christopher Jencks, Hugh Heclo, and others. The collection resulted from a 1984 conference that assessed the anti-poverty efforts of the last twenty years. Though wide in scope, this volume is surprisingly well focused on some central themes to which the essays build in a logical and constructive manner—unlike so many conference editions of this kind. Together with the uniformly high quality of the contributions, these features make this a fine work for a broad audience.

The diversity of the topics and findings in this volume preclude simple synthesis. Sections examine the economic, political, and social effects of anti-poverty efforts, the consequences of economic growth and business cycles for the poor, the politics of policy changes, and other questions that are central to evaluating what has happened. A most interesting finding is that the huge post-1960s effort has achieved much in ameliorating poverty, particularly for certain groups—like the elderly and poor whites—without imposing very significant social costs—such as breaking up families—or reducing individual incentives for self-help. *Fighting Poverty* can only be faulted for limited imagination; it fails to consider what policies and circumstances might have made greater differences compared to what was found and offers as reform what many would judge to be tepid fine-tuning of extant programs.

Rochefort's *American Social Welfare Policy* focuses on assessing the role of social perceptions in shaping different kinds of social welfare programs since the New Frontier. Attempting to correct what he regards as the determinism of the "progressive" and Marxist explanations for the development of social welfare policy, he probes cases of major legislation in mental health, old age, and welfare reform from a "social images" perspective. His findings, which are similar in many respects to Heclo's in the other volume, point to the overwhelming importance of a political consensus in making social policy changes possible; further, the differences in "social images" that different recipient groups have in popular opinion powerfully influence chances for success in the legislative process. Though this work undeniably points to an important source of constraint in welfare politics, Rochefort's theoretical approach is too ambiguous to make much sense of it; his theory does not relate it to other factors and becomes tangled in problems of cause and effect.

PAUL KANTOR

Fordham University
Bronx
New York

HAMILTON, RICHARD F. and JAMES D. WRIGHT. *The State of the Masses.* Pp. xii, 470. New York: Aldine, 1986. $39.95. Paperbound, $18.95.

Hamilton and Wright have studied the results of surveys on how happy and satisfied people in the United States said they were during the 1970s. Even if trendy academics during the 1970s spoke of the greening of America or thought that factory work made people very unhappy with their lives, the people themselves always stated that they were quite satisfied with their work and were happy personally. The state of the masses during the 1970s can best be described as very happy.

From time to time the Gallup poll does show that the public changes its list of concerns. Hamilton and Wright point out that this is an artifact of the methodology and that underlying moods remain constant. Even though the 1970s was a period of stagflation with many segments of the population losing the battle with inflation, none of this affected how happy people were. Even a decline in the standard of living is not correlated with a sense of happiness. If there

is one major conclusion of this book it is that the state of the economy is not correlated with life satisfaction. Neither is race, gender, occupation, education, or total family income. Hamilton and Wright think that people are really satisfied with marriage and the family, since the divorced usually remarry.

During the 1970s the United States was supposed to be moving into a postmaterialist or postindustrialist society. This viewpoint came about, we are told, from too many nights spent at the dining halls of Yale and too few hours talking to the masses. Traditional goals and concerns dominated throughout the period. Hamilton and Wright even feel that leaders who grasp this concept would be likely to be elected. They stop short of stating that Ronald Reagan owes his presidency to his understanding of the true state of the masses.

Are the masses really quietly happy, with no real concerns? Will economic issues never affect how happy people say they are? When the comedian Jimmy Durante started his act by asking the audience, "Is everybody happy?" the audience always yelled back, "Yes." Maybe Jimmy Durante believed that. Perhaps Hamilton and Wright would also.

GEORGE H. CONKLIN

North Carolina Central University
Durham

TODD, EMMANUEL. *The Explanation of Ideology.* Pp. ix, 230. New York: Basil Blackwell, 1985. $24.95.

KAPLAN, MARION A., ed. *The Marriage Bargain: Women and Dowries in European History.* Pp. xi, 182. New York: Institute for Research in History and Haworth Press, 1984. $22.95.

Emmanuel Todd is a research fellow at the Institut national d'études demographiques, Paris. Todd argues that world variations in social ideology and beliefs are conditioned by family structure. He analyzes the distribution of family forms throughout the world and examines the relations between particular structures and, for example, religious values, communism, totalitarianism, and social democracy. He also discusses the links between these forms and a variety of social phenomena: illegitimacy, suicide, infanticide, marital stability, equality between the sexes, and inheritance laws. The hypothesis of the book is that "the ideological system is everywhere the intellectual embodiment of family structure.... One ideological category and only one corresponds to each family type."

This book suffers the problem of any reductionist theory, that is, how to squeeze into the theory the parts that will not fit! Todd is not much disturbed by such problems, however. Unfortunately for Todd, there are many exceptions to his theory. His explanations are ingenious but not convincing. When the theory does not fit, the British Labour Party is fit into the Latin side. When, for example, social indicators are not available for suicide rates in the Soviet Union, he uses other data to suggest information that fits into his theory. When information is not available on Ethiopia, the information on Sudan will do.

He discusses infanticide, age at marriage, the role of women, literacy, suicide rates, religious practices, and education. Undoubtedly some of this is related to family structure. But is family structure shaped by other factors? Perhaps family structure shapes these? Unfortunately, Todd's claim is much grander. He does discuss the role of regional conflicts, the church, the political party, and ethnic variations, but all such factors are reduced to what he calls an anthropological base. He is never clear on what he means by this term. Surely anthropology encompasses more than Todd's theories. Todd asserts that family structure shapes and explains all of social reality. He never attempts to prove the direction of that relationship. He asserts, but does not demonstrate, that family structure causes variations in religious values and economic belief; that family structure causes regional conflicts and ethnic variations. I would not attempt to advise him on how he could prove such relationships; but he does

assume—incorrectly—that he has done so.

Such oversimplifications are inevitable in a book that wishes to explain the entire world on the basis of one theory. The basic premise here is seriously flawed. All complexities are reduced. Why did Christianity fragment while Islam did not? Family structure is the explanation—of course. Why has the black family system suffered in the United States? His explanation is polygamy practices in Africa.

Todd does provide some interesting insights. I found his analysis of the difference between Arab and other forms of socialism worthy of serious consideration. Possibly individualist values shape—or limit—political life. Probably such values are related to family structure. If he had made this kind of argument, and avoided overstatements, he would have made a valuable contribution to an understanding of the role of family structure in shaping political and economic ideology.

Todd is an anthropologist, while I am a political theorist. This book review offers an illustration of the strengths and weaknesses of cross-disciplinary analysis. I am not as concerned with differing family structures as is Todd. I am, however, very concerned about the shallowness of his definitions of politics, democracy, liberty, and equality. As Todd explains in his conclusion, his goal is to attack any beliefs in religious or political truth. Politics is a dream. History is meaningless. What he claims that he values is a high degree of tolerance and a measure of skepticism. What I see in the book is a very ideological diatribe against any values that do not conform to the values of Western European liberal democracies.

The Marriage Bargain: Women and Dowries in European History is a short volume of essays, edited by Marion Kaplan of the Institute for Research in History. The book discusses the dowry in Mediterranean Europe, thirteenth-century Siena, late nineteenth-century Sicily, among the Jews in imperial Germany, and in modern Greece.

The general theme involves the relationship between the dowry and women's position in society. The book demonstrates the importance of linking economics and politics to views of sexuality, marriage, and the role of women. The roles of kin, real property, and money are also linked to love, sex, and marriage.

The dowry has been a payment made by the bride's family in cash, goods, or property to the groom. The dowry was the most significant factor in a young woman's marriageability and, hence, the most significant factor affecting her future. The authors in this volume demonstrate how, through the dowry, the political, economic, and social determinants that limited women's position are revealed. Studies of the dowry address issues of women's status, their roles in the family, the family economy, and the economy at large. Such studies force us to ask questions about women's power and autonomy: about women's relationships to parents, husbands, and their children, and about women's—and men's—marriage and fertility patterns.

Feminist political scientists are continually urging that an adequate understanding of the public must be enlarged to consider family life in an analysis of political life. The traditional liberal distinction between private and public might still be useful in political analysis; perhaps not everything that is personal is political. Nonetheless, while Todd seems to have seriously overstated his case, both books provide valuable evidence of the importance of family in any discussion of politics.

MARY LOU KENDRIGAN
Lansing Community College
Michigan

TOMLINS, CHRISTOPHER L. *The State and the Unions: Labor Relations, Law, and the Organized Labor Movement in America, 1880-1960.* Pp. xvii, 348. New York: Cambridge University Press, 1985. $39.50. Paperbound, $12.95.

CHAISON, GARY N. *When Unions Merge.* Pp. xiii, 186. Lexington, MA: D.C. Heath, 1986. $24.00.

These books were read following the bankruptcy of LTV Corporation and during the strike at USX. In the context of the irrefutable decline in union membership and the demise of our smokestack industries, these two books make valuable contributions to understanding how we got where we are. Christopher L. Tomlins's *State and the Unions* takes a broad view of unionism, its birth, its growth, and its retrenchment. In *When Unions Merge*, Gary Chaison closely examines one aspect of unionism—the merger of unions—to provide us with a clearer understanding of how a changing technology and a changed economy have affected unions, and how changes in unions may affect us.

Tomlins's book is divided into three parts. Part 1 scopes out the changes wrought by the Industrial Revolution, specifically the post-Civil War period, which saw the emergence of large manufacturing enterprises. Part 2 discusses the emergence of "industrial pluralism" during the 1930s and 1940s, characterized by Franklin Roosevelt's New Deal policies, especially the National Labor Relations Act and the National Labor Relations Board. Part 3 analyzes the shift in emphasis prior to World War II from encouraging the growth of unions to postwar efforts to create a balance under the Taft-Hartley Act between the interests of employers and those of unions, and to establish a bill of rights for employees who owed allegiance to the unions and the employers.

The State and the Unions focuses on the premise of industrial pluralism—that the powers and the players in our capitalistic society are so numerous and diverse that change occurs by consensus, rather than via one governing entity or philosophy. Tomlins regards this premise as false. The state—that is, the federal government and its administrative bodies—interacts with employers and unions in such a way, according to Tomlins, that one of the two adversaries must invariably be the loser. Although industrial pluralism argues that management and labor do not always have mutually exclusive interests, state intervention may tip the scales in favor of one side, according to Tomlins.

He cites government actions, legislation, and court decisions that tipped the scales in favor of organized labor during the 1930s and 1940s, and those same state entities acting in favor of management in more recent years. The concept is not without appeal.

Understandably, Tomlins observes, unions are reluctant to admit that "in building their future on industrial pluralism, they have built their future on sand." He concludes that American workers have only been able to obtain a "counterfeit liberty" by working through the state and that they must use their own initiative to create the world they desire.

Tomlins's book covers a broad history and a vast expanse of labor relations law. My one criticism of his premise concerning the falsity of industrial pluralism is that he may have overlooked the self-correcting nature of so complex a mechanism. The oil embargo of 1973-74 illustrated that high prices could make alternative energy sources viable. Similarly, overpaid union workers priced themselves and their industries out of business, by making foreign imports and automated, robot-run manufacturing plants economically feasible. Of course, poor management practices had a part to play, but the unions became the ultimate victims of industrial pluralism. The economy will eventually straighten itself out, and a growth in unionized workers in the service industries is foreseeable. But to say that industrial pluralism is false is to ignore the myriad factors that led to the decline of unions and our heavy industries.

Gary Chaison's *When Unions Merge* is much narrower in scope. His emphasis is on the causes and effects of mergers between national unions. He provides a historical overview of such mergers from 1890 through 1984, including the emergence of the large labor federations. In devising a model of the union merger process, he stresses that merger is not an incident, but a process that happens over a period of time. Chaison provides a realistic look at the obstacles to merger that range from negotiations, to internal and external opposition, to institutional differences.

Chaison acknowledges the changes that have occurred in the 1980s, with concession bargaining, two-tiered wage systems, and the precipitous drop in strike activity. Nevertheless, he seems to adopt Tomlins's philosophy that greater union foresight, creativity, and activism will assist unions in getting out of the doldrums. What has in fact happened is a technological revolution that has significantly and irrevocably changed our manpower needs. No amount of membership innovation will revive unions if a large percentage of members cannot find work.

Chaison correctly perceives the rise of mergers both as growth strategies and as predatory moves. Such raiding tactics have occurred in the past, but the potential for large-scale abuse becomes more likely in his prediction. This aspect of the book hints at a chilling future for the unions. I would have preferred more discussion of this issue. Perhaps Chaison is already in the process of writing his next book along these lines.

Both Tomlins's and Chaison's books are well written and researched. I found them enlightening and educational. They are valuable in what they present, and provocative in what they intimate. They are recommended reading for the serious student of labor relations.

JOSEPH E. KALET
Bureau of National Affairs, Inc.
Washington, D.C.

ECONOMICS

AKIN, JOHN S., CHARLES C. GRIFFIN, DAVID K. GUILKEY, and BARRY M. POPKIN. *The Demand for Primary Health Services in the Third World.* Pp. xiv, 252. Totowa, NJ: Rowman & Allanheld, 1985. $35.00.

This book aims at a "comprehensive description and analysis of the use of primary health care services in the Third World." The authors, three economists and a nutritionist, want to provide information that may be helpful to policymaking. After a brief introduction, they proceed with an overview of existing knowledge on health care utilization in Third World countries. This survey, presented in chapter 2, stresses the coexistence side-by-side of traditional and modern practices, which are adopted depending on the nature and severity of illness. Akin, Griffin, Guilkey, and Popkin note also the importance of self-treatment and the significant role of sellers of pharmaceuticals as a source of medical advice. Chapter 3 discusses the determinants of the health care patterns, using an organizational framework derived from economic demand theory. The emphasis is consequently on economic dimensions, such as prices and incomes, and the behavioral motivation is assumed to be rational maximization of benefits. Although this approach may not be completely convincing to medical sociologists and anthropologists, it has the advantage of focusing on variables that can be quantitatively modeled and that are relevant for policymaking. Another advantage is to demonstrate how much of the noneconomic information can be incorporated into the demand theory framework, although admittedly some knowledge becomes lost in the process.

The formal modeling of the demand for health care is the subject of chapter 4, where various mathematical models, starting from rather simple and proceeding to more elaborate ones, are presented. The discussion includes an introduction to statistical estimation problems, but it is kept at a fairly nontechnical level. In chapter 5 the authors show how theoretical demand models may be used to analyze health care consumption in a specific Third World context. The area studied, the Bicol region of the Philippines, was presumably selected because the necessary data had apparently been generated in connection with economic development projects. In deference to the general reader, Akin and his coauthors relegate the technical aspects of the models and the detailed statistical estimations to separate appendixes. The most important conclusion drawn from the

analysis of the Bicol case is that economic variables explain very little of the prevailing pattern of health care usage. The importance of this negative finding is that, within the prevailing range of prices, low income is not a barrier to health care access in the region. The most important factors affecting the choice of care seem to be seriousness of illness and perceived quality of care. One might argue therefore that economic models are not well suited to explain health care behavior in the Third World. Nevertheless, these models are useful to the extent that they deal with variables that are under the control of policymakers and administrators. For instance, Akin, Griffin, Guilkey, and Popkin are able to argue that since user fees are not a barrier to health care, as is widely assumed, they may be the means to make available higher quality care within given budgetary limitations. This view reflects a certain free-market bias in the book, but it may be seen simply as hard-headed budgeting.

GASTON V. RIMLINGER

Rice University
Houston
Texas

ANDERSON, JAMES E. and JARED E. HAZLETON. *Managing Macroeconomic Policy: The Johnson Presidency.* Pp. xiii, 285. Austin: University of Texas Press, 1986. No price.

As Anderson and Hazleton state, the objective of their research was not to analyze the success or failure of the macroeconomic policies of the Johnson administration, but to discuss the management of institutions and the development of macroeconomic policies. They held steadfast to that objective. Information for their study came mainly from the texts of interviews and memoranda from the cast of players who influenced macroeconomic policies during the Johnson era.

The format of the book is straightforward and systematic. There are two introductory chapters devoted mainly to presidential responsibility and to the style of President Johnson. The substance of the work consists of four chapters on the management of fiscal, monetary, wage-price, and foreign economic policy. These chapters describe the principle institutions and organizations, along with the relevant personnel, that implemented policies in those fields.

For example, there is an explanation of the structure of the Federal Reserve System and why that organization is independent of the executive and legislative branches of government after appointments have been recommended by the president and approved by the Congress. After descriptions of President Johnson's appointments to the Board of Governors of the Federal Reserve System, Anderson and Hazleton correctly explain that coordination of monetary and fiscal policies is usually that of persuasion by the president and members of various executive agencies, and to a lesser extent persuasion by members of Congress. Anderson and Hazleton also correctly note that congressional concern about monetary policy rises with interest rates because short-run political interest in monetary policy is linked to the performance of the economy.

Anderson and Hazleton present little or no empirical information about changes in government spending, the money supply, interest rates, or unemployment over the course of the Vietnam war. I believe that if data had been provided, that information would have helped to explain the great difficulty in coordinating monetary and fiscal policies.

The chapter on wage-price policy and the operation of guideposts is exceptionally good. Although Anderson and Hazleton admit that the guideposts were not very effective, they outline three enforcement techniques used by the Johnson administration to contain price and wage increases. The first consisted of intangible techniques, such as telegrams from Johnson to business and labor leaders. The second comprised the tangible techniques, including such policies as disposing of stockpiles and raising import control levels. Finally, there was government symbolism; the most notable of this type of technique was to keep government wage increases in line with those in the private sector.

There is little doubt that Anderson and Hazleton deliberately wrote the book for historians and other social scientists without formal academic training in economic theory.

MARY A. HOLMAN
George Washington University
Washington, D.C.

CORNES, RICHARD and TODD SANDLER. *The Theory of Externalities, Public Goods, and Club Goods.* Pp. xii, 303. New York: Cambridge University Press, 1986. No price.

Most contemporary economic analysis focuses on private goods. These are commodities that we buy, if we can afford them, when we want or think we need them, the stock of which we reduce when we purchase them, and that we use up when we consume them. We pay for their production when we buy them, we cannot in general get them without paying, and we ourselves get the benefits of consuming them. They include shirts and ties, videocassette recorders and microcomputers, sandwiches, and apartments. Arguably, most commodities are of this sort. But many are not.

We share golf courses, turnpikes, and hospitals. We share ownership of corporations; we share risk through insurance policies. Some clubs we enter voluntarily, like stamp and chess clubs, swimming and tennis clubs, and blood banks, and some we are forced to enter. But whether we pay the fee voluntarily or are taxed for our local elementary schools, these clubs all have characteristics in common. They all give us, in exchange for the fee we pay, a share in something, not the whole thing. We are allocated by time, place or intensity a right to use partially, but not to use up and, in general, not to alienate what it is we share. At base we share things either because the sharing itself is useful or because we feel we cannot individually afford the price of buying one for ourselves alone. The vast majority of commodities are either private or shared, but not all. Arguably, some of the most important are neither.

There are things we produce of which we each get everything that is produced. Physics is an example. It is certainly something we produce, and to produce it costs a lot. Physical knowledge is economically important as an input to the production of other things and, to some people at least, as an item of enjoyable consumption itself. Physics, however, does not have to be shared out among its consumers. Each one can have as much as is produced. Scientific knowledge in general is of this form, as is much of what we call the arts. Beethoven need not write the Ninth twice for two of us each to consume the whole thing. Radio signals and navigational beacons are similar. Each receiver can have the entire program or the entire warning without in any way reducing the amount available to any other receiver. These goods are public in a way private and shared goods are not and cannot be.

Cornes and Sandler have each devoted a large part of their last ten years or so to analyzing club and public goods. This book represents a statement of their cumulative results. The presentation is clear. They begin with the externalities of private consumption and move to thorough consideration first of public and then of club goods. They write well, and their formal presentation is within the range of many nonspecialists. Perhaps the most useful aspect of this book is the way Cornes and Sandler integrate and extend results that they have previously worked out in more limited formats. They consider the full range of questions usually associated with joint and shared supply: equilibrium, optimality of provision, methods of provision, the size of clubs, the range of goods shared in a club of a given type, uncertainty, and risk. They very usefully consider joint

products, one of which is in joint supply or shared, and they comment on a range of methods for estimating demand. Their work amounts to a presentation of current theory—much of which they developed—that is very nearly complete and quite valuable.

Cornes and Sandler do not discuss substantive examples in any depth, and this is a shortcoming. Empirical discussion could certainly integrate different sections of their work in a compelling way. As they admit, they do not sufficiently treat the localness of joint and shared supply, the way in which the value of consumption varies as distance increases from the point of supply. And they do not adequately assess the extent to which problems of voluntary provision arise from differences in preferences rather than from the familiar problem of free riding. All these would make the book more useful—and longer.

Most of our economics may be about private goods, but most of our politics is about the kinds of things Cornes and Sandler analyze in this book. This work contributes to a development of the theory of joint and shared supply more commensurate with the economic importance of the provision of these goods.

THOMAS FOGARTY

Colgate University
Hamilton
New York

RUSSELL, LOUISE B. *Is Prevention Better than Cure?* Pp. x, 129. Washington, DC: Brookings Institution, 1986. $26.95. Paperbound, $9.95.

In this short, readable, worthwhile book, Russell tackles the assumption that prevention costs less than cure and in doing so, uses and improves upon cost-effectiveness analysis. Her work is clearly written and well organized.

The book's design is described in chapter 1. Chapter 2 examines the strategy of the smallpox and measles vaccine, and the major focus of chapter 3 is the screening program for hypertension. In both these substantive chapters, Russell provides excellent summaries of medical studies, alerts the reader to the nuances and complexities of issues, and startles the reader with evidence that prevention is not always the better investment. Her discussion of hypertension is provocative.

Russell's most imaginative chapter is her fourth, where she attempts to build cost-effectiveness models to evaluate exercise as a possible way to improve health. In this chapter, she not only gives a useful summary and critique of existing studies; she also sensitizes the reader to alternative perspectives—are we measuring cost effectiveness for the individual, a subgroup, or society as a whole?—and demonstrates how to approach the data and synthesize the information so that aggregate estimates can be presented in usable form.

For many of us, various biases and anxieties are brought to the health field, where the focus is on well-being and longevity. Russell cuts into the health field material with cold clarity and is able to declare in her overview chapter, chapter 5, that choosing investments in prevention is an economic choice like any other. This is both her strength and weakness, for the book left me feeling that I needed a human balance to it. Russell, after all, leaves it to others to deal with the pain of statistical tragedies—the one case in a million where the preventive inoculation kills.

If there is a criticism to be made, it is that Russell does not grapple sufficiently with the implications of the limits of her economic logic. When numbers and values are plugged into a macro-level balance sheet, there is an unavoidable element of arbitrariness. Russell herself admits this in her examination of the cost of exercise, for example. When discussing the cost of time used in exercise—including travel time, preparation time, and shower time—she points to the problems that arise when the attempt is made to measure time as a major resource cost. When the appropriate value is not a wage rate, but how an individual values his or her time, the concept to be measured is opportunity cost. Not only is there no market price for the leisure given up for exercise, but people value their leisure differently, and some people dislike exercise, which increases the cost to them. One of the practical possibilities Russell suggests for factoring time into a cost equation is to include it without dollar value. But if a dollar value is assigned to exercise time, she suggests using the average wage. Why average wage? It is unexplained decisions like this one that call into question the objectivity of the entire process.

To her credit, Russell develops nonmonetary as well as monetary balance sheets for her major health areas of smallpox and measles inoculation, hypertension treatment, and exercise. The book is worth reading not only by those who specialize in health issues, but also by the many others who study general public policy.

ROBERTA ANN JOHNSON
University of San Francisco
California

OTHER BOOKS

AARON, HENRY J. and CAMERAN M. LOUGY. *The Comparable Worth Controversy.* Pp. ix, 57. Washington, DC: Brookings Institution, 1986. Paperbound, $7.95.

ABRAMSON, JEFFREY B. *Liberation and Its Limits: The Moral and Political Thought of Freud.* Pp. xi, 160. Boston, MA: Beacon Press, 1986. Paperbound, $7.95.

ARONSON, J. RICHARD and JOHN L. HILLEY. *Financing State and Local Governments.* 4th ed. Pp. xviii, 265. Washington, DC: Brookings Institution, 1986. $29.95. Paperbound, $9.95.

BARKUN, MICHAEL. *Crucible of the Millenium: The Burned-Over District of New York in the 1840s.* Pp. xi, 194. Syracuse, NY: Syracuse University Press, 1986. $27.50. Paperbound, $14.95.

BARTH, FREDRIK. *The Last Wali of Swat: An Autobiography as Told to Fredrik Barth.* Pp. 199. New York: Columbia University Press, 1985. $30.00.

BECKER, LAWRENCE C. *Reciprocity.* Pp. xii, 436. New York: Routledge & Kegan Paul in association with Methuen, 1986. $32.50.

BENSTON, GEORGE J. *An Analysis of the Causes of Savings and Loan Association Failures.* Pp. 182. New York: New York University, Graduate School of Business Administration, Solomon Brothers Center for the Study of Financial Institutions, 1986. Paperbound, no price.

BIBERAJ, ELEZ. *Albania and China: A Study of an Unequal Alliance.* Pp. xi, 183. Boulder, CO: Westview Press, 1986. Paperbound, $22.50.

BINKIN, MARTIN. *America's Volunteer Military: Progress and Prospects.* Pp. viii, 63. Washington, DC: Brookings Institution, 1984. Paperbound, no price.

BROWNE, WILLIAM P. and DON F. HADWIGER, eds. *World Food Policies: Toward Agricultural Independence.* Pp. x, 220. Boulder, CO: Lynn Rienner, 1986. $26.50.

BURNHEIM, JOHN. *Is Democracy Possible?* Pp. vii, 205. Berkeley: University of California Press, 1986. $22.50.

BUTLER, J. DOUGLAS and DAVID WALBERT, eds. *Abortion, Medicine, and the Law.* Pp. xvi, 795. New York: Facts on File, 1986. $40.00.

CARLSON, DON and CRAIG COMSTOCK, eds. *Citizen Summitry: Keeping the Peace When It Matters Too Much to Be Left to Politicians.* Pp. 391. Los Angeles: Jeremy Tarcher, 1986. Distributed by St. Martin's Press, New York. Paperbound, $11.95.

CLARK, IAN. *Nuclear Past, Nuclear Present: Hiroshima, Nagasaki, and Contemporary Strategy.* Pp. ix, 146. Boulder, CO: Westview Press, 1985. Paperbound, $15.00.

CLARKE, ROBIN. *London under Attack.* Pp. xi, 397. New York: Basil Blackwell, 1986. $34.95. Paperbound, $14.95.

DOLBEARE, KENNETH M. *The Politics of Economic Renewal.* Rev. ed. Pp. xv, 237. Chatham, NJ: Chatham House, 1986. Paperbound, $11.95.

DUBOFSKY, MELVYN, ed. *Technological Change and Workers' Movements.* Pp. 272. Beverly Hills, CA: Sage, 1985. No price.

EIDELBERG, PAUL. *The Philosophy of the American Constitution: A Reinterpretation of the Intentions of the Founding Fathers.* Pp. xvi, 339. Lanham, MD: University Press of America, 1986. Paperbound, $14.75.

ETHEREDGE, LLOYD S. *Can Governments Learn? American Foreign Policy and Central American Revolutions.* Pp. xii, 227. New York: Pergamon Press, 1985. Paperbound, $13.95.

HELLE, H. J. and EISENSTADT, S. N., eds. *Micro Sociological Theory: Perspectives on Sociological Theory.* Vol. 2. Pp. ix, 170. Beverly Hills, CA: Sage, 1985. Paperbound, no price.

HELLER, PETER S. et al. *Aging and Social Expenditure in the Major Industrial Countries, 1980-2025.* Pp. vii, 76. Washington, DC: International Monetary Fund, 1986. Paperbound, $7.50.

JONES, BRYAN D. et al. *The Sustaining Hand: Community Leadership and Corporate Power.* Pp. xii, 247. Lawrence: University Press of Kansas, 1986. $27.50. Paperbound, $9.95.

KAHLER, MILES, ed. *The Polities of International Debt.* Pp. 272. Ithaca, NY: Cornell University Press, 1986. Paperbound, $9.95.

KATZENSTEIN, PETER J. *Corporatism and Change: Austria, Switzerland, and the Politics of Industry.* Pp. 331. Ithaca, NY: Cornell University Press, 1984. $35.00.

LAL, BRIJ V., ed. *Politics in Fiji.* Pp. xi, 161. Honolulu: University of Hawaii Press, 1986. $18.95.

LANCASTER, JANE B. and BEATRIX A. HAMBURG, eds. *School-Age Pregnancy and Parenthood: Biosocial Dimensions.* Pp. xvii, 403. New York: Walter de Gruyter, Aldine, 1986. $39.95.

LAWSON, RONALD, ed. *The Tenant Movement in New York City, 1904-1984.* Pp. xiv, 289. New Brunswick, NJ: Rutgers University Press, 1986. $35.00. Paperbound, $15.00.

LEBRA, TAKIE SUGIYAMA and WILLIAM P. LEBRA, eds. *Japanese Culture and Behavior: Selected Readings.* Rev. ed. Pp. xix, 428. Honolulu: University of Hawaii Press, 1986. Paperbound, $12.95.

LEVANTROSSER, WILLIAM F., ed. *Harry S. Truman: The Man from Independence.* Pp. x, 427. Westport, CT: Greenwood Press, 1986. $45.00.

LIS, CATHARINA. *Social Change and the Labouring Poor: Antwerp, 1770-1860.* Pp. xiii, 237. New Haven, CT: Yale University Press, 1986. $20.00.

LOWENTHAL, LEO. *Literature and the Image of Man.* Pp. vii, 344. New Brunswick, NJ: Transaction Books, 1986. $24.95.

LUKES, STEVEN, ed. *Power.* Pp. vi, 283. New York: New York University Press, 1986. Distributed by Columbia University, New York. $30.00. Paperbound, $12.50.

MAXWELL, KENNETH, ed. *Portugal in the 1980's: Dilemmas of Direct Consul-* tation. Pp. xiv, 254. Westport, CT: Greenwood Press, 1986. $39.95.

McCLINTOCK, MICHAEL. *State Terror and Popular Resistance in Guatemala.* Vol. 2, *The American Connection.* Pp. 319. London: Zed Press, 1985. Distributed by Biblio Distribution Center, Totowa, NJ: $30.95. Paperbound, $12.25.

MEDVEDEV, ROY. *China and the Superpowers.* Translated by Harold Shukman. Pp. vi, 243. New York: Basil Blackwell, 1986. $19.95.

MILLER, ALDEN D. and LLOYD E. OHLIN. *Delinquency and Community: Creating Opportunities and Controls.* Pp. 208. Beverly Hills, CA: Sage, 1985. No price.

MILLER, J.D.B. *Norman Angell and the Futility of War: Peace and the Public Mind.* Pp. x, 167. New York: St. Martin's Press, 1986. $27.50.

MUSCHAMP, DAVID, ed. *Political Thinkers.* Pp. x, 259. New York: St. Martin's Press, 1986. $29.95.

OSKAMP, STUART, ed. *International Conflict and National Public Policy Issues.* Pp. 312. Beverly Hills, CA: Sage, 1985. Paperbound, no price.

O'SULLIVAN, PATRICK. *Geopolitics.* Pp. 144. New York: St. Martin's Press, 1986. $27.50.

POPE, WHITNEY. *Alexis de Tocqueville: His Social and Political Theory.* Pp. 159. Beverly Hills, CA: Sage, 1986. Paperbound, no price.

PRZEWORSKI, ADAM and JOHN SPRAGUE. *Paper Stones: A History of Electoral Socialism.* Pp. vi, 224. Chicago: University of Chicago Press, 1986. $24.95.

RAMBERG, BENNETT. *Global Nuclear Energy Risks: The Search for Preventive Medicine.* Pp. xv, 128. Boulder, CO: Westview Press, 1986. $22.00.

ROEMER, JOHN, ed. *Analytical Marxism.* Pp. viii, 313. New York: Cambridge University Press, 1986. $39.50. Paperbound, $11.95.

ROGOW, ARNOLD A. *Thomas Hobbes: Radical in the Service of Reaction.* Pp. 287. New York: W. W. Norton, 1986. $19.95.

ROSENBERG, MARK B. and PHILIP L. SHEPHERD, eds. *Honduras Confronts Its Future: Contending Perspectives on Critical Issues.* Pp. xii, 268. Boulder, CO: Lynne Rienner, 1986. $30.00.

RUBIN, H. TED. *Behind the Black Robes: Juvenile Court Judges and the Court.* Pp. 248. Beverly Hills, CA: Sage, 1985. Paperbound, no price.

SHOVER, NEAL. *Aging Criminals.* Pp. 175. Beverly Hills, CA: Sage, 1985. Paperbound, no price.

SIMON, JEFFREY. *Warsaw Pact Forces: Problems of Command and Control.* Pp. xv, 246. Boulder, CO: Westview Press, 1985. Paperbound, $19.50.

STOHL, MICHAEL and GEORGE A. LOPEZ, eds. *Government Violence and Repression: An Agenda for Research.* Pp. viii, 278. Westport, CT: Greenwood Press, 1986. $35.00.

STONE, JOHN. *Racial Conflict in Contemporary Society.* Pp. 191. Cambridge, MA: Harvard University Press, 1986. $18.50. Paperbound, $6.95.

THIO, ALEX. *Sociology: An Introduction.* Pp. xvii, 588. New York: Harper & Row, 1986. No price.

THOMPSON, JUDITH JARVIS. *Rights, Restitution, and Risk: Essays in Moral Theory.* Edited by William Parent. Pp. x, 269. Cambridge, MA: Harvard University Press, 1986. $29.95. Paperbound, $9.95.

TIMMER, C. PETER. *Getting Prices Right: The Scope and Limits of Agricultural Price Policy.* Pp. 160. Ithaca, NY: Cornell University Press, 1986. $25.00. Paperbound, $7.95.

TULLOCK, GORDEN. *The Economics of Wealth and Poverty.* Pp. viii, 210. New York: New York University Press, 1986. Distributed by Columbia University Press, New York. $40.00.

VOLGYES, IVAN. *Politics in Eastern Europe.* Pp. xvii, 368, xxi. Homewood, IL: Dorsey Press, 1986. Paperbound, $20.00.

WILKINSON, PAUL. *Terrorism and the Liberal State.* 2nd ed. Pp. xiv, 322. New York: New York University Press, 1986. Distributed by Columbia University Press, New York. $35.00. Paperbound, $12.50.

WOOD, ELLEN MEIKSINS. *The Retreat from Class: A New "True" Socialism.* Pp. 202. London: Verso, 1986. Distributed by Schocken Books, New York. $24.95. Paperbound, $8.95.

ZIMMER, LYNN E. *Women Guarding Men.* Pp. xiv, 264. Chicago: University of Chicago Press, 1986. $25.00.

INDEX

Here's one reason why you need more life insurance...and three reasons why it should be our group insurance.

Family responsibilities increase and change—a new baby, a job change, a new home. Your family could have a lot to lose unless your insurance keeps pace with these changes.

Now here's why you need our group term life insurance.

First, it's low-cost. Unlike everything else, life rates have gone down over the past 20 years. And, because of our buying power, our group rates are low.

Second, you will continue to receive this protection even if you change jobs, as long as you remain a member and pay the premiums when due.

Third, our wide range of coverage allows you to choose the insurance that's right for you. And you can protect yourself and your entire family.

It's insurance as you need it. So check your current insurance portfolio. Then call or write the Administrator for the extra protection you need.

UP TO $240,000 IN TERM LIFE INSURANCE PROTECTION IS AVAILABLE TO AAPSS MEMBERS.
Plus these other group insurance plans:
Major Medical Expense Insurance
Excess Major Medical
In-Hospital Insurance
High-Limit Accident Insurance
Medicare Supplement

The AAPSS Life Plan is underwritten by New York Life Insurance Company, New York, New York 10010 on form number GT-2-PA-9400.

Contact Administrator, AAPSS Group Insurance Program
Smith-Sternau Organization, Inc
1255 23rd Street, N.W.
Washington, D.C. 20037

800 424-9883 Toll Free
in Washington, D.C. area, 202 296-8030